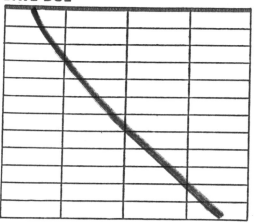

THE EMERGENCE OF AN AMERICAN LEFT

CIVIL WAR TO WORLD WAR I

WILEY SOURCEBOOKS IN AMERICAN SOCIAL THOUGHT

Edited by *David D. Hall and Daniel Walker Howe*

Daniel Walker Howe	THE AMERICAN WHIGS
Staughton Lynd	AMERICAN LABOR RADICALISM: TESTIMONIES AND INTERPRETATIONS
R. Laurence Moore	THE EMERGENCE OF AN AMERICAN LEFT: CIVIL WAR TO WORLD WAR I
Laurence Veysey	THE PERFECTIONISTS: RADICAL SOCIAL THOUGHT IN THE NORTH, 1815–1860
Donald Worster	AMERICAN ENVIRONMENTALISM: THE FORMATIVE PERIOD, 1860–1915
Alan Trachtenberg	LITERATURE AND SOCIETY IN TWENTIETH-CENTURY AMERICA

THE EMERGENCE OF AN AMERICAN LEFT

CIVIL WAR TO WORLD WAR I

Edited by
R. Laurence Moore
Cornell University

John Wiley & Sons, Inc.
New York • London • Sydney • Toronto

Library of Congress Cataloging in Publication Data:
Moore, Robert Laurence, comp.
  The emergence of an American left: Civil War to
World War I.

  (Wiley sourcebooks in American social thought)
  CONTENTS: The First International in American—
labor and radicalism in the post Civil War decade:
Trade unionism and class consciousness: Sylvis, W.H.
What is money? German Marxists and the American liberal
traditions: Sorge, F.A. Socialism and the worker.
Priestess of a counter-culture: Woodhull, V. Tried as
by fire.—Individualism, private property, and the
collective state. [etc.]
  Bibliography: p.

  1. Radicalism—United States. 2. Socialism in the
United States—History. 3. Labor and laboring classes
—United States—History. I. Title. II. Series.

HN90.R3M6   335'.00973   72–14108
ISBN 0–471–61500–5
ISBN 0–471–61501–3 (pbk.)

Printed in the United States of America

10–9 8 7 6 5 4 3 2 1

CONTENTS

Part Three TACTICS FOR A RADICAL MOVEMENT IN THE TWENTIETH CENTURY

Part Four RADICAL CRITIQUES OF PROGRESSIVE AMERICA

THE EMERGENCE OF AN AMERICAN LEFT

CIVIL WAR TO WORLD WAR I

INTRODUCTION

The American presidential campaign of 1864 captured attention in some unexpected quarters. When Abraham Lincoln won a second term in the White House, the International Workingmen's Association (IWA) with headquarters in London forwarded a letter of congratulations through the American minister in England. The message, which was drafted by Karl Marx, commended the American people for their resistance to slavery and, in wording that must have surprised the president, linked the North's struggle against the South to the cause of workingmen in Europe. Just as the American War of Independence had "initiated a new era of ascendancy for the middle class," the American "antislavery war" promised to hasten the victory of the working classes.

The First International, as the International Workingmen's Association is now known, had not in 1864 adopted a strict Marxist program, and Lincoln need not have worried about a possible association of himself with men determined to undermine the institution of private property. Nevertheless Marx, who had in the 1850s eked out an existence as a foreign correspondent for Horace Greeley's *New York Tribune*, attached great significance to the rising industrial power of the United States. Marx anticipated a socialist revolution succeeding somewhere during the nineteenth century and, in a rough way, he expected the country with the highest level of capitalist development to inaugurate the first cooperative commonwealth. If at the time of the Civil War, American industrial strength did not quite make the United States a convincing claimant for that role, the aggressive intrusions of American traders into the world market promised to disrupt European economies sufficiently to provoke a proletarian victory in the Old World.

Before the Civil War political reprisals following the social upheavals of 1848 had already forced a number of German socialists close to Marx to flee to the United States. Many became corrupted by "new world conditions" and renounced a class-based socialist movement in

1

favor of various "bourgeois" reform crusades. Others, however, keeping their eyes focused on events in Europe, maintained their vigilance in this country and organized the first tiny enclaves of people dedicated to the revolutionary overturning of the capitalist system. To one of these, Friedrich A. Sorge, Marx entrusted the direction of the First International when, in 1871, he engineered the removal of its General Council from London to New York City. On that occasion he referred to the United States as "becoming the world of the worker, par excellence" and several weeks later in Amsterdam added that an American socialist victory, in contrast to most countries on the European continent, could be achieved peacefully.

Marx attached no great significance to either of these 1871 remarks. In maneuvering to remove the headquarters of the First International to American soil, Marx intended to kill the organization, which he no longer found useful, before Mikhail Bakunin and other anarchist members took it over. But his interest in the United States was genuine, and it was shared by Friedrich Engels. The latter as late as 1892 remained hopeful that, despite all obstacles, the American socialist movement would move "with an energy and impetuousness compared with which we in Europe shall be mere children."

The material reprinted here documents what happened to Marxist ideas as they struggled for a foothold in this country and mingled with other kinds of radical and collectivist thought. It does not record a triumph. At the end of World War I, the concluding point of this volume, the political fortunes of American radicalism had sunk to zero. The achievement lay in what had been said and written. The student should be aware in reading the documents that despite the legislative misadventures of particular radical programs, radical ideas in the long run, and sometimes in the short run, did modify and influence the dominant strains of American social thought. In the late nineteenth and early twentieth centuries they formed an important part of the struggle to overthrow the ungenerous assumptions of social Darwinism and the rigid laws of classical economic theory. The success of that struggle has made a great difference in our lives.

Part One contains selections from three people involved with the First International in America. In the immediate aftermath of the Civil War there were almost no labor organizations in the United States that seemed likely affiliates of the London-based association. One promising flirtation developed between the International and the National Labor Union, a craft union that, under the brief leadership of William Sylvis in 1868 and 1869, steadily gained strength. However, while a delegate from the American organization, whose passage to

Switzerland was paid by a sympathetic capitalist, did attend the Basle meeting of the International Workingmen's Association in 1869, negotiations for formal affiliation ended with the sudden death of Sylvis in July 1869.

The honor of becoming the first American affiliate of the International went therefore not to an organization of native-born workers, but to one composed largely of German immigrants. Located in New York City, the General German Workingman's Association, which was Local 5 of the National Labor Union, became Section 1 of the American affiliates of the IWA. Friedrich Sorge safely directed Section 1 toward Marxist principles, but he had trouble preventing an influx of middle class reformers into other American sections that were soon added to the International. Sorge interpreted the task of the International as the building of working-class consciousness through trade union activity, and he vehemently opposed labor organizations dissipating energy in behalf of reform measures that were useless to workers even if passed.

In the early 1870s Victoria Woodhull made the most persistent challenge to Sorge's point of view. She, along with her sister Tennessee Claflin and her ardent admirer Stephen Pearl Andrews, organized Section 12 of the American affiliates of the IWA and proceeded to cause the German Marxists of Section 1 no end of trouble. Woodhull, despite the fact that she had been put into the brokerage business by Cornelius Vanderbilt, was unquestionably a radical. She ran as a candidate for president in 1872 on the ticket of the Equal Rights party and espoused a multitude of "anti-establishment" causes including women's suffrage, spiritualism, and free love. Her rejection of the class struggle and the range of her cultural radicalism exasperated Marx, who called her "a banker's woman, free lover, and general humbug." When Sorge carried a complaint to the General Council in London, Marx supported the suspension of Section 12 on the ground that "wage slaves" did not constitute a sufficient proportion of its membership.

The suspension of Section 12 made things easier for Sorge when in 1872 the International moved its central offices to New York City and put Sorge in charge. But the victory came at a cost and had implications for the American socialist movement throughout the rest of the nineteenth century. The International, by rejecting a strain of native American radicalism, reduced itself to an organization of German-speaking members and reinforced in the American consciousness the association of socialism with something foreign. Having repudiated *Woodhull and Claflin's Weekly*, the first paper in

America to print an English translation of *The Communist Manifesto*, the North American Federation of the International had its only newspaper outlet in the German-language *Arbeiter Zeitung*.

Marx and Sorge were aware of the problem. Yet, however lenient they tried to remain with respect to the ideological backwardness of American labor organizations, they had no choice except to reject the middle class leadership of Woodhull and her friends. The tactics of the International made little difference in any case. The difficult economic times of the 1870s led to bitter labor disputes, but there were no compensatory gains in terms of strong and permanent radical labor organizations. The First International died an unnoticed death in Philadelphia in 1876, and although its demise made way for the formation of the Socialist Labor party, a party that has had a more or less continuous existence since 1877, not until the 1890s was there any significant movement of Marxist ideas in the United States. The Socialist Labor party counted only 500 members in 1883 and published no English-language newspaper.

The reluctance of the American labor movement to associate itself with radical foreign doctrines received a solid demonstration in the aftermath of the Haymarket "massacre." On May 4, 1886, someone threw a bomb into a crowd at Haymarket Square in Chicago, where a labor rally was just breaking up, and a policeman was killed. Aroused public opinion put the entire labor movement on the defensive. Though officials never found the actual bomb thrower, a group of anarchists who had had a hand in organizing the rally and who had publicly advocated violence were charged with conspiracy. Four of these men, August Spies, Albert Parsons, George Engel, and Adolph Fischer, eventually were hanged for the crime. Organized labor moved quickly to condemn the indicted anarchists. "The Knights of Labor," declared one labor journal, "are the stoutest opponents yet placed against socialism and anarchy." It did socialists no good to protest that they had long been at odds with anarchist leaders who rejected political action and trade union bargaining in favor of "direct action." Foreign radicalisms blurred in the public mind, and labor worked hard to distinguish foreign radicals from American trade unionists.

In the late 1880s European socialist observers did manage to pick out one or two incidents that they took as hopeful signs of greater class awareness among American working people. One episode that aroused particular enthusiasm came in the same year as Haymarket—the race by Henry George in 1886 to become mayor of New York City. George was neither a Marxist nor a socialist. But for a brief moment both Marxists and other socialists thought that George might provide the spark to draw labor into a radical, independent political movement.

The initial venture of New York's United Labor party was encouraging. George lost, but he received a respectable number of votes and outpolled a young political fledgling named Theodore Roosevelt. The sequel, however, was devastating. Socialists and single taxers found no common ground, the party split, and George's labor support, which had temporarily abandoned the Republican and Democratic parties, returned to the fold.

There are people who would begrudge Henry George the label radical. In objecting only to unearned wealth and not to wages, profits, or competition, he was but a shade removed from a strict laissez-faire conception of state power. Yet that shade made a difference. George did challenge the favorite tenets of classical economic theory. Nature was not niggardly and no iron law of wages doomed laborers to a subsistence existence. George posed a famous paradox—"where population is densest, wealth greatest, and the machinery of production and exchange most highly developed, we find the deepest poverty, the sharpest struggle for existence, and the most enforced idleness"—and used it as the beginning of a far-reaching indictment of American society.

The selections in Part Two represent men who, like George, had a readership, in some cases a large one, among native Americans and who publicized alternative plans to American capitalism that were not directly tied to any socialist or labor school. They owed more to the natural rights formulations of Thomas Jefferson than to the economic determinism of Marx. Except for George, they did not get involved in politics; and, except for Benjamin Tucker, they made strong appeals to Christianity. All rejected the rhetoric of class struggle as inimical to brotherhood. The beliefs of Laurence Gronlund and Edward Bellamy, who favored a strong collective state, were compatible with a socialist point of view, but they were wary of trying to sell the American populace a foreign product. Bellamy chose the term "nationalism" as a substitute for "socialism." The individual imprints made by these men on an American radical tradition have made it something that cannot be summed up totally in the organized struggles of socialists, anarchists, and labor radicals. Their maverick qualities ally them more closely with the Christian socialists who formed a small wing of the Social Gospel Movement and various communitarians both before and after the Civil War.

After the disastrous and fleeting alliance with Henry George and a few unsuccessful overtures to the Populist party in the 1890s, the

Socialist Labor party settled firmly into an uncompromising course that rejected all collaboration with bourgeois reformers. The decision to maintain strict independence, however, did not settle all questions of strategy, and, as the selections in Part Three illustrate, tactical disputes were bitter and numerous enough to cause splits among socialist leaders. Socialist gatherings raised the same questions year after year in the late nineteenth and early twentieth centuries. What attitude should a socialist party adopt toward existing "pure and simple" trade unions? Should it try to "bore from within" and capture the leadership, or should it set up rival unions open only to socialists? What role did political campaigning play in the class struggle? Should a socialist party run candidates and, if so, on what platform? Should a socialist candidate make specific reform demands to win votes or should his platform call only for the end of the capitalist system? Was the purpose of political activity to teach the worker Marxist ideas or was it to win elections? What was a socialist candidate to do, if elected, should he find himself hamstrung by the state legislature and unable to introduce fundamental social changes? What role did extralegal activity, especially sabotage and direct action, have in achieving the cooperative commonwealth?

Daniel DeLeon rose in the early 1890s to the position of top leadership in the Socialist Labor party. DeLeon committed his party equally to political activity and to trade unionism, but after a series of clashes with Samuel Gompers and an unsuccessful bid to capture what was left of the organization of the Knights of Labor, DeLeon renounced the policy of "boring from within." His newspaper *The People* began an unceasing attack on the "labor fakirs," and DeLeon organized the Socialist Trade and Labor Alliance, which he tied closely to his political party, as a rival of the American Federation of Labor.

Because many members of the Socialist Labor party opposed DeLeon's policy of "dual unionism," feeling that the strategy would needlessly alienate many workers from socialism, a split became inevitable. In 1899 dissident members of the Socialist Labor party, who were dubbed the Kangaroos, rejected DeLeon's leadership. This group, which included Hermann Schlüter, Morris Hillquit, Max Hayes, A.M. Simons, and Job Harriman, turned its attention toward effecting a union with the Social Democratic party led by Eugene Debs and Victor Berger. This party had formed in 1897 to further a colonization scheme supported by Debs, but had steadily shifted its position in the direction of Marxism. Jealousies about the name and location of the new party delayed consolidation, but finally in 1901 the two sides agreed on the formation of the Socialist Party of America. At last there was an American socialist party that claimed a majority of native-born members and a number of English-language newspapers.

The next decade went very well for the new party. Expectations remained high because its share of the vote rose in every election. Debs, who became the party's usual presidential candidate, gathered almost a million votes in the election of 1912, and almost all socialists anticipated a quick victory over capitalism. The party did even better in local elections. It captured the government in a number of cities, including Milwaukee, and elected two men to the United States Congress. An increasing emphasis on getting votes alarmed many socialists who worried about the party forgetting its revolutionary goals in the excitement of securing public ownership of a city waterworks. What good, they asked, were elected socialist officials if the only thing that distinguished them from other politicians was a modicum of honesty?

Disquieting as that question was to those socialists who feared the party's capitulation to reformism, the party proceeded through the first decade of the twentieth century without major defections. The activities of William Haywood led to the first permanent rupture in party harmony. When Haywood organized the Industrial Workers of the World in 1905, leaders in both the Socialist party and the Socialist Labor party, which still limped along under DeLeon, praised him. Even some of the trade union socialists who belonged to the American Federation of Labor and who had opposed DeLeon's earlier experiment in dual unionism regarded his attempt to organize the unorganizable as praiseworthy. However, when Haywood began making statements that seemed to reject political action in favor of direct action, socialist sentiment pulled apart. At the 1912 convention of the Socialist party, delegates who feared the effect of Haywood's statements on the party's political campaigns successfully sponsored a resolution that read out of the party any person who advocated direct action and sabotage. A referendum on the basis of that resolution recalled Haywood from his seat on the National Executive Committee, and he left the party.

Haywood's ouster happened to coincide with a change in socialist fortunes. The Socialist party ceased to grow. It did not collapse, but the myth of inevitable victory that had made party activity almost joyous in the first decade of its existence evaporated. New victories in the unlikely state of Oklahoma could not erase the fact that the party had been unable to consolidate its victories anywhere. Debs did not carry the party standard in 1916, and its national vote fell way off. For the first time in a decade party leaders confessed to doubts about their ability to capture the minds of the American people.

The entrance of the United States into World War I gave the Socialist party a renewed opportunity to direct a movement of radical protest. In one way it met the challenge superbly. Alone among the national parties that belonged to the Second International, the American party refused in any way to support its government's decision to go to war. Unlike their counterparts in many European countries, American socialists had never had a role in the national government, and consequently their actions of protest carried no burden of governmental responsibility. Nevertheless their stand was a courageous one based on a fervent conviction that all wars were rooted in capitalist greed, and it cost the party dearly.

Because opposition to American participation in the war was a more popular cause than socialism, the votes received by the party did increase. But gains at the polls proved small compensation for the defection of those party leaders who chose to rally behind Woodrow Wilson and their country. The party lost almost all of its chief publicists and intellectuals. Not all of them repudiated the goals of socialism, but almost without exception they retreated permanently from the arena of radical politics.

The few leaders who remained firm in their opposition to government policies—Morris Hillquit, Victor Berger, and Eugene Debs —faced the severe repression that a state, even a democratic one, can force on its people during wartime. Debs was jailed. Berger won election to Congress, in part because of his opposition to the war, and the House of Representatives refused him his seat. The Post Office Department banned socialist publications from the mails, and the Justice Department brought charges of sedition against the editors of the lively socialist publication *The Masses*. These attacks did not stop with the end of hostilities in Europe. The Bolshevik Revolution of 1917 aroused in the United States new fears about radical activity. Radical leaders of every sort faced harassment during the "Red Scare," and a few were deported.

The Socialist party had its finest hour during the war and also its loneliest. After the guns were silent there were not even pieces to pick up. The Second International had fallen apart without achieving a victory in any of the countries where revolution was considered likely, and western nations were left to stumble along bearing the legacy of the Treaty of Versailles. The stunning success of Lenin and Trotsky in capturing the revolution in Russia gave birth to the Third

International, but it also introduced a new and unbridgeable split in socialist parties around the world. Communists and socialists would henceforth differentiate themselves, not by relatively trivial differences in their attitudes toward private property, but by their bitter disagreements over the nature of democratic government.

Since late in the nineteenth century European and American observers have puzzled over the political failure of radicalism in the United States. Even to non-Marxists it has appeared that in the twentieth century, at the very least, workers should have organized an American labor party along the lines of the English model. There is no completely satisfactory answer to Werner Sombart's classic question, "Why is there no socialism in the United States?"

Strong partisan feeling has been evident in many of the answers that have been given. For example, commentators who have believed wholeheartedly in the American "dream of success" have explained socialism's failure by the general prosperity fostered by American capitalism. On the other hand, critics who have cited capitalism's inability to eliminate poverty and have attacked assumptions about the upward mobility of Americans have attributed the failure of radicalism to savage and persistent repression by a government dedicated to the happiness of the already privileged. Other writers who have expressed a great faith in the consensus demands of the American party system have blamed socialism's poor showing on the apocalyptic mood of radicals that has prevented them from playing a skillful political game. Finally many American socialists have scored particular tactics adopted by their party as responsible for the failure and argued that different tactical decisions would have brought them victory.

All of these answers raise new questions. Certainly there is a historical reality to American prosperity, but that does not explain why great numbers of American poor remained loyal to one of the two major political parties. As experience in this country and elsewhere has demonstrated, strong labor movements are not the product of dire economic hardship. The American government has been guilty of repression, but governments of countries where radical movements have won political success have been far more repressive. Particular moods of radicals and specific tactics adopted by their parties were as much the products of failure as the cause.

The political failure of radical parties in this country forms a part of the story of the general failure of third party movements. In almost all cases Americans rule by the majority, and in the long run, membership in fringe political groups brings no political leverage. In those areas where the majority does not rule, such as the courts, the whole system is weighted heavily against change. Poor immigrants to this country had much more to gain by adhering to a powerful urban machine than by voting for a third party with no reliable organization, no money, and no power. Socialists in Europe did not succeed in becoming a political force simply because of their economic goals. They built organizations that represented working people in their struggle for basic political power and representation. Workingmen joined socialist parties because politically they had nothing to lose and everything to gain. However badly the American system has operated in providing economic justice, the political rights that in this country belonged to white male citizens throughout the nineteenth century did give American working people something to lose.

Still it remains an enigma how radicalism has come to be a word that can terrify the population of a country whose fundamental documents and principles inspire revolutionary aspirations in other parts of the world. Not, as it again should be said, that radicalism has been a complete failure here. Radical critiques of American society, such as those in Part Four, have left their deep impression. If radicals before World War I did not succeed in handing their successors a viable political organization or even a consensus on appropriate tactical ways to proceed, they did in their social thought dramatize the hardship and struggle of people who found themselves poor in a land of plenty. While the idea of class struggle largely miscarried in the United States, the idea of economic injustice as something that can be alleviated has stuck.

Not all the men and women represented here maintained a radical stance throughout their lives. But at the time they made their contributions, they were attacking not just the economic and political conservatism of the late nineteenth century, but benign reformist creeds as well. They should not be confused with progressive Republicans and Democrats whose assaults on social injustice stopped short of advocating a thorough restructuring of social, economic, and political institutions. Some radicals looked to Marx for their principles and others looked to Christ. What gave them a common fighting stance was their abhorrence of unequal competition and of an ethic that measured progress by increased profits. They gave a nation of businessmen, inclined to smugness, something to answer for. Bombs ignited for revolutionary causes make people uncomfortable. Occasionally revolutionary words do too. The smoke and heat that they throw off is not as easily cleared away.

Part One

THE FIRST INTERNATIONAL IN AMERICA—LABOR AND RADICALISM IN THE POST CIVIL WAR DECADE

1

TRADE UNIONISM AND CLASS CONSCIOUSNESS

William H. Sylvis
WHAT IS MONEY?

Early American labor organizations made only modest demands. Often fraternal in purpose, they were locally organized and attracted mainly skilled craftsmen. William Sylvis (1828–1869) was an important transition figure in the labor movement who worked, in the aftermath of Appomattox, to construct a strong national labor organization that could defend the interests of workingmen on both political and economic fronts. A skilled craftsman who won his initial reputation in labor circles as president of the Iron Molders Union, he became head of the National Labor Union in 1868. Despite his wish to affiliate the National Labor Union with the International Working-men's Association, he had no desire to overturn capitalism. Instead, he put his faith in reform measures such as the issuance of greenbacks, the establishment of cooperatives, and the institution of the eight-hour day. Sylvis was a Christian, and he believed that the favorable situation of the American worker called generally for a strategy different from the violent tactics forced on labor leaders in Europe. His remarks on currency reform, printed here, are laced with the most revolutionary utterances he ever made. Sylvis did understand labor to have class interests that had to be defended against the rest of society; and since he had a following among native-born American workers, Marx and his lieutenants watched him with interest. The National Labor Union disintegrated soon after the sudden death of Sylvis on July 27, 1869.

What is money? is a question so frequently asked, especially by workingmen, and so many different answers have been given; all based upon the idea that gold is the only material out of which money can be made, that I have determined to add one more answer to the long list.

SOURCE. William H. Sylvis,"What is Money?" Nos. 1, 4 and 5, *The Workingman's Advocate*, February 27, March 27, April 3, 1869.

13

In taking up this question, I do not expect to present any new idea or to say anything new. My only object is to present the matter in a plain common-sense light, and in doing so I shall use such arguments and illustrations as will be easily understood by every one who reads. What I have to say will be the plain words of a workingman addressed to workingmen.

Money made of gold is a monarchical and aristocratic institution. Kings adopted it as a sure means of keeping the people in subjection, by taking from them all power to control, or in any way interfere with the currency. Princes and nobles were created—special privileges were bestowed upon a few; these few were rich and were of course interested in maintaining the king's money. Thus the king, with his well-fed few, succeeded in robbing the masses, keeping them poor, ignorant, and wholly dependent.

When our ancestors ran away from Europe to escape religious persecution, they came here and set up for themselves; unfortunately for us they did not leave behind them their prejudices and false notions on many of the most vital points in the science of government.

Reared amid the hardships and dangers of a new continent —separated from the "parent government" by a great ocean—thrown upon their own resources, they learned lessons of self-reliance and ideas of self-government that served them well when the struggle for independence came, and for the change in civil government about to take place. It was left for them to present to the world, for the first time, a self-formed government, whose basis was the equal rights of man, civil equality, and common privileges, and whose end was to be the general prosperity, virtue, and happiness of the people. Independence gained, it was natural that joy and satisfaction should be inspired, upon having escaped some of the oppressions of European systems, without feeling much curiosity to ascertain whether the new government was actually so founded as to secure the *happiness of the many, instead of ministering to the benefit of the few.* This could only be learned after a considerable experience, and after that class, out of which came bankers, brokers, bondholders, usurers, and other plunderers of labor, had time to find out and take advantage of the weak places in our system of government.

This point was soon reached, and then began that scramble for wealth and power that has resulted in creating among us a monied aristocracy that is fast sapping the foundation of our government and destroying the liberties of the people.

It is true that compared with the wretched population of despotic Europe and Asia, the people of this country, even under existing unjust relations of man to man, enjoy many things not common to the people of other countries. But comparative superiority may still be a condition fraught with much misery to the human family, and not less repugnant to benevolence, than revolting to justice. Even in Europe and Asia, this superiority forms the boast of one nation over another, throughout the long continued chain of comparative wretchedness among the great mass of the population.

We might run without end through a scale of comparative physical misery and enjoyment, and corresponding moral dignity or degradation, and never attain a principle of justice to reconcile ourselves to a wrong and oppressive system from such examples.

The question is not, what people endure the least misery, but which enjoy the most happiness and real comfort, and having found that point, we are irresistibly forced to another, based upon the susceptibility of the social compact to yield the full amount of happiness to the mass of the people, and to inquire into the reason why this object is not accomplished by our institutions, when it has been so bountifully provided for by a paternal Providence.

The slightest observation will satisfy the most obstinate mind that nature has abundantly supplied the industry of man with the means of universal comfort. We behold it in every form of luxury—every object of magnificence—every refinement of pleasure—every waste of riot and sensuality—every monument of pride—every display of vanity—every gorgeous decoration of wealth, power, and ambition. We behold the proof in the lordly millionaire, tortured on his sick couch by agonies of repletion, while the laborer famishes at his door. We behold it in the luxurious capitalist, swelling with the pride of pampered opulence, while the hearts of those who *labored* to produce his wealth shiver and faint with misery and want, or drag out a protracted life of endless toil. What God has spread before us as the reward and property of him whose labor shall bring it into use, government, unjust, despotic, proud, all-grasping government has ordained shall belong to those who never labor, and for whose exclusive benefit the laborer shall toil forever. Thus do human institutions, founded on tyranny, or turned from their original principle of justice, destroy the beneficence of heaven, robbing the poor and giving to the rich.

Thus do we find our boasted institutions of equal rights to be the merest skeleton of liberty, which by their *letter* declare that equal rights and privileges shall be guaranteed to all, but by their *operation* create aristocracy, special privileges, extortion, monopoly, and robbery.

Such are the defects of organic law, practical government, and property, which are thrown as obstacles in the path of the working-man.

The great mistake made by the founders of our government was in retaining the king's money—in ingrafting into our republican institutions monarchical and aristocratic ideas of currency and finances—in setting up, in our temple of liberty, the golden calf. But the time has come when this idol shall be removed.

Fellow workingmen prepare for the fight. The world's greatest revolution is now at hand. . . .

It was my intention, in the beginning, to have finished this subject in three articles, but I have found it impossible to do so to my own satisfaction. I must therefore ask the indulgence of my readers if I grow tedious, and if these articles are extended beyond what may seem necessary, it must be attributed to an earnest desire to make the whole matter plain to the understanding of every reader.

The power of money to accumulate value by interest is a vast power; so great, indeed, that it is hard to bring it into such proportions as to be easily understood by ordinary minds. When we begin to talk of thousands of millions and billions, etc., the mind of the working-man, who but seldom has more than a week's wages to count over, becomes bewildered, and he doesn't care to listen. I have already said that interest acts like the tax collector, it gathers up the products of labor; taking them from the laborer and giving them to the capitalists. Money loaned at ten percent, will double in seven years, three months, and five days; at nine percent, in eight years and fifteen days; at eight percent, in nine years and two days; at seven percent, in ten years, two months, and twenty-six days; at six percent, in eleven years, ten months, and twenty-one days; at five percent in fourteen years, two months, and thirteen days; at four percent in seventeen years and eight months; at three percent, in twenty-three years, five months, and ten days; and at two percent, in about thirty-five years. The average rate of interest for seventy years has been about eight percent per annum. At the beginning property was more equally distributed than it is now. We will suppose one-eighth of the population to have owned one-fourth of the value of the property, and to have loaned it on interest, or rented their property at this rate, collecting and reloaning the interest annually for the seventy years, the amount would be $54,639,310,622, or over three times the amount of the value of the whole property of the nation in 1860.

Now, cannot the simplest mind see something wrong in this? The rate of interest amounting in seventy years, to more than *three times* the entire value of all the property in the nation. All that labor produced went to capitalists, a few men, all nonproducers, and this balance of interest over production is a lien upon labor, productive labor, physical labor, a vast load of debt heaped upon the backs of the toiling millions, a mortgage upon the bone and muscle of the nation, the very heart's blood of the workingman is mortgaged from the cradle to the grave.

Had the rate of interest been *three percent*, instead of *eight percent*, it would have amounted, in seventy years, to $1,980,000,000, or less than one twenty-seventh part of the amount at eight percent. Thus, it will be seen that, at three percent, labor would have retained over seven-eighths of all it produced, while at eight percent, capital got over three times more than the value of all the property in the nation, besides ALL that labor produced. This seven-eighths, which would have been labor's share, would have been divided among the producers in the shape of wages, and every workingman in the nation could be in the possession of a comfortable home, and in circumstances entirely independent. We would have no Vanderbilts, Drews, Astors, Stewarts, Belmonts and Cookes, worth their hundreds of millions and exercising an influence and power over the government and people such as was never before known since creation, while the dismal cries of poverty-stricken labor, shivering with cold and hunger, come up from every part of the land. Just think of it, fellow workingmen, there are ten men in the city of New York whose combined wealth is *over three hundred millions of dollars*, and in the same city there are over one hundred thousand working men and women whose daily wages do not bring them the commonest necessaries of life, and during last winter, many honest, industrious working men and women were compelled to apply for public or private charity to keep themselves and their loved ones from starvation, and many died from want of proper food, clothes, and shelter. While these ten men were worth millions, there were nearly 63,000 paupers supported by the city of New York during the year 1867, and a much larger number during 1868. Let it be remembered that a large proportion of these poor people, called paupers by newspapers and officials, are honest working men and women, the profits of whose toil go to make up the fortunes—the millions—of the few whose costly equipages jostle the starving mechanic in the same street.

Nowhere in the world is so high a rate of interest maintained; nowhere in the world is labor more completely under the control of the money power, and nowhere in the world is all wealth so surely and so rapidly concentrating in the hands of the few, as in the United States.

It is a first principle that no man can become rich without making another one poor, and that all accumulations of great fortunes necessarily produce poverty somewhere. The course is plain. It is not in the power of man to produce a sum of labor so immense as to make everyone rich, but he does produce enough to make all comfortable. If some, therefore, acquire large fortunes from the pile produced by labor, it must leave others without any. To make this still plainer, we will suppose there are one hundred men whose combined, or aggregate, production is $100,000; an equal division would give to each one $1,000. If one of these men got one dollar more than his share, ninety-nine would get less. But suppose ten of them got $5,000 each, then there would be but $555.55 apiece for the other ninety; but if twenty of the ninety take $2,500 each, then seventy would be left without any. A truth so plain requires no further demonstration.

Wealth, seated in the midst of her golden paradise, often sends her attendant—false benevolence—among the wretched, who are famishing from hunger and cold, to exhort them to economy and temperance, or alarmed by their cries of anguish and suffering, she gathers the poor into alms houses, and eases her conscience by feeding them upon offals, and selling their dead bodies to the dissecting rooms to defray a portion of the expense. The most pernicious character in society is the miser, the accumulator, the man who will garner up the product of labor beyond his needs, the man who steals from honest toil and leaves the toiler to starve. He is one of the moral extremes that meet on the verge of misery, worthlessness, and nonproduction. The accumulator is a tyrant, whose every step inflicts anguish, crushes the heart, or slays his victim. . . .

"Money creates no wealth; it only gathers up and appropriates to its owner things already produced."

Money is not wealth; it only gives to its owner power over the productions of labor. Wealth is accumulated labor. Money creates nothing, and has no value whatsoever to its owner, except as he exchanges it for what labor produces. A man may have a million of dollars and be very poor; if he keeps it in his possession, he will starve—he will be destitute of food, clothing, and shelter. Money has no value, only as we part with it for something we need. This is, of course, plain to every mind.

A centralization of wealth is a centralization of power. When the few possess themselves of everything, and the many are reduced to that condition of dependence when it is compulsory to work or starve, then it is that the power of wealth and the rule of the few is absolute.

The most pernicious effect of wealth is that it hardens the heart, blunts the sensibilities, deadens the conscience, deforms the moral nature, and makes a tyrant of its possessors.

For money, men sacrifice domestic comfort, health, character, and even hazard life itself; for it, they are guilty of fraud, deception, and robbery. For money, they sacrifice friendship, gratitude, natural affection, and every holy and divine feeling. For money, man becomes a creeping, crawling, miserable thing, instead of walking upright, as God intended he should. Mammon and manhood are incompatible.

When wealth accumulates in the hands of the few, the spirit of vindictiveness—a desire to rule, to get more, to reduce labor to a condition of vassalage, and to make pliant tools and helpless, obedient slaves of all who toil at physical labor—develops itself more and more, and widens the breach between the rich and the poor. As the one goes up, the other must go down. The one feels secure in its power, the other grows restless under fraud and persecution.

Here is the fountain from which flow all the social eruptions that blacken the body politic. Here is the cause of all strikes and revolutions. So tight has the hold of these money changers upon the industry of the country become, that we will find it a hard job to shake them off. We must not waste our time in parleying, in trying to coax them to let go, or thinking we can frighten them away. All this has been tried. There is but one way left. We must take them by the neck, with a grasp like a vice and squeeze the life out of them.

There are but two ways by which this can be done. The first is by our power at the ballot box; we can vote them out of existence, if we will. If we fail to do this, they will continue to suck at our vitals, until, in a fit of desperation, we cut their heads off with the sword.

If out of the vast wealth we produce, we are to receive but a miserable subsistence, and no prospect before us but eternal toil, and starvation or an almshouse in old age; if the ballot box is not a sufficient remedy for these evils, if a few men will appropriate all to themselves while labor toils and starves, then the time will come when an outraged and enslaved people will rise in their physical power, and force a more equitable division of the products of their labor, by other means than a lower rate of interest.

What we want and what we propose to have is a general leveling up. I do not mean by this that we desire to pull anybody down, not even if they are up with a rope around their necks—as a considerable number of them ought to be; but we do desire and intend to get up.

The work of accumulation on the one hand and degradation on the other *must stop*. The millions of little streams of wealth put into motion by our hands must find their way into other and a larger number of pockets. We have no desire to disturb any man in the possession of what he now has; we are willing the thieves shall escape with their plunder, but we say the work of plunder must stop. This is what we mean by a leveling up, and this leveling up must be effected by a lower rate of interest, and an entire change in our monetary system. This change we will have by one means or another. The bleeding operation has been going on long enough, the patient is tired of it and demands that it be abandoned. We are for a peaceable solution of this problem; but if there must be bloodletting, it shall be on the other side.

Confiscation, or organism is no part of our plan, but it does not require a very great stretch of the imagination to picture the lamp posts in Wall Street, ornamented with the bloated carcasses of the money shavers, gold gamblers and land sharks who are robbing the government and the people. Labor is forced into an unnatural and degrading position. It is at the bottom of the hill instead of at the top. The products of labor are sifted like corn through a ladder; labor gets what sticks to the rings. Out of this unnatural position we desire to get—through the ballot box—and by peaceable means if possible; but we mean to get out, even if to do so involves the cutting off of a few heads. If this is a digression from the subject, I ask the reader's pardon.

2

GERMAN MARXISTS AND
THE AMERICAN LIBERAL TRADITION

Friedrich A. Sorge
SOCIALISM AND THE WORKER

Friedrich Sorge (1828–1906) had some bad luck as a young man. His part in the unsuccessful uprisings of 1848 led to his expulsion from Germany, Switzerland, and Belgium, and in 1852, unable to find work in London, he became a reluctant immigrant to the United States. Taking up residence in New York City, he emerged at the end of the 1860s as the principal interpreter of Marxism in this country. He remained more interested in the revolutionary situation in Europe than in the one in the United States; and, as in this defense of socialism to workers, he advised American labor organizations to imitate those in Europe. Despite his attempts to influence Sylvis' National Labor Union and his sincere wish to tailor Marx's ideas to the American environment, his struggles to preserve his hegemony over sections of the First International in America led to ideological disputes that severely restricted his influence. Opposing the establishment of the Socialist Labor party in 1877 because he thought working-class consciousness in the United States too undeveloped to make a socialist political party useful, Sorge found himself without a forum and remained thereafter on the sidelines of the American labor movement. However, until his death, he reported regularly on American developments to his colleagues in Europe.

Socialism has been attacked and incriminated at all times, but never with more animosity than recently. Socialists are reproached with every kind of wickedness; of the tendency to do away with property, marriage, family, to pollute everything that is sacred; they have even been accused of arson and murder. And why not? If we look at the originators of these incriminations we are not the least astonished, for they have to defend privileges and monopolies which in reality are in danger, if drawn to the broad daylight and handled by the socialist.

SOURCE. Friedrich A. Sorge, *Socialism and the Worker* (New York, 1876).

They act according to the old jesuitic stratagem: invent lies, pollute your enemy in every way you can; something will stick. But if we find those reproaches repeated and echoed even by workingmen whose interests are quite different, we must wonder indeed.

If the workers, however, hate and attack socialism, it is not a clear perception of the wickedness of the aims of socialism by which their judgment is guided, but by a dim and vague idea, and it is well known that specters are awful things in the dark for people who believe in them.

But everybody who hates and persecutes other people for their purposes and pursuits should be convinced that he is right in doing so. For, if we hate and persecute persons whose purposes and pursuits are reasonable and right, we are wrong.

For this reason let us examine the real aims of the socialists. I think I know them pretty well, and I promise to tell the truth and nothing but the truth about them.

When you have read this to the end you may persecute the socialists with renewed hatred if you find they are bad; on the other hand, you will think favorably of them if you find their views good and right. For I am convinced that you, dear reader, whoever you are, have not a mind to love the bad and hate the good.

Foremost and above all it seems to be certain that the socialists intend to divide all property. Everybody who owns anything must give up what he owns; this whole mass has to be divided equally among all the people, and each person may use his part just as he likes. After a while, when some have used up their allotted part and a new disproportion of property has arisen, a new division will be made; and so on. Especially the money and the soil are to be divided—this is what some people say concerning socialism.

Now, honestly, reader, have you ever seen or heard of a man of sound mind who really demanded such nonsense? No, you have not! Such a demand involves the highest degree of craziness. Just reflect, dear reader, to whose lot, for instance, should a railroad fall? Who should have the rails, or a locomotive, or a carriage? And since everybody would have a right to demand an equal share all these things would have to be broken and smashed up, and one would get a broken axletree, another the door of a carriage, or perhaps some bolts. Not even lunatics could recommend such a state of things.

A division of money or soil might possibly be thought of, but money and soil form only a small part of the wealth of a country. The ready money forms even a very small part. And if the soil should be divided, all the new owners would be in need of houses, barns, stables, agricultural implements of all kinds. Such a distribution of the soil is, therefore, utterly impossible, and the socialists know well enough that such a proceeding would benefit nobody. During the great French Revolution in 1789 something similar was tried; large estates were divided among poor country people to make them happy. What is the result? The French peasantry, generally, are so poor that thousands of them live in dwellings with only a door and no window at all, or with only one small window at the side of the door. And small farmers are not much better off in any country, except, perhaps, in the vicinity of large cities. The small farmer must, as a rule, toil harder than any other person to make a living, and a very scanty and poor one in any case. Farming in our age only pays well if done on a large scale, if large tracts of land can be cultivated with the aid of machinery and the application of all modern improvements. And this knowledge and doctrine of the socialists is strictly opposed to a division of the soil. On the contrary, the socialists are of the opinion that there will be a time when a number of small farmers will unite to cultivate their farms in common and divide the products among themselves, seeing that farming on a small scale cannot compete with farming on a large scale, just as manufacturing on a small scale cannot compete with manufacturing on a large scale. Therefore, what has been said about the intention of the socialists with respect to dividing the soil is an apparent falsehood.

Concerning the division of money I must relate an anecdote invented to ridicule people who are represented to have such intentions. One day in 1848, as the story goes, Baron Rothschild took a walk on the Common of Frankfort-on-the-Main. Two laborers met him and accosted him thus: "Baron, you are a rich man; we want to divide with you." Baron Rothschild, not the least puzzled, took out his purse good-humouredly and answered: "Certainly! We can do that business on the spot. The account is easily made. I own 40 millions of florins; there are 40 millions of Germans. Consequently each German has to receive one florin; here is your share"; and giving one florin to each of the laborers, who looked at their money quite confused, he walked off smiling.

This teaches that the division of money is but an idle invention.

And with a little brain and thought everybody must easily come to the conclusion that the great number of those who confess to the principles of socialism cannot possibly consist of blockheads or rather lunatics, which they would prove to be if they demanded such nonsense. In Germany 700,000 voters (more than 1,000,000 at the last election) voted for socialist candidates. Can they all be crazy?

Therefore there must be something else in socialism. The number of socialists in Germany is constantly growing. Even Prince Bismarck confesses that. There must be something in it.

Now if we go to the meetings of the socialists, if we read their papers and pamphlets, what do we find?

They do not intend to introduce division of property; on the contrary, they are for abolishing its division.

This sounds strange, but it is so.

The socialists are of the opinion that division of property is flourishing in our society at present, and further they are of the opinion that this division is carried on in a very unjust manner. If you doubt, only think of our millionaires, and say whether those fellows did or did not understand how to divide and to appropriate to themselves large sums of money. Think of those swindling railroad and other companies. How many honest mechanics, farmers, laborers, have been swindled by them out of the little sums of money they had gathered by hard work and saving?

The socialists do not claim the honor of being the first to discover that this kind of distribution is going on everywhere throughout the world: they have learned it. Men who belong to their adversaries taught them. John Stuart Mill, who was opposed to socialism, said in one of his writings: "As we now see, the produce of labor is in an almost inverse ratio to the labor—the largest portions to those who have never worked at all, the next largest to those whose work is almost nominal, and so on in a descending scale, the remuneration dwindling as the work grows harder and more disagreeable, until the most fatiguing and exhausting bodily labor cannot count with certainty on being able to earn even the necessaries of life."

This sounds really dreadful, but if you look around and consult your own experience, is it not so? Certainly it is!

There are people who have a princely income, who plunge from one pleasure into another—and perhaps they have never in their life done the least useful thing; they need not work, they do not work themselves, but—they draw the proceeds of the work of other people and enjoy them.

On the other hand, look at him who "eats his bread in the sweat of his brow," look at the laborer who works for wages. If he is skillful, industrious, and strong, and if he is lucky enough to find employment, he may even be able to save a little. But the large majority of laborers cannot even think of that, in spite of all the hardships they undergo. When they have to stop work, they are as poor as when they began it. And many, many laborers, hard toiling men, are not able to protect themselves and their families from exposure and hunger. You need not go far, reader; you will find them everywhere. Ragged, pale-faced, despairing people will meet your gaze, and on inquiring you will learn that they were industrious, orderly workers, and that there are thousands, aye, hundreds of thousands of people living in the same miserable condition, in the cities as well as in the country.

Now look at the mechanics. A few of them may succeed; they may be able to reach a state in which they are safe from sorrow and care for the necessaries of life. The greater number of mechanics who have a little shop of their own and work on a small scale have to battle with poverty and care. Thousands, hundreds of thousands of mechanics fail in this battle; they give up their small establishments and turn wage-laborers. One manufacturer on a large scale deprives hundreds of small mechanics of their independent existence; one large shop or "cooperative store" crushes out fifty small shopkeepers. As things stand today, only those will succeed in the great struggle for life, in the universal competition, who command large means, a great amount of capital.

In commerce it is the same; merchants with small means rarely do a good business; many go bankrupt. Merchants with large means grow richer and richer. It is similar with farmers throughout the civilized countries of Europe and America. Owners of small farms just eke out a scanty living and have to work very hard; many gradually fall off; in general the peasantry get poorer. There is the usurer, who knows how to make a profit of a poor crop. Very frequently, we find that small farms are bought by owners of large farms to be united with them. Only the latter understand the business and are able to farm with profit.

Thus we see how the large class of those who work hard and assiduously do not make money, do not amass riches—on the contrary, many of them must suffer from want and care. But now, who creates these riches which fall to those who never worked, or whose work hardly deserves the name of work? Who else, but that selfsame working class?

For industry and work scarcely a living! Riches for those who never or seldom did anything useful! Do you call that just? Can you approve of such a state of things? I know you cannot. No sensible man can approve of it. And now say what you may against socialists—in this point they are right. This state of things cannot and must not continue. It is wrong, and therefore it must be changed. Socialists do not object to acquisitions made by honest work; on the contrary, they try to secure the product of work to the worker himself, and to protect it from the clutches of those who hitherto have been accustomed, not to work themselves, but only to draw profit from the work of others, and who, in doing so, are not content with a small part, but try to take the lion's share as it is in the fable.

But do the socialists not go too far in their zeal? It would, certainly, be well and just if it could be accomplished, that those who toil and work should be liberated from care and want, and those who have been idle so far should be forced to work also. But are not the socialists enemies of the property holders, and is not everybody who owns property threatened to lose it by the socialists, should they come into power—so much so that he would have to face penury and want? *Are they not Communists?*

These objections and reproaches have been made and are made. Let us not make light of them, but let us consider them quietly, in order to judge rightly and justly.

Before we go on we must explain two conceptions:

I. What is communism?

II. What is property?

About communism many lies have been set afloat, especially by people whose interest it was to do so, viz., by those money-making idlers, so that most people cannot but connect with the word communism the idea of rascality; communist and scoundrel of the worst kind appear to them to be synonymous terms. Therefore it is not an easy matter to speak of communism without running the risk of being condemned before one commences. Many people in such a case will not hear, will not see, will not judge. Their verdict is formed. All social prejudices are awakened and called forth by this expression. For that reason it is very difficult to come to a quiet understanding about it. But the reader, who has followed us so far, will follow us farther, not blindfolded, but using good common sense.

If we open our eyes and look around us, we find many beneficent and useful institutions established by many or by the whole people *in common*. In one place associations are formed, for instance, to save and shelter shipwrecked persons; at another place the *community* erect a school, or the State, the commonwealth, builds a harbor or a canal. In ordinary life everybody cares for himself, but in such cases as those just mentioned, people unite for advancing a *common, social* purpose. Experience teaches that in doing so they do admirably well; everyone of them who will reflect a little must confess that his own welfare is greatly advanced by such institutions of *common* usefulness. What would people be without *common* roads, *common* schools, etc., that is, such as are built and instituted at the cost of the *community* for *common* use? We should be in a terrible situation if all at once the different insurance companies were to cease to exist, whose object is to transfer a calamity, by which a person might be struck heavily, or perhaps be ruined, from his shoulders to the shoulders of many. If I chose I could mention here a thousand other things, but the above named *common* institutions will be sufficient. Now all these institutions are nothing but *communism*. For *communism* is nothing but the principle of the *common interests* of society. In everyday life everybody looks out for his own interest, even at the cost of his fellowmen; here cold, ugly egoism is dominant. The large cotton mills have ruined thousands and thousands of weavers; but who cares for hundreds of honest, industrious, happy people who are ruined by one mill? Who cares how many honest shoemakers are deprived of a living by the large shoe manufacturers? What does the usurer care for the victims of his avarice? What do the speculating swindlers care for the fate of the shareholders after their hard-earned savings are gone? Nobody ever thought of caring for such things, and it is my firm belief that a business man in our days who should show any consideration for the welfare of his fellowmen in his transactions would be certain to become a laughing stock. Egoism rules supreme. Everybody thinks of his own welfare, and does not care whether by doing so he destroys the welfare of others. "What business have I to care for others if I am comfortable?" In spite of the prevalence of egoism, the *common* interest of mankind is irrepressibly gaining ground. More and more people unite to cultivate it, more and more associations are formed, the activity of the state and the community is extending its influence over more and more objects. Who would have thought in former times of all the different associations which are formed today to advance any number of *common* interests of every description? Who had an idea in former years, that whole countries would be cut in all directions by railroads, that telegraphs would communicate news to the remotest parts of the world in an instant? Who could have predicted the admirable development of our postal system? Who thought of waterworks or of gas? Who had an idea of the modern arrangement of the fire brigades? The root of all these is *communism*. They represent the victory of *common* interests over hideous egoism.

To turn institutions of *common* interest to the use of all is the tendency of the age, and however people may curse at communism, they are bound to obey its mandates. Everywhere *common* interests press their claims, and *communism,* proudly elevating its head, marches on triumphantly with all conditions of human life in its train.

He who declares himself an enemy of communism declares himself an enemy of common interest, an enemy of society and mankind! Whoever wishes to annihilate communism will have to destroy the common roads, the schools, he will have to destroy the public gardens and parks, he will have to abolish the public baths, the theaters, the waterworks, all the public buildings; for instance, town halls, courts, all the hospitals, the alms houses; he will have to destroy the railroads, the telegraphs, the post office! For all these belong to *communism.*

Communism cannot be annihilated. It has its origin and root in human nature, like egoism. Everybody who will open his eyes must see that in the present time we are in full sail to land in its sheltering harbor. Sheltering? Yes, sheltering! Sheltering for the great majority of mankind for whom a better time will come, must come, when the common interest, the interest of all, will be the rule governing all our social conditions, when a barrier will be erected against egoism by the regard for the common or public welfare. If it happens nowadays that rich speculators make people in hard times pay exorbitant prices, and take advantage of a common calamity to double their wealth; or if railway shareholders make their own rates for freight, injuring by high prices producers as well as consumers, in order to gain a large dividend; or if manufacturers prefer running short time to selling at lower prices—those proceedings are considered "all right," for everybody can do with his own as he chooses. But everybody must see that such egoism is opposed to the common interest; and there will be a time when people will know how to protect the common interest against egoism. When that time has come it will be better for all; all will enjoy life, not those only who do so now at the cost of their fellow beings.

If you define communism in this way, some of my readers will say, we do not object to it; quite on the contrary, we must confess we belong to the communists ourselves. But this is not what people generally understand by the word "communism." We were to consider the communism which the socialists want to introduce, the communism with regard to property. We admit that they do not intend to divide, but do they not intend to abolish property? That is what we oppose; otherwise we would not object to it.

What is property? "To be sure that which a person owns, possesses!" Well! But now tell me, are you certain that the socialists are, or ever were, opposed to what Peter or Paul owns? Can you show me a sentence or passage from any of the writings or pamphlets of socialists which justifies the supposition that they intend to attack the property of any person?

You cannot, because such an idea never entered the head of a socialist. I should not wonder if you yourself have not thought sometimes that, considering the means and ways by which many amass their riches, it would be only just and right to take that ill-gotten wealth from their rascally owners. But it is a firm principle of socialism never to interfere with personal property in order to investigate its origin or to arrange it in a different way. Never and nowhere! And whoever asserts to the contrary either does not know the principles of socialism or willingly and knowingly asserts an untruth. The socialists deem an investigation into the origin of an acknowledged personal property an unnecessary trouble. They do not envy the Duke of Westminster or Lord Brassey their wealth. Although they perceive very well the constant changes with regard to property; although they investigate and are acquainted with the causes producing those changes; although they are well aware that fraud and meanness and violence in a great many instances are among those causes, they forbear to investigate how much these causes, how much others, have influenced the state of property of this or that single person. They consider the personal property an accomplished fact, and respect it; so much so that they consider stealing a crime. Every time revolution was victorious in Paris, bills were seen at the street corners threatening death to thieves. A remarkable fact is that Baron Rothschild fled suddenly from Paris as soon as these bills were posted. At Lyons during an insurrection in 1832 a man who had appropriated another man's property was shot by a laborer in command. During the reign of the Commune of 1871 Paris had no thieves, no prostitutes.

On the other hand, the right of the owner is not always respected in our time, but they are not socialists who violate the sanctity of property in these cases, although it must be confessed that in many instances an abrogation of the right of a property holder becomes necessary. Socialists cannot be reproached with ever having condemned houses or tracts of land for the purpose of building a street or opening a railroad. They certainly are not socialists who seize and sell houses or lots at auction for unpaid taxes. Nor will you find socialists who connive at those shamefully unjust appropriations of the property of others which however go on in a lawful form.

One thing, however, calls forth all the energy of the socialists, and they will try with all their might to remedy it. I have stated already, they do not care whether a person owns hundreds of thousands or millions of pounds, whether that person makes use of his money one way or the other, whether he spends it wisely or foolishly. He may spend his own as he chooses. But—these sums of money are not used simply to be spent, but to bring interest, to increase, if possible, the wealth of the possessor. Does he himself want to work, to do something useful? Far from it. His money works for him, his money makes money, as the saying is; or in plain English, his money is the channel through which the earnings of other industrious people flow into his pockets. Socialists call all kinds of property in this respect "capital," this expression comprising all means for production. And because one class of the people possess, by their wealth, these means—that is, capital—another, and by far the largest class, have only their physical or mental strength and skill for labor. Hence capital becomes a means for enslaving workers, forcing them to give up the greater part of their produce to him who owns the capital. They themselves obtain hardly enough to support themselves and their families, while the capitalists enjoy life and get richer without working at all. This is the point: dead property deprives living work of its fruits. Now since work should, by rights, own what it produces as its sole and legitimate earning, dead property becomes the bitter enemy of working life.

Hence the struggle of labor against capital.

Returning to the question, "What is property?" the answer given above appears unsatisfactory. We must add another question: To whom justly belongs what the working part of the human race produces?

The answer to this question is of greatest importance. Now it is capital which appropriates the greater part of it, leaving to the workers, who form by far the greater number, only so much of it that they may keep alive. They are treated like bees; they are robbed of the honey they make. This class is excluded from enjoying the blessings of civilization; the greater part of their product is taken by capital.

What right has the owner of a beehive to rob the bees of the fruit of their industry and labor ? They are his property, his is the might. What right has capital to rob the working class of the greater part of the fruit of their industry and labor? The wage-laborers, the mechanics, the farm hands, are they the property of the capitalist? Are they his slaves?

As things stand today, they are! Might is right, and by the title of such right the slaveowner considers the fruit of the work of his slaves his property; by this right, in former times, the feudal landowner made his serfs work for his employment and benefit. Slavery is injustice; sefdom is injustice; so the right which capital claims to the work of the worker is injustice. I would not like to be misunderstood here. As far as anything is the personal property of a person he may enjoy it as he chooses; nobody has a right to interfere. But as soon as he tries to use this property to enslave other people, he steps over his domain and must be checked. For I think it is acknowledged among civilized people that nobody has a right of ownership over his fellow men. Slavery has been abolished, serfdom has been abolished, so the power which capital exercises now will be abolished: its place will be occupied by the natural and sacred right of the worker to the proceeds of his work.

But—is not capital as necessary as labor? Can labor produce anything without capital? There must be raw material, there must be tools, there must be machines, there must be workshops, warehouses, and so forth; there must be soil to be tilled, etc. What can mere labor do without all these? But labor existed before capital, and made the tools, workshops, etc. Is it necessary that capital, now the foundation of successful labor, which has been produced by labor, should be owned by a few individuals? Has this minority a right to continue to take the best part of what labor produces?

The socialists take the side of labor. They maintain that it is everybody's duty to work, unless he be sick or crippled. They maintain that whoever is able to work and is not willing to do it, has no right to enjoy the fruits of the industry and labor of others.

If capitalists attempt to justify their way of making profit by saying that they have to run risks sometimes, that a part of their property might occasionally be lost, we answer that labor has nothing to do with that. The real cause of it is the competition among the employers, the custom to produce at random without investigating whether what is produced is really wanted. For the class of capitalists there is no risk, because its wealth increases every day. But there is a great risk for the working class. When business is slack, when wages go down, when many workers are out of employment—when, in consequence of this, mechanics, grocers, and even farmers suffer, the condition of the working part of the people is pitiable, and many suffer. The newspapers tell about that. Have they not had startling accounts of people starving to death in our great cities? Look at the local columns of the daily papers, and it is exceptional if there is no account of some family or other being poverty-stricken, of people driven to despair, driven to commit suicide by want. And all this in cities that have stores and warehouses crowded with goods. Is this no risk?

But how could this state of things be changed?

This, certainly, cannot be done of a sudden. There is a natural process of development in this, as in all changes that history has recorded so far. According to the reasoning of the socialists this development will be as follows:

Some time ago the middle class formed the firm and solid foundation of society and state. Machinery was invented and a change occurred. Manufacturing, and even farming to a certain extent, were conducted on a large scale; the middle-class people were pressed down into a class of wage-laborers, and were employed in large numbers by the manufacturers or employers. More and more this middle class ceases to be property holders; it is getting more and more difficult for the mechanics and small farmers to hold their ground; thus the middle class is constantly decreasing, the class of wage-laborers increasing, until there will be only two classes of people—rich and poor. In this process the number of rich people is diminishing, wealth becoming concentrated in the hands of comparatively few persons who are getting enormously rich.

But this process must soon have its limit. There will be a time when the large mass of the working people will feel its consequences unbearable, and will abolish it. That will be the time when communism will enter into its rights. Labor will then be organized according to a certain reasonable plan, and since, for that purpose, the use of the existing capital—comprising soil, houses, railways, shipping, manufactories, machines, etc.—will be necessary, those comparatively few possessors of all the wealth of the nations will have to be expropriated. Perhaps they then will consent themselves to such a measure, and give up everything necessary for production of their own accord, honored and praised for their patriotism and humanity, and remunerated deservedly; perhaps they will use their ample means to resist the common demand, and will perish, overwhelmed by the newly formed organization of the state. As I hinted before, in the new order of things all branches of labor will be organized in a similar way to the arrangements we see today in large factories, large estates, or institutions of the government. Unnecessary work will be avoided, and the reward for work done will be greater. Labor will not be wasted in making luxuries for the idle, but will be usefully employed in making the necessaries of life for other workers. It will be everybody's duty to work, hence everybody will have ample leisure for recreation and mental development. All will strive to ameliorate the conditions of the community they belong to; for, by doing so, everybody will improve his own private situation.

The basis of this state of things will be abolition of private property of individuals in such things as are necessary for production and transportation, such as land, factories, machines, railroads, etc., or which have been created for instruction and amusement, such as schools, colleges, museums, parks, etc. Personal property will be what is necessary or useful for private life. These are the outlines of a picture of future times. Nobody is able to state whether the development will go on exactly in the way we sketch out; but that does not matter, if only the underlying idea of communism is right. When Stephenson more than fifty years ago built the first railroad, he certainly did not plan all the locomotives, rails, signals, stations, etc., such as we find them today; but his idea was right, and it conquered the world. Thus the idea of socialism will conquer the world, for this idea is nothing but the real, well understood interest of mankind. It is an injustice that a large majority today must work hard and suffer want in order to procure a superabundance of enjoyment for a small minority of people who do not work. And who would deny that, if it is everybody's duty to work, if the production of unnecessary, nay even of injurious, articles is abolished, if production is organized in conformity with the real wants and pleasures of mankind—who would deny, I ask, that the standard of life of the whole human race might be raised infinitely above its present grade, that the great mass of human beings might enter into that sphere of life worthy of a human being, from which they have been rigorously excluded so far?

Let me point out to you an example of organized labor in one branch, to show the benefit of such an arrangement. How would it be possible to send a letter to any place in the United Kingdom for a penny, a postcard for a half-penny, a letter to America for 2 1/2d., if the postmasters in the different parts of the world were private contractors like the merchants and manufacturers of today, if we had not the communistic arrangement of the post? Formerly the post was also a private business in nearly all the countries of Europe, like our railroads, and the owners of this institution derived a princely income from it, although its use was very limited. And well arranged as our post office may be, it might be better yet, and will be more convenient in time.

Similar benefits would arise from the reorganization of all branches of human activity. Look at our railroads—might they not be the property of the community at large as well as the high roads, instead of being a monopoly in the hands of private persons, whose sole object is to enrich themselves at the cost of their fellow citizens? If so, it has been proved that you could go to any part of these islands with a shilling ticket, just as a letter goes now by post with a penny stamp. In this manner one branch after the other will be organized according to the ideas of communism, perhaps by classes of people who are far from admitting the truth of the principles of socialism, of communism, by classes who are inimical to it—because they do not understand it—and who are still narrow-minded enough to shut their ears and their eyes to everything that does not tend to their private interest.

This is not yet enough. All means for transportation, such as ships, etc., must come into the hands of the community at large; so must all means for production. This demand of socialism has caused people to accuse the socialists of hostility to property, even to the property of those who own but a little. But who is it that actually drives the owner of small means from his house, from his soil? Is it the socialist? It is the large capitalist, the large landowner! As the magnet attracts iron filings, so large capital attracts the small sums round it. And the same capitalists who in all directions seize what they can get, try to persuade the small owners to beware of socialism, because it is ready to tear their property from them. What a shameful falsehood! Socialism only teaches the way in which in a future time people will try to reestablish justice and a more equal condition of life for the whole community; while the owners of small property are being robbed of the little they own, not by socialists—they have neither the power nor the desire to do so—but by the rich capitalists.

And this way is well-organized labor.

This certainly includes expropriation of those who have expropriated the mass of the people, and restitution of all means of production to those who made them. Socialism is the true and only friend of the man of small means, for it is the party of the working people. Large property is the natural enemy of small property, as long as it has not been able to seize and devour it.

Moreover, socialism, far from intending to abolish any property today or tomorrow, only predicts that there will be a time, not suddenly provoked, but brought on by historical development, when the working people will insist upon their right to the product of their own work, against the privilege which property enjoys with regard to the work of others.

The conception of "property of capital" will be transformed gradually into the conception of "property of work."

Nowhere, you will perceive, is abolition of property thought of by socialists, and nobody, I trust, will object to the change just mentioned. The development of mankind to greater perfection never was and never will be arrested by the prevailing laws concerning property. For instance, it was not arrested, when humanity demanded abolition of slavery, by the pretended divine right of the slaveowners. And if such rights and laws demand that humanity stop its progress, such demand is madness. Laws and rights concerning property are subjected to constant changes, when such changes are in the interest of progress. But even in our better institutions injustice is ruling, and the change just spoken of will abolish that injustice and lead mankind to a higher state of perfection. At the bottom of our institutions there is a remnant of slavery; as soon as capital shall cease to govern, wage-labor and the rest of slavery will be abolished.

Freedom and equality will then be no longer empty and cheap phrases, but will have a meaning; when all men are really free and equal, they will honor and advance one another. The working man will then no longer be deprived of the fruit of his work, his property, and everybody who will work will be able to spend a good deal more in food, clothing, lodging, recreation, pleasure, and instruction than he can spend at present.

If the socialists had nothing to offer to the suffering people but the consolation that communism will bring help at some future time, when the condition of life, nearly unbearable now, will have become quite so, this consolation would be poor. Long enough a future state of bliss has been held out to suffering mankind, in which they would be rewarded for all the wants and sufferings and pains of this world, and now most people have lost confidence in such empty promises. They demand an amelioration: not words, not promises, but facts. They do not want to expect, with resignation, what may come after death: they demand a change of their unfortunate situation while living on earth.

The interests of all workers are the same! This is best shown by the fact that in many strikes working shopkeepers are in favor of the wage-laborers. Low wages are unfavorable to the farmer as well as to the mechanic, for when wages are low the struggle for economical independence is more difficult; large capital increases at the expense of small property. If the working people would only learn to comprehend the solidarity of their interests!

As it is with the increase of wages, so it is with the decrease of working hours. Eight hours' work a day is judged sufficient by physicians. A person who has worked properly eight hours a day ought to have done his duty, and has a right to request some hours for recreation, for instruction, and for his family. Those who are the loudest in complaining of the laziness of the working men would soon make wry faces if they were compelled to work only six hours a day. This decreasing of the working hours will better the condition of the whole of the working class. Everybody can easily see that. Even in the country it could be done, although there such a shortening will meet with the greatest objections, but it will be done. What a great benefit will be achieved by this measure alone! Whole armies of paupers, tramps, etc., will find useful employment. They will disappear, and with them a great deal of mischief and crime.

Now if the wage-laborers of the cities and manufacturing places will be ready to lead the van in the struggle for the interest of labor, the rest of the whole working class have no right to put themselves in the position of idle, indifferent, or even grudging and hostile spectators. On the contrary, it is the duty of the whole working class to participate in this struggle, for this war is carried on in the interest of all workers, and the wage-laborers who have taken up the gauntlet are the pioneers for the human race.

But in order to carry on this war successfully, the workers must be organized. Singly and isolated they are powerless; if all would unite for the same purpose, they would be a formidable power which nothing could resist. You may easily break many single matches, but you may try in vain to break a whole bundle of them tied together.

With regard to this, the socialists have the gratification of seeing that their endeavors have not been fruitless. In Germany socialism already forms a respectable power, which has puzzled even the great Bismarck. They have been able to elect twenty-four (now more than thirty) representatives into the German Parliament, who, by their untiring activity, by the speeches they have delivered, have opened the eyes of hundreds of thousands of people in Germany. And who would venture to pretend that those men strove for something that was bad, that they betrayed the interests of their constituents? But not only in Parliament, but in a great many municipal assemblies also we find members belonging to the working class or representing its interests.

And all this has been accomplished in a few years. It is only twenty-four years since the labor party unfurled its banner there. And what has been tried and done during those twenty-two years to suppress the labor movement! It has been ridiculed, scorned, incriminated. Many of its prominent leaders have been put into prison. Many were deprived of their offices and situations, and customers. In spite of all this it grew and thrived. In France, Belgium, Holland, Denmark, Austria, Russia, Italy, Spain, and now in England—everywhere throughout the civilized world socialism has taken root. Everywhere it has begun the struggle against capital, monopoly, and class rule, and its victory is assured. Concerning socialism there might be said what was said in olden times about Christianity: if it is bad it will die of its own badness; if it is good it will conquer the world in spite of all persecutions!

And socialism will conquer the world. Its principles will carry the whole human race to a higher state of perfection.

Reader, you may judge for yourself and decide either in favor of or against socialism. If you think the aims and endeavors of the socialists deserve your hatred, try to crush them; if, on the contrary, you are convinced that they are good, that the socialists endeavor to promote the happiness and welfare of mankind, join them! And if you do not like to act publicly, help them secretly. Try to propagate their principles among your acquaintances, explaining them in your intercourse, destroying the falsehoods brought against them. Tell them that the socialists form the true and only party of the working people. And if you are a capitalist yourself, reflect how much nobler it is to help to promote the welfare of the many than to serve only your own interest, ugly and hideous egoism.

3
PRIESTESS OF A COUNTERCULTURE

Victoria Woodhull
TRIED AS BY FIRE

*The sort of cultural radicalism espoused by Victoria Woodhull (1838–1927)
and her circle won favor among Bohemian New Yorkers, but German Marxists trying to establish some reasonable version of scientific socialism on this
soil treated it with a disdain matched only by that of Anthony Comstock, the
self-appointed guardian of American sexual purity in the late nineteenth
century. Although the sins of Section 12 of the American affiliates of the
International Workingmen's Association were numerous and included its
heavily bourgeois and intellectual membership, nothing in the activities of
Woodhull more offended Sorge than her treatment of the women's question as
more important than the emancipation of workers. Woodhull's radicalism
was not single-minded enough to fit a Marxist program of revolution. Her
defense of "free love" in the following selection took straight aim at the
hypocrisy of Victorian society; and if many radicals decried her indifference
to economic questions, others have praised her position, arguing that any
revolution must remain a myth until dominant cultural values have been
crumpled along a wide front.*

The sexual relations of humanity are fundamental to its continuous
existence, and are, therefore, the most important into which men and
women enter. It is vital that they should be entered into properly, that
they should be understood clearly, and, still more so, that they should
be lived rightly. Nevertheless, the world has virtually declared that
this shall not be. It denies all knowledge of them to the young, and
permits the youth and the maiden to walk blindfolded into their
exploration, ignorant even of their own functions, only taking special
care that the journey, once begun, may never be retraced or stopped. It
has left the travelers, as it were, in the mid-ocean of what may be their

source. Victoria Woodhull, *Tried as by Fire; or the True and the False,
Socially.* (New York, 1874) pp. 5–8, 23–25, 39–44.

eternal happiness, if the course pursued be right; or their certain destruction if the chosen way be wrong, without chart or compass, subjected to winds which drive them, they know not where, and to currents and countercurrents, for which no haven of safety is provided; and, alas! they too often go down to untimely graves, victims to a willful ignorance. Such are the results of modern social regulations.

I am conducting a campaign against marriage, with the view of revolutionizing the present theory and practice. I have strong convictions that, as a bond or promise to love another until death, it is a fraud upon human happiness; and that it has outlived its day of usefulness. These convictions make me earnest, and I enter the fight meaning to do the institution all possible harm in the shortest space of time; meaning to use whatever weapons may fall in my way with which to stab it to the heart, so that its decaying carcass may be buried, and clear the way for a higher and a better institution.

I speak only what I know, when I say that the most intelligent and really virtuous people of all classes have outgrown this institution; that they are constantly and systematically unfaithful to it; despise and revolt against it as a slavery; and only submit to a semblance of fidelity to it, from the dread of a falsely educated public opinion and a sham morality, which are based on the ideas of the past, but which no longer really represent the convictions of anybody.

Nor is this hypocritical allegiance the only or the greatest or gravest consideration that is capturing the opinions of the really intelligent. It is rapidly entering into the public thought, that there should be, at least, as much attention given to breeding and rearing children, as is given to horses, cattle, pigs, fowls and fruit. A little reflection shows that the scientific propagation of children is a thing of paramount importance; as much above and beyond that of personal property as children are above dogs and cats. And this conviction, practically considered, also shows that the union of the sexes, for propagation, should be consummated under the highest and best knowledge, and in such manner and by such methods as will produce the best results. These considerations are so palpable that they cannot be ignored; and they look to the early supercedure of the institution of marriage by some better system for the maintenance of women as mothers, and children as progeny. This is as much a foregone conclusion with all the best thinkers of today as was the approaching dissolution of slavery, no more than ten years before its final fall.

But in the meantime men and women tremble on the verge of the revolution, and hesitate to avow their convictions; but aware of their rights, and urged by the impulses of their natures, they act upon the new theories while professing allegiance to the old. In this way an organized hypocrisy has become a main feature of modern society, and poltroonery, cowardice, and deception rule supreme in its domain. The continuation of such falsity for a generation, touching one of the most sacred interests of humanity, will eradicate the source of honesty from the human soul. Every consideration of expediency, therefore, demands that someone lead the van in a relentless warfare against marriage, so that its days may be made short.

This is my mission. I entered the contest, bringing forward, in addition to the wise and powerful words of others, such arguments as my own inspirations and reflections suggested. No sooner had I done this, however, than the howl of persecution sounded in my ears. Instead of replying to my arguments, I was assaulted with shameful abuse; and I was astonished to find that the most persistent and slanderous and foulmouthed accusations came from precisely those whom I happened often to know should have been, from their practices, the last to raise their voices against anyone, and whom, if I had felt so disposed, I could have easily silenced. But simply as personality or personal defense or spiteful retort, I have almost wholly abstained during these years of sharp conflict from making use of the rich resources at my command for this kind of attack and defense, and, passing the vile abuse which has beset me, have steadfastly pressed on in the warfare.

In a single instance only have I departed from this course.[1] Circumstances conspired to put me in possession of certain facts regarding the most prominent divine in the land, and from him I learned that he too was not only false to the old dispensation, but unfaithful to the new—a double hypocrisy, over which I hesitated many months, doubting if I should use it. It was not that I desired or had any right to personally attack this individual; but something had to be done to break down the partition walls of prejudice that prevented public consideration of the sexual problem, and fully to launch it upon the tide of popular discussion. This revolution, like every other that ever preceded it, and as every other that ever will follow it, must have its terrific cost, if not in blood and treasure, then still in the less tangible but equally real sentimental injury of thousands of sufferers. It was

---

[1]Woodhull refers in this passage to her role in raising the charge of adultery against Henry Ward Beecher, pastor of the Plymouth Church in Brooklyn, New York. Beecher was acquitted of the charges in a church trial, but the scandal left a permanent mark on the reputation of this clergyman. Ed.

necessary that somebody should be hurt. I cast the thunderbolt into the very center of the socio-religio-moralistic camp of the enemy and struck their chieftain, and the world trembled at the blow. In twenty years not anybody will say that I was wrong, any more than anybody now says that the old leaders of the antislavery revolution were wrong in attacking slavery in the concrete.

My purpose was accomplished. Whereas before none had dared to broach the sexual question, it is now on everybody's lips; and where it would have been impossible for a man, even, to address a public, promiscuous audience anywhere without being mobbed, a woman may now travel the country over, and from its best rostrums, speak the last truth about sexuality, and receive respectful attention, even enthusiastic encouragement. The world has come to its senses—has been roused to the real import and meaning of this terrible question, and to realize that only through its full and candid examination may we hope to save the future from utter demoralization.

But why do I war upon marriage? I reply frankly: first, because it stands directly in the way of any improvement in the race, insisting upon conditions under which improvement is impossible; and second, because it is, as I verily believe, the most terrible curse from which humanity now suffers, entailing more misery, sickness, and premature death than all other causes combined. It is at once the bane of happiness to the present, and the demon of prophetic miseries to the future—miseries now concealed beneath its deceptive exterior, gilded over by priestcraft and law, to be inwrought in the constitutions of coming generations to mildew and poison their lives.

Of what in reality does this thing consist, which, while hanging like a pall over the world, is pretendedly the basis of its civilization? The union of the opposites in sex is an instinct inherent in the constitutions of mankind; but legal marriage is an invention of man, and so far as it performs anything, it defeats and perverts this natural instinct. Marriage is a license for sexual commerce to be carried on without regard to the consent or dissent of this instinct. Everything else that men and women may desire to do, except to have sexual commerce, may be and is done without marriage.

Marriage, then, is a license merely—a permission to do something that it is inferred or understood ought not to be done without it. In other words, marriage is an assumption by the community that it can regulate the sexual instincts of individuals better than they can themselves; and they have been so well regulated that there is scarcely such a thing known as a natural sexual instinct in the race; indeed, the regulations have been so at war with nature that this instinct has become a morbid disease, running rampant or riotous in one sex, and feeding its insatiable maw upon the vitality of the other, finally resulting in disgust or impotency in both.

Isn't this a pretty commentary on regulation? Talk of Social Evil bills! The marriage law is the most damnable Social Evil bill—the most consummate outrage on woman—that was ever conceived. Those who are called prostitutes, whom these bills assume to regulate, are free women, sexually, when compared to the slavery of the poor wife. They are at liberty, at least to refuse; but she knows no such escape. "Wives, submit yourselves to your husbands," is the spirit and the universal practice of marriage.

Of all the horrid brutalities of this age, I know of none so horrid as those that are sanctioned and defended by marriage. Night after night there are thousands of rapes committed, under cover of this accursed license; and millions—yes, I say it boldly, knowing whereof I speak —millions of poor, heartbroken, suffering wives are compelled to minister to the lechery of insatiable husbands, when every instinct of body and sentiment of soul revolts in loathing and disgust. All married persons know this is truth, although they may feign to shut their eyes and ears to the horrid thing, and pretend to believe it is not. The world has got to be startled from this pretense into realizing that there is nothing else now existing among pretendedly enlightened nations, except marriage, that invests men with the right to debauch women, sexually, against their wills. Yet marriage is held to be synonymous with morality! I say, eternal damnation sink such morality!

When I think of the indignities which women suffer in marriage, I cannot conceive how they are restrained from open rebellion. Compelled to submit their bodies to disgusting pollution! Oh, Shame! where hast thou fled, that the fair face of womanhood is not suffused with thy protesting blushes, stinging her, at least into self-respect, if not into freedom itself! Am I too severe? No, I am only just!

Prate of the abolition of slavery! There was never servitude in the world like this one of marriage. It not only holds the body to whatever polluting use—abstracting its vitality, prostituting its most sacred functions, and leaving them degraded, debauched, and diseased—but utterly damning the soul for all aspiration, and sinking it in moral and spiritual torpor. Marriage not slavery! Who shall dare affirm it? Let woman practically assert her sexual freedom and see to what it will lead! It is useless to mince terms. We want the truth; and that which I have about this abomination I will continue to give, until it is abolished. . . .

When a limit is placed upon anything that by nature is free, its action becomes perverted. All the various attractions in the world are but so many methods by which love manifests itself. The attraction which draws the opposites in sex together is sexual love. The perverted action of sexual love, when limited by law or otherwise, is lust. All sexual manifestations that are not free are the perverted action of love—are lust. So, logically, the methods enforced by man to ensure purity convert love into lust. Legal sexuality is enforced lust. All the D.D.'s and LL.D.'s in the world, though they have all the mental gifts and the tongues of angels, cannot controvert the proposition.

This brings us to a still more serious part of my subject. Remember I am to withhold nothing—no fact, no advice. We are now face to face with the most startling and the most common fact connected with the miseries of marriage. But I know of no author, no speaker, who has dared to call attention to, or to suggest a remedy for it, or even to hint at it as needing a remedy, or to recognize its existence in any manner.

It will be remembered that early in the evening I showed that marriage when analyzed, is a license to cohabit sexually. Now I am going to show that the enforcement of this method eventually defeats the original object. I state it without fear of contradiction by fact or of refutation by argument that it is the common experience among the married who have lived together strictly according to the marriage covenant, for from five to ten years, that they are sexually estranged. There may be, I know there are, exceptions to this rule, but they are the exceptions and not the rule. It is a lamentable fact that all over this country there is a prolonged wail going up on account of this condition. Sexual estrangement in from five to ten years! Think of it, men and women whom Nature has blessed with such possibilities for happiness as are conferred on no other order of creation—your God-ordained capacity blasted, prostituted to death, by enforced sexual relations where there is neither attraction or sexual adaptation; and by ignorance of sexual science!

Some may assert, as many do, that failure in sexual strength is intellectual and spiritual gain. Don't harbor the unnatural lie. Sexuality is the physiological basis of character and must be preserved as its balance and perfection. To kill out the sexual instinct by any unnatural practice or repression, is to emasculate character; is to take away that which makes what remains impotent for good—fruitless, not less intellectually and spiritually than sexually.

It is to do even more than this. From the moment that the sexual instinct is dead in any person, male or female, from that moment such person begins actually to die. It is the fountain from which life proceeds. Dry up the fountain and the stream will disappear. It is only a question of time, and of how much is obtained from other fountains, when the stream will discharge its last waters into the great ocean of life.

Others again seem to glory over the fact that they never had any sexual desire, and to think that this desire is vulgar. What! Vulgar! The instinct that creates immortal souls vulgar! Who dare stand up amid Nature, all prolific and beautiful, whose pulses are ever bounding with the creative desire, and utter such sacrilege! Vulgar, indeed! Vulgar, rather, must be the mind that can conceive such blasphemy. No sexual passion, say you ? Say, rather, a sexual idiot, and confess that your life is a failure, your body an abortion, and no longer bind your shame upon your brow or herald it as purity. Call such stuff purity. Bah! Be honest, rather, and say it is depravity.

It is not the possession of strong sexual powers that is to be deprecated. They are that necessary part of human character which is never lacking in those who leave their names standing high in the historic roll. The intellect, largely developed, without a strong animal basis is never prolific of good in any direction. Evenly balanced natures, in which there are equal development and activity of all departments, are those which move the world palpably forward for good; but if superiority of any kind is desirable at all, let it be in the animal, since with this right, the others may be cultivated to its standard. If this be wanting, however, all possible cultivation, intellectually, will only carry the individual further away from balance, and make the character still more "out of tune" with nature. These are physiological facts inherent in the constitution of mankind, and they cannot be ignored with impunity. No reliable theory of progressive civilization can ever be established that does not make them its chief cornerstone, because they are the foundation upon which civilization rests.

It is the misuse, the abuse, the prostitution of the sexual instinct that is to be deprecated. Like all other capacities, it needs to be educated, cultivated, exercised rightly, and to do this is to live in accordance with nature and as commanded by the higher law, that law which everyone finds deep-seated in his soul, and whose voice is the truest guide. When the world shall rise from its degradation into the sphere of this law, when the sexual act shall be the religion of the world, as it is now my religion, then, and then only, may we reasonably hope that its redemption is nigh.

What other religion so near alike to God—the all-loving, all-creating Father; or so much in harmony with Nature—the ever-receptive and ever-evolving Mother. Let your religious faith be what it may if it does not include the sexual act it is impotent. Make that act the most divine of all your worship. Let it be unto you without spot or blemish. Let it rise unto God a continual incense of piety and holiness, and be henceforth resurrected from the debauch in which the ages have sunk it. This is my religion—the fundamental principles for the generation of the race. Let it be yours and all mankind's, and with no other, the salvation long sought, long prayed for, long prophesied and long sung will soon be found. Discard it, put its life and health-giving blessings aside, and all the other religions ever conceived or dreamed, or that may be conceived of, dreamed, combined, will be impotent to usher in the glad time. . . .

I make the claim boldly, that from the very moment woman is emancipated from the necessity of yielding the control of her sexual organs to man to ensure a home, food, and clothing, the doom of sexual demoralization will be sealed. From that moment there will be no sexual intercourse except such as is desired by women. It will be a complete revolution in sexual matters, in which men will have to take a back seat and be content to be servants where they have been masters so long. The present system is at variance with everything in nature. Everywhere, except among men and women, the female has supreme authority in the domain of sex, and the male never pretends to oppose it, nor to appeal from its decisions. Compare men and women with the animals and see how far below them they have fallen in this regard. Yet among animals the principle of freedom is thoroughly exemplified. Why are they not degraded, debauched and diseased? Simply because the female is the dominant power in sex. What would be the result among animals were the barbarous rule of marriage enforced; were the female to be compelled to submit herself without reserve to the lecherous instincts of the male? It would be the same that has obtained among women—disease everywhere, until there is scarcely a sexually healthy woman past the age of puberty to be found. This is the purity, this the morality, this the divinity of mariage. Oh, God! is there no power that can restore woman to the level of the brutes? Is their nothing that can rescue her from this shameless condition, from this pollution, this nastiness?

To woman, by nature, belongs the right of sexual determination.

When the instinct is aroused in her, then, and then only, should commerce follow. When woman rises from sexual slavery into freedom, into the ownership and control of her sexual organs, and man is obliged to respect this freedom, then will this instinct become pure and holy; then will woman be raised from the iniquity and morbidness in which she now wallows for existence, and the intensity and glory of her creative functions be increased a hundredfold; then may men and women, like the beasts or the birds, if they will, herd together, and the instinct in woman, by the law of natural attraction and adaptation, rouse in man its answering counterpart, and its counterpart only.

This is the purity at which I aim; this is the holiness to which I would have woman and, through her functions, the sexual relations elevated; this is the glory with which I would have woman crowned; this is what it means to be virtuous; this what it means to be pure. Again I ask, is there a man or woman who hears me who will ever dare hereafter to associate this doctrine with the debased and the low, and call it an attempt to descend further into lust and license?

Oh, woman! would that the beautiful, the shining, the redeemed of heaven could come to you in their white-robed purity and sing in your ears the blessed song of the angels who "neither marry nor are given in marriage," and who live in their own natural element of freedom. Oh! that they could come to you as they have to me, and show how, through you, as represented by Eve—through your sexual slavery to men—has sin and misery and crime been introduced into the world; and how through the assertion and maintenance of your sexual freedom and purity only can "the seed of the woman bruise the serpent's head," and humanity be restored to its original sexual purity, the Scripture fulfilled and the millennium ushered in.

Instead of opposing this doctrine, the churches should see that through its propagation only can their sacred prophecies be realized. Instead of denouncing me the ministers ought to be my most earnest advocates, not merely because through the theory of free love only can their lives be justified, but because by its practice alone can salvation come to the world. They have been working at the wrong end of salvation; they have been trying to save souls while their bodies were damned. Now let them save bodies, and the souls will take care of themselves. I should be glad to believe that these clerical persons are honest, but I cannot. They know the sad lives of thousands of women, suffering and yearning for comfort and sympathy; these women go to their pastors for relief, and I have the very best of reasons for believing, indeed, I know that in numerous instances, they not only get that for which they yearn, but also that further comfort and sympathy to which the others naturally lead, and which the ministers know they can so safely administer. This is another reason to be added to the matter of fees, which I have already mentioned, why this class do not wish the marriage relations disturbed. The ministers, lawyers, and doctors have a monopoly of this field, and they intend to keep it.

The world will have a genuine surprise some day when it shall awaken to the truth, as I know it, about the churches; to a knowledge of the kind of currency in which lawyers often receive their divorce fees. As this, however, is none of my business, I shall let the world take its own time about it. But I sometimes think it would be only a just reward for their stupidity were husbands to be shown why it is that their wives are so earnest in religious matters. Everybody knows that the churches would totter and tumble if it were not for the women. Men have mostly grown out of churches and attend them because their families wish it, so that the "pew rent" may be paid. There are many churches besides Plymouth in which half the women are in love with their pastors; and in these cases I think it safe to say, as it is in that of Plymouth, it is usually reciprocated.

But as to the difficulty of freedom for woman: there is but one, and that is pecuniary independence. I know that opposers refer to the condition of women in Greece and Rome, when there were few restrictions sexually, and use it as an argument against freedom now. But it doesn't apply, and I will show you why. In those times it mattered not whether there were marriage laws or not. In either case woman was dependent upon her sex for support; if married, then upon her husband; if not married, then upon her lover.

So the mere abolition of marriage does not necessarily mean sexual freedom for woman. I do not hesitate to admit that marriage has played its necessary part in the evolution of society; nor that among a people where women have a very limited position in the industrial organization, that it provides them a support. I will go so far even as to say that, so long as women prefer to depend upon the sale of their sexual favors rather than upon their industrial capacities for support, that marriage may be deemed a sort of protection. But I also hold that, to a woman who prefers rather to rely upon her own talent for support, marriage is intolerable.

This is the same argument that was used by the slaveholders. "Slaves," they said, "were better off as slaves than they could be, free. They need to be taken care of; and until they are capable of self-support it is best that slavery continue." The slaves themselves generally coincided with this idea. Only a few of the more intelligent saw that the argument was a deceit.

So now do most women coincide with the same argument as applied to marriage. Only a few who have solved the question for themselves, see that it is fallacious. In spite of the argument the antislavery revolution came, and violently cast the slaves upon their own resources. Who is there who now dare say their condition is not improved? So will it be with women. They will hesitate to take the responsibility of freedom. They will say: "I prefer to rely upon my sex a little longer." But the revolution will come eventually, and thrust them upon their own resources; and in ten years nobody will be found to doubt that their condition has been improved.

But the old argument as applied to women is fallacious in still another way, as I will show. Suppose that all the women in the land, on a given day, should rise and throw off the yoke of marriage, and declare and hold themselves free, how long would it be before the men would accede to any terms? Do you think it would be a month—three weeks—two weeks? I haven't the slightest idea that they would hold out a single week. Women are entirely unaware of their power. Like an elephant led by a string, they are subordinated by a writing, drawn up by just those who are most interested in holding them in slavery. I am sometimes almost out of patience at the servility with which women fawn upon their masters, when they might lead them by the nose wherever they please.

It is sometimes asked: "If what you say is true, and that marriage is a curse, why did not the deprecated results obtain years ago?" I will show you why. It will be remembered that it used to be said by the slaveholders that the moment a slave got the freedom crotchet into his head he was no longer of any account. A negro was a good slave so long as the idea of freedom was not born in his soul. Whenever this birth occurred, he began to feel the galling of his chains.

It is the same with women. So long as they entertain the idea that their natural destiny is to be owned and cared for by some man, whom they are to repay by the surrender of their person, they are good, legal wives; but from the moment the notion that they have an individual right to themselves—to the control of their bodies and maternal functions—has birth in their souls, they become bad wives. They rebel in their souls, if not in words and deeds; and the legal claims of their husbands become a constant source of annoyance, and the enforcement of their legal rights an unbearable thing. . . .

I said at the outset that I am endeavoring to effect a revolution in marriage, or rather to replace the institution by a better method of providing for women as mothers and children as progeny. Everybody admits that our social system is far from perfect. Society, like everything else in the universe, evolves by natural laws. Marriage is not the perfect condition. It will be replaced by another and more perfect, which will be a legitimate outcome of the old. As republicanism in politics is a legitimate child of constitutional monarchy, so in socialism shall personal freedom be the offspring of legal limitation; and when it shall come, not anybody will doubt its parentage or question its legitimacy.

Sexual freedom, then, means the abolition of prostitution both in and out of marriage; means the emancipation of woman from sexual slavery and her coming into ownership and control of her own body; means the end of her pecuniary dependence upon man, so that she may never, even seemingly, have to procure whatever she may desire or need by sexual favors; means the abrogation of forced pregnancy, of ante-natal murder, of undesired children; means the birth of love-children only, endowed by every inherited virtue that the highest exaltation can confer at conception, by every influence for good to be obtained during gestation, and by the wisest guidance and instruction onto manhood, industrially, intellectually, and sexually.

It means no more sickness, no more poverty, no more crime: it means peace, plenty, and security, health, purity, and virtue; it means the replacement of money-getting as the aim of life by the desire to do good; the closing of hospitals and asylums, and the transformation of prisons, jails, and penitentiaries into workshops and scientific schools; and of lawyers, doctors, and ministers into industrial artisans; it means equality, fraternity, and justice raised from the existence which they now have in name only, into practical life; it means individual happiness, national prosperity and universal good.

Ultimately, it means more than this even. It means the establishment of cooperative homes, in which thousands who now suffer in every sense shall enjoy all the comforts and luxuries of life, in the place of the isolated households which have no care for the misery and destitution of their neighbors. It means for our cities, the conversion of innumerable huts into immense hotels, as residences; and the combination of all industrial enterprises upon the same plan; and for the country, the cooperative conduct of agriculture by the maximum of improvements for labor-saving, and the consequent reduction of muscular toil to the minimum. And it means the inter-cooperation of all these in a grand industrial organization to take the places of the present governments of the world, whose social basis shall be all people united in the great human family as brothers and sisters.

So after all I am a very promiscuous free lover. I want the love of you all, promiscuously. It makes no difference who or what you are, old or young, black or white, pagan, Jew, or Christian, I want to love you all and be loved by you all; and I mean to have your love. If you will not give it to me now, these young, for whom I plead, will in after years bless Victoria Woodhull for daring to speak for their salvation. It requires a strong and a pure woman to go before the world and attack its most cherished institution. No one who has not passed through the fiery furnace of affliction and been purged of selfishness by the stern hand of adversity and become emancipated from public opinion could stand the load of opprobium that I have been forced to carry. I sometimes grow weary under its weight and sigh for rest, but my duty to my sex spurs me on. Therefore I want your sympathy, your sustaining love, to go with me and bless me; and when I leave you for other fields of labor and stand upon other rostrums, fearing I may not be able to do my duty, I want to feel the yearnings of your hearts following me with prayers that my efforts may be blessed. I want the blessings of these fathers, the affections of these sons, the benedictions of these mothers, and the prayers of these daughters to follow me everywhere, to give me strength to endure the labor, courage to speak the truth, and a continued faith that the right will triumph.

And may the guardian angels who are hovering over you carry the benign light of freedom home to your souls to bless each sorrowing heart, to relieve each suffering body, and to comfort each distressed spirit as it hath need, is the blessing which I leave with you.

Part Two

INDIVIDUALISM, PRIVATE PROPERTY, AND THE COLLECTIVE STATE—SOME NINETEENTH CENTURY VIEWS

1

LAISSEZ-FAIRE AS A RADICAL MANIFESTO

Henry George
PROGRESS AND POVERTY

Henry George (1839-1897) believed in the sanctity of most forms of private property. He saw no invidious distinctions in a certain measure of economic inequality, valued competition, and insisted, in keeping with traditional liberal fears of a strong state, that government should as much as possible stay out of the affairs of ordinary Christian citizens. But George could not abide poverty in a country where there were resources for all to share affluence. After the publication of Progress and Poverty *in 1879, from which this selection is taken, George emerged as the best-known opponent of the Malthusian notion that population pressures made general prosperity an impossible ideal. George hoped through the imposition of his single tax on rent, a measure that aimed at the least possible extension of state authority, to make private gain impossible except through the personal exertion of labor and talent. His formula to preserve individual sovereignty while advancing the cause of social justice passed over a host of economic problems; but however much socialists condemned the inadequacy of his single tax idea, George accomplished what a moribund socialist movement in the 1880s could never have done. In arousing many Americans to the ills of industrial society, he did as much to change the direction of reform thought as the efforts of any one man could.*

When it is proposed to abolish private property in land, the first question that will arise is that of justice. Though often warped by habit, superstition, and selfishness into the most distorted forms, the sentiment of justice is yet fundamental to the human mind, and whatever dispute arouses the passions of men, the conflict is sure to rage, not so much as to the question "Is it wise?" as to the question "Is it right?"

SOURCE. Henry George, *Progress and Poverty* (New York, 1881), pp. 299–308, 362–366, 489–490, 493–496.

This tendency of popular discussions to take an ethical form has a cause. It springs from a law of the human mind; it rests upon a vague and instinctive recognition of what is probably the deepest truth we can grasp. That alone is wise which is just; that alone is enduring which is right. In the narrow scale of individual actions and individual life this truth may be often obscured, but in the wider field of national life it everywhere stands out.

I bow to this arbitrament, and accept this test. If our inquiry into the cause which makes low wages and pauperism the accompaniments of material progress has led us to a correct conclusion, it will bear translation from terms of political economy into terms of ethics, and as the source of social evils show a wrong. If it will not do this, it is disproved. If it will do this, it is proved by the final decision. If private property in land be just, then is the remedy I propose a false one; if, on the contrary, private property in land be unjust, then is this remedy the true one.

What constitutes the rightful basis of property? What is it that enables a man to justly say of a thing, "It is mine!" From what springs the sentiment which acknowledges his exclusive right as against all the world? Is it not, primarily, the right of a man to himself, to the use of his own powers, to the enjoyment of the fruits of his own exertions? Is it not this individual right, which springs from and is testified to by the natural facts of individual organization—the fact that each particular pair of hands obey a particular brain and are related to a particular stomach; the fact that each man is a definite, coherent, independent whole—which alone justifies individual ownership? As a man belongs to himself, so his labor when put in concrete form belongs to him.

And for this reason, that which a man makes or produces is his own, as against all the world—to enjoy or to destroy, to use, to exchange, or to give. No one else can rightfully claim it, and his exclusive right to it involves no wrong to any one else. Thus there is to everything produced by human exertion a clear and indisputable title to exclusive possession and enjoyment, which is perfectly consistent with justice, as it descends from the original producer, in whom it [is] vested by natural law. The pen with which I am writing is justly mine. No other human being can rightfully lay claim to it, for in me is the title of the producers who made it. It has become mine, because transferred to me by the stationer, to whom it was transferred by the importer, who obtained the exclusive right to it by transfer from the manufacturer, in whom, by the same process of purchase, vested the rights of those who dug the material from the ground and shaped it into a pen. Thus, my exclusive right of ownership in the pen springs from the natural right of the individual to the use of his own faculties.

Now, this is not only the original source from which all ideas of exclusive ownership arise—as is evident from the natural tendency of the mind to revert to it when the idea of exclusive ownership is questioned, and the manner in which social relations develop—but it is necessarily the only source. There can be to the ownership of anything no rightful title which is not derived from the title of the producer and does not rest upon the natural right of the man to himself. There can be no other rightful title, because (1) there is no other natural right from which any other title can be derived, and (2) because the recognition of any other title is inconsistent with and destructive of this.

For (1) what other right exists from which the right to the exclusive possession of anything can be derived, save the right of a man to himself? With what other power is man by nature clothed, save the power of exerting his own faculties? How can he in any other way act upon or affect material things or other men? Paralyze the motor nerves, and your man has no more external influence or power than a log or stone. From what else, then, can the right of possessing and controlling things be derived? If it spring not from man himself, from what can it spring? Nature acknowledges no ownership or control in man save as the result of exertion. In no other way can her treasures be drawn forth, her powers directed, or her forces utilized or controlled. She makes no discriminations among men, but is to all absolutely impartial. She knows no distinction between master and slave, king and subject, saint and sinner. All men to her stand upon an equal footing and have equal rights. She recognizes no claim but that of labor, and recognizes that without respect to the claimant. If a pirate spread his sails, the wind will fill them as well as it will fill those of a peaceful merchantman or missionary bark; if a king and a common man be thrown overboard, neither can keep his head above water except by swimming; birds will not come to be shot by the proprietor of the soil any quicker than they will come to be shot by the poacher; fish will bite or will not bite at a hook in utter disregard as to whether it is offered them by a good little boy who goes to Sunday school, or a bad little boy who plays truant; grain will grow only as the ground is prepared and the seed is sown; it is only at the call of labor that ore can be raised from the mine; the sun shines and the rain falls, alike upon just and unjust. The laws of nature are the decrees of the Creator. There is written in them no recognition of any right save that of labor; and in them is written broadly and clearly the equal right of all men to the use and enjoyment of nature; to apply to her by their exertions, and to receive and possess her reward. Hence, as nature gives only to labor, the exertion of labor in production is the only title to exclusive possession.

(2) This right of ownership that springs from labor excludes the possibility of any other right of ownership. If a man be rightfully entitled to the produce of his labor, then no one can be rightfully entitled to the ownership of anything which is not the produce of his labor, or the labor of someone else from whom the right has passed to him. If production give to the producer the right to exclusive possession and enjoyment, there can rightfully be no exclusive possession and enjoyment of anything not the production of labor, and the recognition of private property in land is a wrong. For the right to the produce of labor cannot be enjoyed without the right to the free use of the opportunities offered by nature, and to admit the right of property in these is to deny the right of property in the produce of labor. When nonproducers can claim as rent a portion of the wealth created by producers, the right of the producers to the fruits of their labor is to that extent denied.

There is no escape from this position. To affirm that a man can rightfully claim exclusive ownership in his own labor when embodied in material things, is to deny that anyone can rightfully claim exclusive ownership in land. To affirm the rightfulness of property in land, is to affirm a claim which has no warrant in nature, as against a claim founded in the organization of man and the laws of the material universe.

What most prevents the realization of the injustice of private property in land is the habit of including all the things that are made the subject of ownership in one category, as property, or, if any distinction is made, drawing the line, according to the unphilosophical distinction of the lawyers, between personal property and real estate, or things movable and things immovable. The real and natural distinction is between things which are the produce of labor and things which are the gratuitous offerings of nature; or to adopt the terms of political economy, between wealth and land.

These two classes of things are in essence and relations widely different, and to class them together as property is to confuse all thought when we come to consider the justice or the injustice, the right or the wrong of property.

A house and the lot on which it stands are alike property, as being the subject of ownership, and are alike classed by the lawyers as real estate. Yet in nature and relations they differ widely. The one is produced by human labor, and belongs to the class in political economy styled wealth. The other is a part of nature, and belongs to the class in political economy styled land.

The essential character of the one class of things is that they embody labor, are brought into being by human exertion, their existence or nonexistence, their increase or diminution, depending on man. The essential character of the other class of things is that they do not embody labor, and exist irrespective of human exertion and irrespective of man; they are the field or environment in which man finds himself; the storehouse from which his needs must be supplied, the raw material upon which, and the forces with which, his labor alone can act.

The moment this distinction is realized, that moment is it seen that the sanction which natural justice gives to one species of property is denied to the other; that the rightfulness which attaches to individual property in the produce of labor implies the wrongfulness of individual property in land; that, whereas the recognition of the one places all men upon equal terms, securing to each the due reward of his labor, the recognition of the other is the denial of the equal rights of men, permitting those who do not labor to take the natural reward of those who do.

Whatever may be said for the institution of private property in land, it is therefore plain that it cannot be defended on the score of justice.

The equal right of all men to the use of land is as clear as their equal right to breathe the air—it is a right proclaimed by the fact of their existence. For we cannot suppose that some men have a right to be in this world and others no right.

If we are all here by the equal permission of the Creator, we are all here with an equal title to the enjoyment of his bounty—with an equal right to the use of all that nature so impartially offers. This is a right which is natural and inalienable; it is a right which vests in every human being as he enters the world, and which during his continuance in the world can be limited only by the equal rights of others. There is in nature no such thing as a fee simple in land. There is on earth no power which can rightfully make a grant of exclusive ownership in land. If all existing men were to unite to grant away their equal rights, they could not grant away the right of those who follow them. For what are we but tenants for a day? Have we made the earth, that we should determine the rights of those who after us shall tenant it in their turn? The Almighty, who created the earth for man and man for the earth, has entailed it upon all the generations of the children of men by a decree written upon the constitution of all things—a decree which no human action can bar and no prescription determine. Let the parchments be ever so many, or possession ever so long, natural justice can recognize no right in one man to the possession and enjoyment of land that is not equally the right of all his fellows. Though his titles have been acquiesced in by generation after generation, to the landed estates of the Duke of Westminster the poorest child that is born in London today has as much right as has his eldest son. Though the sovereign people of the state of New York consent to the landed possessions of the Astors, the puniest infant that comes wailing into the world in the squalidest room of the most miserable tenement house, becomes at that moment seized of an equal right with the millionaires. And it is robbed if the right is denied.

Our previous conclusions, irresistible in themselves, thus stand approved by the highest and final test. Translated from terms of political economy into terms of ethics, they show a wrong as the source of the evils which increase as material progress goes on.

The masses of men, who in the midst of abundance suffer want; who, clothed with political freedom, are condemned to the wages of slavery; to whose toil labor-saving inventions bring no relief, but rather seem to rob them of a privilege, instinctively feel that "there is something wrong." And they are right.

The wide-spreading social evils which everywhere oppress men amid an advancing civilization, spring from a great primary wrong—the appropriation, as the exclusive property of some men, of the land on which and from which all must live. From this fundamental injustice flow all the injustices which distort and endanger modern development, which condemn the producer of wealth to poverty and pamper the nonproducer in luxury, which rear the tenement house with the palace, plant the brothel behind the church, and compel us to build prisons as we open new schools.

There is nothing strange or inexplicable in the phenomena that are now perplexing the world. It is not that material progress is not in itself a good; it is not that nature has called into being children for whom she has failed to provide; it is not that the Creator has left on natural laws a taint of injustice at which even the human mind revolts, that material progress brings such bitter fruits. That amid our highest civilization men faint and die with want is not due to the niggardliness of nature, but to the injustice of man. Vice and misery, poverty and pauperism are not the legitimate results of increase of population and industrial development; they only follow increase of population and industrial development because land is treated as private property—they are the direct and necessary results of the violation of the supreme law of justice, involved in giving to some men the exclusive possession of that which nature provides for all men.

The recognition of individual proprietorship of land is the denial of the natural rights of other individuals—it is a wrong which *must* show itself in the inequitable division of wealth. For as labor cannot produce without the use of land, the denial of the equal right to the use of land is necessarily the denial of the right of labor to its own produce. If one man can command the land upon which others must labor, he can appropriate the produce of their labor as the price of his permission to labor. The fundamental law of nature, that her enjoyment by man shall be consequent upon his exertion, is thus violated. The one receives without producing; the others produce without receiving. The one is unjustly enriched; the others are robbed. To this fundamental wrong we have traced the unjust distribution of wealth which is separating modern society into the very rich and the very poor. It is the continuous increase of rent—the price that labor is compelled to pay for the use of land, which strips the many of the wealth they justly earn, to pile it up in the hands of the few, who do nothing to earn it.

Why should they who suffer from this injustice hesitate for one moment to sweep it away? Who are the landholders that they should thus be permitted to reap where they have not sown?

Consider for a moment the utter absurdity of the titles by which we permit to be gravely passed from John Doe to Richard Roe the right to exclusively possess the earth, giving absolute dominion as against all others. In California our land titles go back to the Supreme Government of Mexico, who took from the Spanish king, who took from the Pope, when he by a stroke of the pen divided lands yet to be discovered between the Spanish or Portuguese—or if you please they rest upon conquest. In the eastern states they go back to treaties with Indians and grants from English kings; in Louisiana to the government of France; in Florida to the government of Spain; while in England they go back to the Norman conquerors. Everywhere, not to a right which obliges, but to a force which compels. And when a title rests but on force, no complaint can be made when force annuls it. Whenever the people, having the power, choose to annul those titles, no objection can be made in the name of justice. There have existed men who had the power to hold or to give exclusive possession of portions of the earth's surface, but when and where did there exist the human being who had the right?

The right to exclusive ownership of anything of human production is clear. No matter how many the hands through which it has passed, there was, at the beginning of the line, human labor—someone who, having procured or produced it by his exertions, had to it a clear title as against all the rest of mankind, and which could justly pass from one to another by sale or gift. But at the end of what string of conveyances or grants can be shown or supposed a like title to any part of the material universe? To improvements such an original title can be shown; but it is a title only to the improvements, and not to the land itself. If I clear a forest, drain a swamp, or fill a morass, all I can justly claim is the value given by these exertions. They give me no right to the land itself, no claim other than to my equal share with every other member of the community in the value which is added to it by the growth of the community.

But it will be said: there are improvements which in time become indistinguishable from the land itself! Very well; then the title to the improvements becomes blended with the title to the land; the individual right is lost in the common right. It is the greater that swallows up the less, not the less that swallows up the greater. Nature does not proceed from man, but man from nature, and it is into the bosom of nature that he and all his works must return again.

Yet, it will be said: as every man has a right to the use and enjoyment of nature, the man who is using land must be permitted the exclusive right to its use in order that he may get the full benefit of his labor. But there is no difficulty in determining where the individual right ends and the common right begins. A delicate and exact test is supplied by value, and with its aid there is no difficulty, no matter how dense population may become, in determining and securing the exact rights of each, the equal rights of all. The value of land, as we have seen, is the price of monopoly. It is not the absolute, but the relative, capability of land that determines its value. No matter what may be its intrinsic qualities, land that is no better than other land which may be had for the using can have no value. And the value of land always measures the difference between it and the best land that may be had for the using. Thus, the value of land expresses in exact and tangible form the right of the community in land held by an indivdual; and rent expresses the exact amount which the individual should pay to the community to satisfy the equal rights of all other members of the community. Thus, if we concede to priority of possession the undisturbed use of land, confiscating rent for the benefit of the community, we reconcile the fixity of tenure which is necessary for improvement with a full and complete recognition of the equal rights of all to the use of land. . . .

We have traced the want and suffering that everywhere prevail among the working classes, the recurring paroxysms of industrial depression, the scarcity of employment, the stagnation of capital, the tendency of wages to the starvation point, that exhibit themselves more and more strongly as material progress goes on, to the fact that the land on which and from which all must live is made the exclusive property of some.

We have seen that there is no possible remedy for these evils but the abolition of their cause; we have seen that private property in land has no warrant in justice, but stands condemned as the denial of natural right—a subversion of the law of nature that as social development goes on must condemn the masses of men to a slavery the hardest and most degrading.

We have weighed every objection, and seen that neither on the ground of equity or expediency is there anything to deter us from making land common property by confiscating rent.

But a question of method remains. How shall we do it? . . .

It is an axiom of statesmanship, which the successful founders of tyranny have understood and acted upon—that great changes can best be brought about under old forms. We, who would free men, should heed the same truth. It is the natural method. When nature would make a higher type, she takes a lower one and develops it. This, also, is the law of social growth. Let us work by it. With the current we may glide fast and far. Against it, it is hard pulling and slow progress.

I do not propose either to purchase or to confiscate private property in land. The first would be unjust; the second, needless. Let the individuals who now hold it still retain, if they want to, possession of what they are pleased to call *their* land. Let them continue to call it *their* land. Let them buy and sell, and bequeath and devise it. We may safely leave them the shell, if we take the kernel. *It is not necessary to confiscate land; it is only necessary to confiscate rent.*

Nor to take rent for public uses is it necessary that the State should bother with the letting of lands, and assume the chances of the favoritism, collusion, and corruption that might involve. It is not necessary that any new machinery should be created. The machinery already exists. Instead of extending it, all we have to do is to simplify and reduce it. By leaving to landowners a percentage of rent which would probably be much less than the cost and loss involved in attempting to rent lands through State agency, and by making use of this existing machinery, we may, without jar or shock, assert the common right to land by taking rent for public uses.

We already take some rent in taxation. We have only to make some changes in our modes of taxation to take it all.

What I, therefore, propose as the simple yet sovereign remedy, which will raise wages, increase the earnings of capital, extirpate pauperism, abolish poverty, give remunerative employment to whoever wishes it, afford free scope to human powers, lessen crime, elevate morals, and taste, and intelligence, purify government and carry civilization to yet nobler heights, is—*to appropriate rent by taxation.*

In this way, the State may become the universal landlord without calling herself so, and without assuming a single new function. In form the ownership of land would remain just as now. No owner of land need be dispossessed, and no restriction need be placed upon the amount of land anyone could hold. For, rent being taken by the State in taxes, land, no matter in whose name it stood, or in what parcels it was held, would be really common property, and every member of the community would participate in the advantages of its ownership.

Now, insomuch as the taxation of rent, or land values, must necessarily be increased just as we abolish other taxes, we may put the proposition into practical form by proposing—

To abolish all taxation save that upon land values.

As we have seen, the value of land is at the beginning of society nothing, but as society develops by the increase of population and the advance of the arts, it becomes greater and greater. In every civilized country, even the newest, the value of the land taken as a whole is sufficient to bear the entire expenses of government. In the better developed countries it is much more than sufficient. Hence it will not be enough to merely place all taxes upon the value of land. It will be necessary, where rent exceeds the present governmental revenues, to commensurately increase the amount demanded in taxation, and to continue this increase as society progresses and rent advances. But this is so natural and easy a matter, that it may be considered as involved, or at least understood, in the proposition to put all taxes on the value of land. That is the first step, upon which the practical struggle must be made. When the hare is once caught and killed, cooking him will follow as a matter of course. When the common right to land is so far appreciated that all taxes are abolished save those which fall upon rent, there is no danger of much more than is necessary to induce them to collect the public revenues being left to individual landholders.

Experience has taught me (for I have been for some years endeavoring to popularize this proposition) that wherever the idea of concentrating all taxation upon land values finds lodgment sufficient to induce consideration, it invariably makes way, but that there are few of the classes most to be benefited by it, who at first, or even for a long time afterwards, see its full significance and power. It is difficult for workingmen to get over the idea that there is a real antagonism between capital and labor. It is difficult for small farmers and homestead owners to get over the idea that to put all taxes on the value of land would be to unduly tax them. It is difficult for both classes to get over the idea that to exempt capital from taxation would be to make the rich richer, and the poor poorer. These ideas spring from confused thought. But behind ignorance and prejudice there is a powerful interest, which has hitherto dominated literature, education, and opinion. A great wrong always dies hard, and the great wrong which in every civilized country condemns the masses of men to poverty and want, will not die without a bitter struggle. . . .

In the short space to which this latter part of our inquiry is necessarily confined, I have been obliged to omit much that I would like to say, and to touch briefly where an exhaustive consideration would not be out of place.

Nevertheless, this, at least, is evident, that the truth to which we were led in the politico-economic branch of our inquiry, is as clearly apparent in the rise and fall of nations and the growth and decay of civilizations, and that it accords with those deep-seated recognitions of relation and sequence that we denominate moral perceptions. Thus have been given to our conclusions the greatest certitude and highest sanction.

This truth involves both a menace and a promise. It shows that the evils arising from the unjust and unequal distribution of wealth, which are becoming more and more apparent as modern civilization goes on, are not incidents of progress, but tendencies which must bring progress to a halt; that they will not cure themselves, but, on the contrary, must, unless their cause is removed, grow greater and greater, until they sweep us back into barbarism by the road every previous civilization has trod. But it also shows that these evils are not imposed by natural laws; that they spring solely from social maladjustments which ignore natural laws, and that in removing their cause we shall be giving an enormous impetus to progress.

The poverty which, in the midst of abundance, pinches and embrutes men, and all the manifold evils which flow from it, spring from a denial of justice. In permitting the monopolization of the natural opportunities which nature freely offers to all, we have ignored the fundamental law of justice—for so far as we can see, when we view things upon a large scale, justice seems to be the supreme law of the universe. But by sweeping away this injustice and asserting the rights of all men to natural opportunities, we shall conform ourselves to the law—we shall remove the great cause of unnatural inequality in the distribution of wealth and power; we shall abolish poverty; tame the ruthless passions of greed; dry up the springs of vice and misery; light in dark places the lamp of knowledge; give new vigor to invention and a fresh impulse to discovery; substitute political strength for political weakness; and make tyranny and anarchy impossible.

The reform I have proposed accords with all that is politically, socially, or morally desirable. It has the qualities of a true reform, for it will make all other reforms easier. What is it but the carrying out in letter and spirit of the truth enunciated in the Declaration of Independence—the "self-evident" truth that is the heart and soul of the Declaration—"*That all men are created equal; that they are endowed by their Creator with certain inalienable rights; that among them are life, liberty, and the pursuit of happiness!*"

These rights are denied when the equal right to land—on which and by which men alone can live—is denied. Equality of political rights will not compensate for the denial of the equal right to the bounty of nature. Political liberty, when the equal right to land is denied, becomes, as population increases and invention goes on, merely the liberty to compete for employment at starvation wages. This is the truth that we have ignored. And so there come beggars in our streets and tramps on our roads; and poverty enslaves men whom we boast are political sovereigns; and want breeds ignorance that our schools cannot enlighten; and citizens vote as their masters dictate; and the demagogue usurps the part of the statesman; and gold weighs in the scales of justice; and in high places sit those who do not pay to civic virtue even the compliment of hypocrisy; and the pillars of the republic that we thought so strong already bend under an increasing strain. . . .

In our time, as in times before, creep on the insidious forces that, producing inequality, destroy liberty. On the horizon the clouds begin to lower. Liberty calls to us again. We must follow her further; we must trust her fully. Either we must wholly accept her or she will not stay. It is not enough that men should vote; it is not enough that they should be theoretically equal before the law. They must have liberty to avail themselves of the opportunities and means of life; they must stand on equal terms with reference to the bounty of nature. Either this, or Liberty withdraws her light! Either this, or darkness comes on, and the very forces that progress has evolved turn to powers that work destruction. This is the universal law. This is the lesson of the centuries. Unless its foundations be laid in justice the social structure cannot stand.

Our primary social adjustment is a denial of justice. In allowing one man to own the land on which and from which other men must live, we have made them his bondsmen in a degree which increases as material progress goes on. This is the subtle alchemy that in ways they do not realize is extracting from the masses in every civilized country the fruits of their weary toil; that is instituting a harder and more hopeless slavery in place of that which has been destroyed; that is bringing political despotism out of political freedom, and must soon transmute democratic institutions into anarchy.

It is this that turns the blessings of material progress into a curse. It is this that crowds human beings into noisome cellars and squalid tenement houses; that fills prisons and brothels; that goads men with want and consumes them with greed; that robs women of the grace and beauty of perfect womanhood; that takes from little children the joy and innocence of life's morning.

Civilization so based cannot continue. The eternal laws of the universe forbid it. Ruins of dead empires testify, and the witness that is in every soul answers, that it cannot be. It is something grander than benevolence, something more august than charity—it is Justice herself that demands of us to right this wrong. Justice that will not be denied; that cannot be put off—Justice that with the scales carries the sword. Shall we ward the stroke with liturgies and prayers? Shall we avert the decrees of immutable law by raising churches when hungry infants moan and weary mothers weep?

Though it may take the language of prayer, it is blasphemy that attributes to the inscrutable decrees of Providence the suffering and brutishness that come of poverty; that turns with folded hands to the All-Father and lays on Him the responsibility for the want and crime of our great cities. We degrade the Everlasting. We slander the Just One. A merciful man would have better ordered the world; a just man would crush with his foot such an ulcerous anthill! It is not the Almighty, but we who are responsible for the vice and misery that fester amid our civilization. The Creator showers upon us his gifts—more than enough for all. But like swine scrambling for food, we tread them in the mire—tread them in the mire, while we tear and rend each other!

In the very centers of our civilization today are want and suffering enough to make sick at heart whoever does not close his eyes and steel his nerves. Dare we turn to the Creator and ask Him to relieve it? Supposing the prayer were heard, and at the behest with which the universe sprang into being there should glow in the sun a greater power; new virtue fill the air; fresh vigor the soil; that for every blade of grass that now grows two should spring up, and the seed that now increases fiftyfold should increase a hundredfold! Would poverty be abated or want relieved? Manifestly no! Whatever benefit would accrue would be but temporary. The new powers streaming through the material universe could only be utilized through land. And land, being private property, the classes that now monopolize the bounty of the Creator would monopolize all the new bounty. Landowners would alone be benefited. Rents would increase, but wages would still tend to the starvation point!

This is not merely a deduction of political economy; it is a fact of experience. We know it because we have seen it. Within our own times, under our very eyes, that power which is above all, and in all, and through all; that power of which the whole universe is but the manifestation; that power which maketh all things, and without which is not anything made that is made, has increased the bounty which men may enjoy, as truly as though the fertility of nature had been increased. Into the mind of one came the thought that harnessed steam for the service of mankind. To the inner ear of another was whispered the secret that compels the lightning to bear a message round the globe. In every direction have the laws of matter been revealed; in every department of industry have arisen arms of iron and fingers of steel, whose effect upon the production of wealth has been precisely the same as an increase in the fertility of nature. What has been the result? Simply that landowners get all the gain. The wonderful discoveries and inventions of our century have neither increased wages nor lightened toil. The effect has simply been to make the few richer; the many, more helpless!

Can it be that the gifts of the Creator may be thus misappropriated with impunity? Is it a light thing that labor should be robbed of its earnings while greed rolls in wealth—that the many should want while the few are surfeited? Turn to history, and on every page may be read the lesson that such wrong never goes unpunished; that the Nemesis that follows injustice never falters nor sleeps! Look around today. Can this state of things continue? May we even say, "After us the deluge!" Nay; the pillars of the state are trembling even now, and the very foundations of society begin to quiver with pent-up forces that glow underneath. The struggle that must either revivify, or convulse in ruin, is near at hand, if it be not already begun.

The fiat has gone forth! With steam and electricity, and the new powers born of progress, forces have entered the world that will either compel us to a higher plane or overwhelm us, as nation after nation, as civilization after civilization, have been overwhelmed before. It is the delusion which precedes destruction that sees in the popular unrest with which the civilized world is feverishly pulsing, only the passing effect of ephemeral causes. Between democratic ideas and the aristocratic adjustments of society there is an irreconcilable conflict. Here in the United States, as there in Europe, it may be seen arising. We cannot go on permitting men to vote and forcing them to tramp. We cannot go on educating boys and girls in our public schools and then refusing them the right to earn an honest living. We cannot go on prating of the inalienable rights of man and then denying the inalienable right to the bounty of the Creator. Even now, in old bottles the new wine begins to ferment, and elemental forces gather for the strife!

But if, while there is yet time, we turn to Justice and obey her, if we trust Liberty and follow her, the dangers that now threaten must disappear, the forces that now menace will turn to agencies of elevation. Think of the powers now wasted; of the infinite fields of knowledge yet to be explored; of the possibilities of which the wondrous inventions of this century give us but a hint. With want destroyed; with greed changed to noble passions; with the fraternity that is born of equality taking the place of the jealousy and fear that now array men against each other; with mental power loosed by conditions that give to the humblest comfort and leisure; and who shall measure the heights to which our civilization may soar? Words fail the thought! It is the Golden Age of which poets have sung and high-raised seers have told in metaphor! It is the glorious vision which has always haunted man with gleams of fitful splendor. It is what he saw whose eyes at Patmos were closed in a trance. It is the culmination of Christianity—the City of God on earth, with its walls of jasper and its gates of pearl! It is the reign of the Prince of Peace!

2

AMERICAN ANARCHISM

Benjamin Tucker
STATE SOCIALISM AND ANARCHISM

Anarchists have a worse reputation in this country than socialists. Their names have been more easily linked to acts of violence and terror than those of parliamentary-minded radicals who worked toward their goals through political processes. Benjamin Tucker (1854–1939), however, following the teachings of the American anarchist Josiah Warren, remained as far away as possible from bombs and sabotage. Moreover he viewed his individualist anarchism as something very distinct from the anarchist communism of Mikhail Bakunin. Tucker regularly denounced Henry George, but he shared with the champion of the single tax a fear of state power. The future society that he envisaged, as is clear in this selection, bore little resemblance to a socialist republic. In an age of growing business consolidation, Tucker hoped to resolve social conflict by smashing the privileges that any government invariably extended to the dominant economic class. In so doing, he imagined a society where, in effect, all men were capitalists.

Probably no agitation has ever attained the magnitude, either in the number of its recruits or the area of its influence, which has been attained by modern socialism, and at the same time been so little understood and so misunderstood, not only by the hostile and the indifferent, but by the friendly, and even by the great mass of its adherents themselves. This unfortunate and highly dangerous state of things is due partly to the fact that the human relationships which this movement—if anything so chaotic can be called a movement —aims to transform, involve no special class or classes, but literally all mankind; partly to the fact that these relationships are infinitely more varied and complex in their nature than those with which any

SOURCE. Benjamin Tucker, "State Socialism and Anarchism: How Far They Agree, and Wherein They Differ," *Instead of a Book by a Man Too Busy to Write One* (New York, 1893), pp. 3–16.

special reform has ever been called upon to deal; and partly to the fact that the great molding forces of society, the channels of information and enlightenment, are well-nigh exclusively under the control of those whose immediate pecuniary interests are antagonistic to the bottom claim of socialism that labor should be put in possession of its own.

Almost the only persons who may be said to comprehend even approximately the significance, principles, and purposes of socialism are the chief leaders of the extreme wings of the socialistic forces, and perhaps a few of the money kings themselves. It is a subject of which it has lately become quite the fashion for preacher, professor, and penny-a-liner to treat, and, for the most part, woeful work they have made with it, exciting the derision and pity of those competent to judge. That those prominent in the intermediate socialistic divisions do not fully understand what they are about is evident from the positions they occupy. If they did; if they were consistent, logical thinkers; if they were what the French call *consequent* men—their reasoning faculties would long since have driven them to one extreme or the other.

For it is a curious fact that the two extremes of the vast army now under consideration, though united, as has been hinted above, by the common claim that labor shall be put in possession of its own, are more diametrically opposed to each other in their fundamental principles of social action and their methods of reaching the ends aimed at than either is to their common enemy, the existing society. They are based on two principles the history of whose conflict is almost equivalent to the history of the world since man came into it; and all intermediate parties, including that of the upholders of the existing society, are based upon a compromise between them. It is clear, then, that any intelligent, deep-rooted opposition to the prevailing order of things must come from one or the other of these extremes, for anything from any other source, far from being revolutionary in character, could be only in the nature of such superficial modification as would be utterly unable to concentrate upon itself the degree of attention and interest now bestowed upon modern socialism.

The two principles referred to are *authority* and *liberty*, and the names of the two schools of socialistic thought which fully and unreservedly represent one or the other of them are, respectively, *State socialism* and *anarchism*. Whoso knows what these two schools want and how they propose to get it understands the socialistic movement. For, just as it has been said that there is no halfway house between Rome and reason, so it may be said that there is no halfway house between State socialism and anarchism. There are, in fact, two currents steadily flowing from the center of the socialistic forces which are concentrating them on the left and on the right; and, if socialism is to prevail, it is among the possibilities that, after this movement of separation has been completed and the existing order has been crushed out between the two camps, the ultimate and bitterer conflict will be still to come. In that case all the eight-hour men, all the trades-unionists, all the Knights of Labor, all the land nationalizationists, all the greenbackers, and, in short, all the members of the thousand and one different battalions belonging to the great army of labor, will have deserted their old posts, and these being arrayed on the one side and the other, the great battle will begin. What a final victory for the State socialists will mean, and what a final victory for the anarchists will mean, it is the purpose of this paper to briefly state.

To do this intelligently, however, I must first describe the ground common to both, the features that make socialists of each of them.

The economic principles of modern socialism are a logical deduction from the principle laid down by Adam Smith in the early chapters of his "Wealth of Nations"—namely, that labor is the true measure of price. But Adam Smith, after stating this principle most clearly and concisely, immediately abandoned all further consideration of it to devote himself to showing what actually does measure price, and how, therefore, wealth is at present distributed. Since his day nearly all the political economists have followed his example by confining their function to the description of society as it is, in its industrial and commercial phases. Socialism, on the contrary, extends its function to the description of society as it should be, and the discovery of the means of making it what it should be. Half a century or more after Smith enunciated the principle above stated, socialism picked it up where he had dropped it, and, in following it to its logical conclusions, made it the basis of a new economic philosophy.

This seems to have been done independently by three different men, of three different nationalities, in three different languages: Josiah Warren, an American; Pierre J. Proudhon, a Frenchman; Karl Marx, a German Jew. That Warren and Proudhon arrived at their conclusions singly and unaided is certain; but whether Marx was not largely indebted to Proudhon for his economic ideas is questionable. However this may be, Marx's presentation of the ideas was in so many respects peculiarly his own that he is fairly entitled to the credit of originality. That the work of this interesting trio should have been done so nearly simultaneously would seem to indicate that socialism was in the air, and that the time was ripe and the conditions favorable for the appearance of this new school of thought. So far as priority of time is concerned, the credit seems to belong to Warren, the American—a fact which should be noted by the stump orators who are so fond of declaiming against socialism as an imported article. Of the purest revolutionary blood, too, this Warren, for he descends from the Warren who fell at Bunker Hill.

From Smith's principle that labor is the true measure of price—or, as Warren phrased it, that cost is the proper limit of price—these three men made the following deductions: that the natural wage of labor is its product; that this wage, or product, is the only just source of income (leaving out, of course, gift, inheritance, etc.); that all who derive income from any other source abstract it directly or indirectly from the natural and just wage of labor; that this abstracting process generally takes one of three forms—interest, rent, and profit; that these three constitute the trinity of usury, and are simply different methods of levying tribute for the use of capital; that, capital being simply stored-up labor which has already received its pay in full, its use ought to be gratuitous, on the principle that labor is the only basis of price; that the lender of capital is entitled to its return intact, and nothing more; that the only reason why the banker, the stockholder, the landlord, the manufacturer, and the merchant are able to exact usury from labor lies in the fact that they are backed by legal privilege, or monopoly; and that the only way to secure to labor the enjoyment of its entire product, or natural wage, is to strike down monopoly.

It must not be inferred that either Warren, Proudhon, or Marx used exactly this phraseology, or followed exactly this line of thought, but it indicates definitely enough the fundamental ground taken by all three, and their substantial thought up to the limit to which they went in common. And, lest I may be accused of stating the positions and arguments of these men incorrectly, it may be well to say in advance that I have viewed them broadly, and that, for the purpose of sharp, vivid, and emphatic comparison and contrast, I have taken considerable liberty with their thought by rearranging it in an order, and often in a phraseology, of my own, but, I am satisfied, without, in so doing, misrepresenting them in any essential particular.

It was at this point—the necessity of striking down monopoly—that came the parting of their ways. Here the road forked. They found that they must turn either to the right or to the left—follow either the path of authority or the path of liberty. Marx went one way; Warren and Proudhon, the other. Thus were born State socialism and anarchism.

First, then, state socialism, which may be described as *the doctrine*

*that all the affairs of men should be managed by the government,
regardless of individual choice.*

Marx, its founder, concluded that the only way to abolish the class
monopolies was to centralize and consolidate all industrial and commercial interests, all productive and distributive agencies, in one vast
monopoly in the hands of the State. The government must become
banker, manufacturer, farmer, carrier, and merchant, and in these
capacities must suffer no competition. Land, tools, and all instruments of production must be wrested from individual hands, and
made the property of the collectivity. To the individual can belong
only the products to be consumed, not the means of producing them.
A man may own his clothes and his food, but not the sewing machine
which makes his shirts or the spade which digs his potatoes. Product
and capital are essentially different things; the former belongs to
individuals, the latter to society. Society must seize the capital which
belongs to it, by the ballot if it can, by revolution if it must. Once in
possession of it, it must administer it on the majority principle,
through its organ, the State, utilize it in production and distribution,
fix all prices by the amount of labor involved, and employ the whole
people in its workshops, farms, stores, etc. The nation must be transformed into a vast bureaucracy, and every individual into a State
official. Everything must be done on the cost principle, the people
having no motive to make a profit out of themselves. Individuals not
being allowed to own capital, no one can employ another, or even
himself. Every man will be a wage-receiver, and the State the only
wage-payer. He who will not work for the State must starve, or, more
likely, go to prison. All freedom of trade must disappear. Competition
must be utterly wiped out. All industrial and commercial activity
must be centered in one vast, enormous, all-inclusive monopoly. The
remedy for *monopolies* is *monopoly.*

Such is the economic program of State socialism as adopted from
Karl Marx. The history of its growth and progress cannot be told here.
In this country the parties that uphold it are known as the Socialistic
Labor party, which pretends to follow Karl Marx; the Nationalists,
who follow Karl Marx filtered through Edward Bellamy; and the
Christian Socialists, who follow Karl Marx filtered through Jesus
Christ.

What other applications this principle of authority, once adopted in
the economic sphere, will develop are very evident. It means the
absolute control by the majority of all individual conduct. The right of
such control is already admitted by the State socialists, though they
maintain that, as a matter of fact, the individual would be allowed a

much larger liberty than he now enjoys. But he would only be allowed it; he could not claim it as his own. There would be no foundation of society upon a guaranteed equality of the largest possible liberty. Such liberty as might exist would exist by sufferance and could be taken away at any moment. Constitutional guarantees would be of no avail. There would be but one article in the constitution of a State socialist country: "The right of the majority is absolute."

The claim of the State socialists, however, that this right would not be exercised in matters pertaining to the individual in the more intimate and private relations of his life is not borne out by the history of governments. It has ever been the tendency of power to add to itself, to enlarge its sphere, to encroach beyond the limits set for it; and where the habit of resisting such encroachment is not fostered, and the individual is not taught to be jealous of his rights, individuality gradually disappears and the government or State becomes the all-in-all. Control naturally accompanies responsibility. Under the system of State socialism, therefore, which holds the community responsible for the health, wealth, and wisdom of the individual, it is evident that the community, through its majority expression, will insist more and more on prescribing the conditions of health, wealth, and wisdom, thus impairing and finally destroying individual independence and with it all sense of individual responsibility.

Whatever, then, the State socialists may claim or disclaim, their system, if adopted, is doomed to end in a State religion, to the expense of which all must contribute and at the altar of which all must kneel; a State school of medicine, by whose practitioners the sick must invariably be treated; a State system of hygiene, prescribing what all must and must not eat, drink, wear, and do; a State code of morals, which will not content itself with punishing crime, but will prohibit what the majority decide to be vice; a State system of instruction, which will do away with all private schools, academies, and colleges; a State nursery, in which all children must be brought up in common at the public expense; and, finally, a State family, with an attempt at stirpiculture, or scientific breeding, in which no man and woman will be allowed to have children if the State prohibits them and no man and woman can refuse to have children if the State orders them. Thus will authority achieve its acme and monopoly be carried to its highest power.

Such is the ideal of the logical State socialist, such the goal which lies at the end of the road that Karl Marx took. Let us now follow the fortunes of Warren and Proudhon, who took the other road—the road of liberty.

This brings us to anarchism which may be described as *the doctrine that all the affairs of men should be managed by individuals or voluntary associations, and that the State should be abolished.*

When Warren and Proudhon, in prosecuting their search for justice to labor, came face to face with the obstacle of class monopolies, they saw that these monopolies rested upon authority, and concluded that the thing to be done was, not to strengthen this authority and thus make monopoly universal, but to utterly uproot authority and give full sway to the opposite principle, liberty, by making competition, the antithesis of monopoly, universal. They saw in competition the great leveler of prices to the labor cost of production. In this they agreed with the political economists. The query then naturally presented itself why all prices do not fall to labor cost; where there is any room for incomes acquired otherwise than by labor; in a word, why the usurer, the receiver of interest, rent, and profit, exists. The answer was found in the present one-sidedness of competition. It was discovered that capital had so manipulated legislation that unlimited competition is allowed in supplying productive labor, thus keeping wages down to the starvation point, or as near it as practicable; that a great deal of competition is allowed in supplying distributive labor, or the labor of the mercantile classes, thus keeping, not the prices of goods, but the merchants' actual profits on them, down to a point somewhat approximating equitable wages for the merchants' work; but that almost no competition at all is allowed in supplying capital, upon the aid of which both productive and distributive labor are dependent for their power of achievement, thus keeping the rate of interest on money and of house-rent and ground-rent at as high a point as the necessities of the people will bear.

On discovering this, Warren and Proudhon charged the political economists with being afraid of their own doctrine. The Manchester men were accused of being inconsistent. They believed in liberty to compete with the laborer in order to reduce his wages, but not in liberty to compete with the capitalist in order to reduce his usury. *Laissez faire* was very good sauce for the goose, labor, but very poor sauce for the gander, capital. But how to correct this inconsistency, how to serve this gander with this sauce, how to put capital at the service of businessmen and laborers at cost, or free of usury—that was the problem.

Marx, as we have seen, solved it by declaring capital to be a different thing from product, and maintaining that it belonged to society and should be seized by society and employed for the benefit of all alike. Proudhon scoffed at this distinction between capital and product. He maintained that capital and product are not different kinds of wealth, but simply alternate conditions or functions of the same wealth; that all wealth undergoes an incessant transformation from capital into product and from product back into capital, the process repeating itself interminably; that capital and product are purely social terms; that what is product to one man immediately becomes capital to another and *vice versa*; that, if there were but one person in the world, all wealth would be to him at once capital and product; that the fruit of A's toil is his product, which, when sold to B, becomes B's capital (unless B is an unproductive consumer, in which case it is merely wasted wealth, outside the view of social economy); that a steam engine is just as much product as a coat, and that a coat is just as much capital as a steam engine; and that the same laws of equity govern the possession of the one that govern the possession of the other.

For these and other reasons Proudhon and Warren found themselves unable to sanction any such plan as the seizure of capital by society. But, though opposed to socializing the ownership of capital, they aimed nevertheless to socialize its effects by making its use beneficial to all instead of a means of impoverishing the many to enrich the few. And when the light burst in upon them, they saw that this could be done by subjecting capital to the natural law of competition, thus bringing the price of its use down to cost—that is, to nothing beyond the expenses incidental to handling and transferring it. So they raised the banner of Absolute Free Trade; free trade at home, as well as with foreign countries; the logical carrying out of the Manchester doctrine; *laissez faire* the universal rule. Under this banner they began their fight upon monopolies, whether the all-inclusive monopoly of the State socialists, or the various class monopolies that now prevail.

Of the latter they distinguished four of principal importance: the money monopoly, the land monopoly, the tariff monopoly, and the patent monopoly.

First in the importance of its evil influence they considered the money monopoly, which consists of the privilege given by the government to certain individuals, or to individuals holding certain kinds of property, of issuing the circulating medium, a privilege which is now enforced in this country by a national tax of ten percent upon all other persons who attempt to furnish a circulating medium and by State laws making it a criminal offence to issue notes as currency. It is claimed that the holders of this privilege control the rate of interest, the rate of rent of houses and buildings, and the prices of goods—the first directly, and the second and third indirectly. For, say Proudhon and Warren, if the business of banking were made free to all, more and more persons would enter into it until the competition should become sharp enough to reduce the price of lending money to the labor cost, which statistics show to be less than three-fourths of one percent. In that case the thousands of people who are now deterred from going into business by the ruinously high rates which they must pay for capital with which to start and carry on business will find their difficulties removed. If they have property which they do not desire to convert into money by sale, a bank will take it as collateral for a loan of a certain proportion of its market value at less than one percent discount. If they have no property, but are industrious, honest, and capable, they will generally be able to get their individual notes endorsed by a sufficient number of known and solvent parties; and on such business paper they will be able to get a loan at a bank on similarly favorable terms. Thus interest will fall at a blow. The banks will really not be lending capital at all, but will be doing business on the capital of their customers, the business consisting in an exchange of the known and widely available credits of the banks for the unknown and unavailable, but equally good, credits of the customers, and a charge therefore of less than one percent, not as interest for the use of capital, but as pay for the labor of running the banks. This facility of acquiring capital will give an unheard-of impetus to business, and consequently create an unprecedented demand for labor—a demand which will always be in excess of the supply, directly the contrary of the present condition of the labor market. Then will be seen an exemplification of the words of Richard Cobden that, when two laborers are after one employer, wages fall, but when two employers are after one laborer, wages rise. Labor will then be in a position to dictate its wages, and will thus secure its natural wage, its entire product. Thus the same blow that strikes interest down will send wages up. But this is not all. Down will go profits also. For merchants, instead of buying at high prices on credit, will borrow money of the banks at less than one percent, buy at low prices for cash, and correspondingly reduce the prices of their goods to their customers. And with the rest will go house-rent. For no one who can borrow capital at one percent with which to build a house of his own will consent to pay rent to a landlord at a higher rate than that. Such is the vast claim made by Proudhon and Warren as to the results of the simple abolition of the money monopoly.

Second in importance comes the land monopoly, the evil effects of which are seen principally in exclusively agricultural countries, like Ireland. This monopoly consists in the enforcement by government of land titles which do not rest upon personal occupancy and cultivation. It was obvious to Warren and Proudhon that, as soon as individuals should no longer be protected by their fellows in anything but personal occupancy and cultivation of land, ground-rent would disappear, and so usury have one less leg to stand on. Their followers of today are disposed to modify this claim to the extent of admitting that the very small fraction of ground-rent which rests, not on monopoly, but on superiority of soil or site, will continue to exist for a time and perhaps forever, though tending constantly to a minimum under conditions of freedom. But the inequality of soils which gives rise to the economic rent of land, like the inequality of human skill which gives rise to the economic rent of ability, is not a cause for serious alarm even to the most thorough opponent of usury, as its nature is not that of a germ from which other and graver inequalities may spring, but rather that of a decaying branch which may finally wither and fall.

Third, the tariff monopoly, which consists in fostering production at high prices and under unfavorable conditions by visiting with the penalty of taxation those who patronize production at low prices and under favorable conditions. The evil to which this monopoly gives rise might more properly be called *mis*usury than usury, because it compels labor to pay, not exactly for the use of capital, but rather for the misuse of capital. The abolition of this monopoly would result in a great reduction in the prices of all articles taxed, and this saving to the laborers who consume these articles would be another step toward securing to the laborer his natural wage, his entire product. Proudhon admitted, however, that to abolish this monopoly before abolishing the money monopoly would be a cruel and disastrous policy, first, because the evil of scarcity of money, created by the money monopoly, would be intensified by the flow of money out of the country which would be involved in an excess of imports over exports, and, second, because that fraction of the laborers of the country which is now employed in the protected industries would be turned adrift to face starvation without the benefit of the insatiable demand for labor which a competitive money system would create. Free trade in money at home, making money and work abundant, was insisted upon by Proudhon as a prior condition of free trade in goods with foreign countries.

Fourth, the patent monopoly, which consists in protecting inventors and authors against competition for a period long enough to enable them to extort from the people a reward enormously in excess of the labor measure of their services—in other words, in giving certain people a right of property for a term of years in laws and facts of Nature, and the power to exact tribute from others for the use of this natural wealth, which should be open to all. The abolition of this monopoly would fill its beneficiaries with a wholesome fear of competition which would cause them to be satisfied with pay for their services equal to that which other laborers get for theirs, and to secure it by placing their products and works on the market at the outset at prices so low that their lines of business would be no more tempting to competitors than any other lines.

The development of the economic program which consists in the destruction of these monopolies and the substitution for them of the freest competition led its authors to a perception of the fact that all their thought rested upon a very fundamental principle, the freedom of the individual, his right of sovereignty over himself, his products, and his affairs, and of rebellion against the dictation of external authority. Just as the idea of taking capital away from individuals and giving it to the government started Marx in a path which ends in making the government everything and the individual nothing, so the idea of taking capital away from government-protected monopolies and putting it within easy reach of all individuals started Warren and Proudhon in a path which ends in making the individual everything and the government nothing. If the individual has a right to govern himself, all external government is tyranny. Hence the necessity of abolishing the State. This was the logical conclusion to which Warren and Proudhon were forced, and it became the fundamental article of their political philosophy. It is the doctrine which Proudhon named An-archism, a word derived from the Greek, and meaning, not necessarily absence of order, as is generally supposed, but absence of rule. The anarchists are simply unterrified Jeffersonian Democrats. They believe that "the best government is that which governs least," and that that which governs least is no government at all. Even the simple police function of protecting person and property they deny to governments supported by compulsory taxation. Protection they look upon as a thing to be secured, as long as it is necessary, by voluntary association and cooperation for self-defense, or as a commodity to be purchased, like any other commodity, of those who offer the best article at the lowest price. In their view it is in itself an invasion of the individual to compel him to pay for or suffer a protection against invasion that he has not asked for and does not desire. And they further claim that protection will become a drug in the market, after poverty and consequently crime have disappeared through the realization of their economic program. Compulsory taxation is to them the life-principle of all the monopolies, and passive, but organized, resistance to the tax collector they contemplate, when the proper time comes, as one of the most effective methods of accomplishing their purposes.

Their attitude on this is a key to their attitude on all other questions of a political or social nature. In religion they are atheistic as far as their own opinions are concerned, for they look upon divine authority and the religious sanction of morality as the chief pretexts put forward by the privileged classes for the exercise of human authority. "If God exists," said Proudhon, "he is man's enemy." And, in contrast to Voltaire's famous epigram, "If God did not exist, it would be necessary to invent him," the great Russian Nihilist, Mikhail Bakunin, placed this antithetical proposition: "If God existed, it would be necessary to abolish him." But although, viewing the divine hierarchy as a contradiction of anarchy, they do not believe in it, the anarchists nonetheless firmly believe in the liberty to believe in it. Any denial of religious freedom they squarely oppose.

Upholding thus the right of every individual to be or select his own priest, they likewise uphold his right to be or select his own doctor. No monopoly in theology, no monopoly in medicine. Competition everywhere and always; spiritual advice and medical advice alike to stand or fall on their own merits. And not only in medicine, but in hygiene, must this principle of liberty be followed. The individual may decide for himself not only what to do to get well, but what to do to keep well. No external power must dictate to him what he must and must not eat, drink, wear, or do.

Nor does the anarchistic scheme furnish any code of morals to be imposed upon the individual. "Mind your own business" is its only moral law. Interference with another's business is a crime and the only crime, and as such may properly be resisted. In accordance with this view the anarchists look upon attempts to arbitrarily suppress vice as in themselves crimes. They believe liberty and the resultant social well-being to be a sure cure for all the vices. But they recognize the right of the drunkard, the gambler, the rake, and the harlot to live their lives until they shall freely choose to abandon them.

In the matter of the maintenance and rearing of children the anarchists would neither institute the communistic nursery which the State socialists favor nor keep the communistic school system which now prevails. The nurse and the teacher, like the doctor and the preacher, must be selected voluntarily, and their services must be paid for by those who patronize them. Parental rights must not be taken away, and parental responsibilities must not be foisted upon others.

Even in so delicate a matter as that of the relations of the sexes the anarchists do not shrink from the application of their principle. They acknowledge and defend the right of any man and woman, or any men and women, to love each other for as long or as short a time as they can, will, or may. To them legal marriage and legal divorce are equal absurdities. They look forward to a time when every individual, whether man or woman, shall be self-supporting, and when each shall have an independent home of his or her own, whether it be a separate house or rooms in a house with others; when the love relations between these independent individuals shall be as varied as are individual inclinations and attractions; and when the children born of these relations shall belong exclusively to the mothers until old enough to belong to themselves.

Such are the main features of the anarchistic social ideal. There is wide difference of opinion among those who hold it as to the best method of obtaining it. Time forbids the treatment of that phase of the subject here. I will simply call attention to the fact that it is an ideal utterly inconsistent with that of those Communists who falsely call themselves anarchists while at the same time advocating a *régime of anarchism* fully as despotic as that of the State socialists themselves. And it is an ideal that can be as little advanced by the forcible expropriation recommended by John Most and Prince Kropotkin as retarded by the brooms of those Mrs. Partingtons of the bench who sentence them to prison; an ideal which the martyrs of Chicago did far more to help by their glorious death upon the gallows for the common cause of socialism than by their unfortunate advocacy during their lives, in the name of anarchism, of force as a revolutionary agent and authority as a safeguard of the new social order. The anarchists believe in liberty both as end and means, and are hostile to anything that antagonizes it.

3

EXPANDING THE SPHERE OF THE STATE

Laurence Gronlund
THE COOPERATIVE COMMONWEALTH

Laurence Gronlund (1846–1899), who came to the United States in 1867, has borne the reputation of being Marx's foremost American interpreter and popularizer in the late nineteenth century. The Cooperative Commonwealth was one of the few English works written in America that borrowed heavily from Marxist economic ideas. Also, in contrast to George and Tucker, Gronlund argued for a strong collective state. Nevertheless he was no Marxist. He rejected out of hand the class struggle and insisted that socialism, while inevitable, could only succeed if the revolution was peaceful and was not tied to the interests of any particular class. He opposed women's suffrage, favored a protective tariff, and supported measures to restrict immigration. Unworried about possible restrictions on liberty imposed by future bureaucracies, Gronlund looked forward to the establishment of an efficient government run by an elite corps of experts. In his last book, The New Economy, it became clear that Christianity had exerted as great an influence on Gronlund as had the writings of any economic thinker.

We have concluded the socialist critique of the present order of things. In a nutshell it is this: the fleecings increase in our country and in all industrial countries at a very great rate. In order that capital (the sum of these fleecings) may be simply *maintained*, (mark that!) it must be constantly employed in production and a market must be found for the products which it enables labor to create. Foreign markets will soon dry up; our autocrats, therefore, will be confined to their respective home markets. But the masses at home are more and more becoming wage-workers from the operation of "individualism"; wage-workers receive in wages only about half of what they produce; the masses, consequently, are becoming more and more unable to buy

SOURCE. Laurence Gronlund, *The Cooperative Commonwealth* (Boston, 1884), pp. 75–99.

back the values they create. Thus for lack of consumption, capital will be more and more threatened with depreciation. The more capital, the more "overproduction." The wage system and private "enterprise" *will*, indeed, involve capitalists and laborers in one common ruin.

This is the foundation for what may be called: "constructive" socialism. We are not under the delusion that nations can be *persuaded* by the grandeur, excellence, and equity of our system. The future is ours, because the present system will soon be *unbearable;* because, as we said, we might fold our arms and calmly wait to see the established order fall to pieces by its own weight. Our conception of value, therefore, truly comprises the *whole* of socialism.

When the culmination has been reached, the reins will drop from the impotent hands of our autocrats and will be taken up by an impersonal power, coeval with human nature: the State.

It is a pity that we must commence by guarding ourselves against the corrupt American use of the term "State", but, writing mainly for our American countrymen, we cannot help ourselves.

The "state" of Pennsylvania and the other thirty-seven "states" are not, and never were, *States*. By State we mean with Webster "a whole people, united in one body politic." That is the meaning of *State* in all languages, English included—except the American language. Now, not one of our American "states" was ever for one moment a "whole people." They either were subjects to the crown of England, or parts of the Confederation, or of the Union. The Union then is a *State*, just as France and Spain are States, and it is emphatically so since the American people commenced to call themselves a Nation with a big N. This, however, by no means excludes local centers of authority, what we are wont to call "local self-government."

"The State" is a stumbling block to many very worthy persons. They apprehend—a fear very honorable in them—that State supremacy would be prejudicial to freedom. We hope to make it apparent that State action and individual freedom, far from being antagonistic, are really complementary of each other.

The reason why "the State" is nowadays such a bugbear to so many is that this word has quite another meaning in the mouth of an individualist, wherever you find him, than when used by a socialist. Indeed, the fundamental distinction between "individualism" and socialism must be sought in the opposition of these two conceptions.

Individualists, and foremost amongst them our autocrats, cherish this degrading notion of the State: that it is merely an organ of society, synonymous with "government"—with the political machinery of society. We claim—to quote Webster once more—that the State is "a whole people, united in one body politic," in other words, that

The State is the organized society.

We cannot better contrast these two conceptions than by comparing the views of Herbert Spencer when he was a young philosopher with his present views now that he is a mature one.

Young Spencer wrote a book called *Social Statics*, which to a great extent has become a manual to our "let-alone" politicians. In that work he starts out with a "first principle" from which he proposes to reason out, deductively, the whole science of government—a method, by the way, that is thought rather precarious by scientific men of today. This assumed axiom which, undoubtedly, looks very captivating at first sight, is that "every man has freedom to do all that he wills, provided he infringes not *the like freedom* of any other man." From this "principle"—of which we shall presently have more to say—he proves with flawless logic that society is simply a *voluntary* association of men for mutual protection and the State merely its organ to that end. The business of the State, therefore, is only to secure to each citizen unlimited freedom to exercise his faculties. Then, to be sure, the State has no right to tax men of property for educating other men's children, or for feeding the poor or even for looking after the public health. In taking upon itself these functions the State is acting the part of an aggressor instead of that of a protector.

The State is a policeman—nothing more. By and by, when the millennium arrives, the State will lose even that function; it will become a rudimentary organ. The State will then disappear altogether. As long as it exists, it is nothing but a necessary evil; only instituted for the bad, and only a burden to the good. If the facts do not verify that conclusion, so much the worse for the facts. If the State's activity does spread more and more, even in Spencer's own country—in response to the pressure of the "logic of events," and in spite of the frantic struggles of its ruling class: the wealthy middle class—so much the worse for the State.

Such was the reasoning of Spencer in 1850; and these views are accepted and practiced by the ruling powers of our country, as far as in them lies. Our capital-holders cry out: "You, State! You government! Your whole business, you know, consists in securing us unlimited freedom to exercise our faculties. That is all we are doing here; the whole crowd of us are exercising our faculties, each to the extent of his ability. It does not concern you a bit whom or how many we are able to fleece or how much we fleece them; or how many fall and are trampled upon. Let us alone, then, and simply see to it that we are not interfered with! That is what you are paid for, you know. 'Every one look out for himself, and the devil take the hindmost,' is our and your rule of action." And the "government" lets them alone. That is to say, it allows itself to be made into a peace officer of a singular sort. For suppose a policeman should see a bully attack a weaker man, and should say to himself: "It is not my business to protect that weak man or to interfere with the combatants at all. I take it to be my duty, just to see to it that no one interferes with them. So I will make a ring round them and let the best man win." That is what our so-called governments virtually do, and so the shrewd, greedy individuals who can exercise their faculties do so to their heart's content and grow fat at the expense of other individuals. Probably in no other age did individuals have such a power over their neighbors as they have now in consequence of this "let-alone" policy. Every factory, mine, workshop, and railroad shows the working of it. The individual Vanderbilt has acquired two hundred millions, while another individual—perhaps the producer of part of his fortune—is sent to prison as a tramp.

But that is all in order. For hear young Spencer: "The shouldering aside the weak by the strong, which leaves so many in shallows and miseries, is the decree of a large, farseeing benevolence, regarded not separately, but in connection with the interests of universal humanity. To step in between weakness and its consequences suspends the progress of weeding out those of lower development"—and Vanderbilt and Gould, of course, are the "strong," and men of "*higher* development!"

Why do not those men of property—of "higher development"—abolish this good-for-nothing "State" altogether? Would it not be a good speculation for them to let courts of justice to the highest bidder, and farm out the prosecution of wars to stock companies? Can they not buy protection against violence, as well as insurance against fire, and more cheaply too, on the glorious free-competition plan? Why do they not do it?

Well, perhaps the State is something else than *an organ* after all.

Herbert Spencer, the *mature* and profound philosopher, pursues the far more scientific method of studying society, as it is, and the process of its development, instead of evolving it, as young Spencer did, out of his own inner consciousness.

His results now are that the body politic, instead of being a "voluntary" association is, what socialists claim that it is, an *organism*.

Beside arguments in his other works he devotes a very able and ingenious essay to the drawing of parallels between a highly developed State and the most developed animals, and sums up:

"That they gradually increase in mass; that they become, little by little more complex; that at the same time their parts grow more mutually dependent; and that they continue to live and grow as wholes, while successive generations of their units appear and disappear—are broad peculiarities, which bodies politic display, in common with all living bodies, and in which they and other living bodies differ from everything else."

In several striking passages Spencer further shows with what singular closeness correspondences can be traced in the details between the two kinds of organisms, as, for instance, between the distributing system of animal bodies and the distributing system of bodies politic, or between our economic division of labor, and that prevailing in organic bodies, "so striking, indeed, that the expression 'physiological division of labor' has been suggested by it."

And some of the leading contrasts between the two kinds of organisms, he shows, are far less important than appears at first glance. Thus, the distinction that the living elements of society do not, as in individual organisms, form one continuous mass, disappears when we consider that the former are not separated by intervals of dead space, but diffused through space, covered with life of a lower order, which ministers to their life. And thus with this other peculiarity, that the elements of a social organism are capable of moving from place to place, is obviated by the fact, that as farmers, manufacturers, and traders, men generally carry on business in the same localities; that, at all events, each great center of industry, each manufacturing town or district, continues always in the same place.

There is then but one distinction left that may be deemed material. In the social organism the living units are conscious, while in the animal organism it is the *whole* that possesses consciousness.

But then those other highly developed organisms—to wit: the vegetable ones—have no consciousness at all. Society could then be considered a mighty plant whose units are highly developed animals.

Again, though the social organism has no consciousness of its own, it certainly has a distinctive character of its own; a corporate *individuality*, a corporate "oneness." As a unit of that organism every individual certainly displays a wholly different character from that of the organism itself. Every nation has its own spirit, which the Germans call the "*Volksgeist*"; a spirit which has its life in the national history, which produces specific traits of nationality, differing from the common traits of humanity. It generally lies deep, hidden, unsuspected until such a moment arrives as that with us, when Fort Sumter was fired upon; then rising, as it were, out of an abyss it urges thinkers and actors resistlessly on to pursue, unwittingly, the loftiest ideal of the race. This corporate individuality is far from being identical with average "public opinion." It is *sui generis* and makes the social organism an organism *sui generis.*

We therefore insist, with even greater force than Spencer did, that the State is a living organism, differing from other organisms in no essential respect. This is not to be understood in a simply metaphorical sense; it is not that the State merely resembles an organism, but that it, including with the people the land and all that the land produces, literally is *an organism*, personal and territorial.

The "government"—the punishing and restraining authority—may possibly be dispensed with at some future time. But the State—*never.* To dispense with the State would be to dissolve society.

It follows that the relation of the State, the body politic, to us, its citizens, is *actually* that of a tree to its cells, and *not* that of a heap of sand to its grains, to which it is entirely indifferent how many other grains of sand are scattered and trodden under foot.

This is a conception of far-reaching consequence.

In the *first* place, it, together with the modern doctrine of *evolution*, as applied to all organisms, deals a mortal blow to the theory of "man's natural rights," the theory of man's "inalienable right" to life, liberty, property, "happiness," etc., the theory of which mankind during the last century has heard and read so much; the theory that has been so assiduously preached to our dispossessed classes, and which has benefited them so little!

Natural rights! The highest "natural right" we can imagine is for the stronger to kill and eat the weaker, and for the weaker to be killed and eaten. One of the "natural rights" left "man" now is to act the brute toward wife and children, and that "right" the State has already curtailed and will by-and-by give it the finishing stroke. Another "natural right," very highly prized by our autocrats, is the privilege they now possess of "saving" for themselves what other people produce. In brief, "natural rights" are the rights of the muscular, the cunning, the unscrupulous.

These so-called natural rights and an equally fictitious "law of nature" were invented by Jean Jacques Rousseau (who followed Luther and the other Reformers in the work of making breaches in the old petrified system of the Middle Ages) as a metaphysical expedient to get some sanction to legitimate resistance to absolute authority in kings, nobility, and clergy. He derived them from a supposed "state of nature" which he and his disciples as enthusiastically praised as if they had been there and knew all about it. Now, modern historical comparative methods prove conclusively that this "state of nature" never existed. A man, living from the moment of his birth outside organized society, if this were possible, would be no more a man than a hand would be a hand without the body. *Civil society is man's natural state.* This "state of nature," on the other hand, would be for man the most unnatural state of all, and fortunately so, for in it we should not have been able to make the least headway against our conditions, but must have remained, till the present moment, hungry, naked savages, whose "rights" would not procure us a single meal. And as to a "law of nature," if it is proper to use that term at all, it is nothing but the conscience and reason of civil society.

No, Rousseau did say several things worth notice—as any author who is being refuted a century after his death must have done. These speculations of his are indeed worth notice, to us Americans especially, since they formed the logical basis of our own "epoch-making" Revolution—as a German might happily call it—though we cannot help remarking that the conclusion here justified the premises, rather than the reverse. And, further, they also furnished the justification, the steampower, for the great French Revolution. The incidents of the latter event, however, showed that Rousseau could, under certain circumstances, be a very unsafe guide; they demonstrated that the "natural rights of man" were good tools to tear down rotten systems with, but sandy foundations on which to erect new systems.

We have been outspoken on this matter, because it is so important that thoughtful people should know that philosophic socialists repudiate that theory of "natural rights," and insist that the lesson taught by Rousseau and repeated (why not say so outright?) in our own Declaration of Independence must be unlearned before any firm foundation can be reached. Unfortunately nearly all our "reformers"—men with the noblest and often truly socialist hearts—cling to it and build on man's "God-given rights" as if they were the special confidants of God.

But Carlyle is emphatically right when he says "Nothing solid can be founded on shams; it must conform to the realities, the verities of things."

Here is such a reality:

It is society, organized society, the State that gives us all the rights we have. To the State we owe our freedom. To it we owe our living and property, for outside of organized society man's needs far surpass his means. The humble beggar owes much to the State, but the haughty millionaire far more, for outside of it they both would be worse off than the beggar now is. To it we owe all that we are and all that we have. To it we owe our civilization. It is by its help that we have reached such a condition as man individually never would have been able to attain. Progress is the struggle with nature for mastery, is war with the misery and inabilities of our "natural " condition. The State is the organic union of us all to wage that war, to subdue nature, to redress natural defects and inequalities. The State therefore, so far from being a burden to the "good," a "necessary evil, " is man's greatest good.

This conception of the State as an organism thus consigns the "rights of man" to obscurity and puts *duty* in the foreground.

In the *second* place, we now can ascertain the true sphere of the State. That is, we now can commence to build something solid.

We say *sphere* on purpose; we do not ask what are the "rights," "duties" or 'functions" of the State, for if it truly is an organism it is just as improper to speak of *its* rights, duties, or functions towards its citizens as it is to speak of a man's rights, duties, and functions in relation to his heart, his legs, or his head. The State has rights, duties, and functions in relation to other organisms, but toward its own members it has only a sphere of activities.

The sphere of the State simply consists in caring for its own welfare, just as a man's sphere, as far as himself is concerned, consists in caring for his own well-being. If that be properly done, then his brain, his lungs, and his stomach will have nothing to complain of.

So with the State. Its whole sphere is the making all special activities work together for one general end: its own welfare, or the *public good*. Observe that the public good, the general welfare, implies far more than "the greatest good to the greatest number" on which our "practical" politicians of today base their trifling measures. Their motto broadly sanctions the sacrifice of minorities to majorities, while the "general welfare" means the greatest good of every individual citizen.

To that end the State may do anything whatsoever which is shown to be expedient.

It may, as it always has done, limit the right of a person to dispose of himself in marriage as he pleases.

The State is, in the words of J.S. Mill, "fully entitled to abrogate or alter any particular right of property which it judges to stand in the way of the public good."

The State may tomorrow, if it judges it expedient, take all the capital of the country from its present owners, without any compensation whatsoever, and convert it into social capital.

In Chapter 1 we showed that the whole wealth of the country (i.e., not natural wealth but the sum of all values) is the result of labor. As against capitalists the producers, therefore, would clearly be entitled to it. But as against the State, the organized society; even labor does not give us a particle of title to what our hands and brain produce.

One need not be a socialist to acknowledge that.

Wm. B. Weeden, a manufacturer in Providence, R.I., says in a criticism on Henry George's book in the *Atlantic Monthly* for December 1880: "The axe you use is not yours, though you may have made it, instead of buying it in the market. The idea of the axe, its potentiality, which enables it to prevail over nature, does not belong to you. This is the result of long generations of development, from the rudest stone-tool to the elegant steelblade which rings through the pinewoods of Maine. This belongs to society. Neither the laborer nor the capitalist owns that principle. So everywhere. Neither labor nor capital employs the other. It is society which employs both."

To whom does the telegraph belong? To society. Neither Professor Morse nor any other inventor can lay sole claim to it. It *grew* little by little.

With still greater force the State may reclaim possession of all the land within its limits, all laws, customs and deeds to the contrary notwithstanding.

We say "with still greater force," not because the ownership of land is on a different footing from that of other capital. Its value, like that of other capital, is partly real, arising from the labor of this and former generations, and partly unreal, due to the monopoly of it and the constantly increasing necessities of the community. It therefore is the creation of society as much as other capital. We say so because the common law of Great Britain and our country has always claimed, and still does claim that the State is the sole landlord:

"The first thing the student has to get rid of is the absolute idea of ownership. Such an idea is quite unknown to the English law. No man is, in law, the absolute owner of lands; he can only hold an estate in them." Williams: *On the Law of Real Property.*

When, therefore, the Trinity Church Corporation of New York City claims to *own* city property of sufficient value to pay all the debts of the state of New York, its cities and villages, a value mainly created by the tenants who have covered that tract of land with buildings, graded and paved the streets, and built the sewers, it is simply a glaring usurpation.

When, therefore, the increased values of real estate, due simply to the progress of the country, are permitted, in the form of increased rents "to drop into the mouths of landowners as they sleep instead of being applied to the public necessities of the Society which created it" in the words of Mill, it is only because the too "enterprising" individual has got the better of the State.

For the same reason the landowner has been permitted to possess whatever treasure may be hidden in it, even treasure of which no man knew anything, when the owner entered into possession—an allowance, than which no one more foolish or absurd could be imagined.

For the same reason the splendid opportunities which our country had, both in the reconstruction of the Southern states and in the settlement of our public lands, for making the nation the sole landlord, were not so much as thought of.

Our landowners ought to admit with Blackstone: "We seem to fear, that our titles are not quite good; it is well the great mass obey the laws without inquiring why they were made so and not otherwise."

But there is no need to devote more space here to discuss the supreme title of the State to the land since the appearance of Henry George's book, *Progress and Poverty*, which we hope all our readers have read. The main criticism which socialists have to make on this work is that it pushes the land question—in our country a secondary question in importance—so much into the foreground, that sight is entirely lost of the principal question: who should control the instruments of production and transportation? Furthermore, George seems to have written his book for Englishmen, Scotchmen and Irishmen, rather than for Americans. To start the solution of the social problem in our country, where as yet the great majority of farmers own the land which they cultivate, with a proposition to divest all landowners of their titles, is to commence by making a very large portion of the workers to be benefited hostile to all social change.

The State is thus fully entitled to take charge of *all* instruments of labor and production, and to say that all social activities shall be carried on in a perfectly different manner.

Undoubtedly the whole fleecing class will interpose their socalled "vested rights." That is to say because the State for a long time tacitly allowed a certain class to divide the common stock of social advantages among themselves and appropriate it to their own individual benefit therefore the State is estopped, they say, from ever recovering it. And not alone will they claim undisturbed possession of what they have, but also the right to use it in the future as they have in the past; that is, they will claim a "vested right" to fleece the masses to all eternity.

But such a protest will be just as vain as was that of the Pope against the loss of his temporal sovereignty. The theory of "vested rights" never applies when a revolution has taken place; when the whole structure of society is changed. The tail of a tadpole that is developing into a frog may protest as much as it pleases; nature heeds it not. And when the frog is an accomplished fact, there is no tail to protest.

This whole doctrine of "vested rights," moreover, has its reason in the fact that from the dawn of history to the present time we have had and have *privileged* classes. Henry George remarks very pointedly: "When we allow 'vested rights' we still wear the collar of the Saxon thrall." The only "vested right" any man has is the right to such institutions as will best promote the public good. A man has no other right whatever in a civilized community. If he is not satisfied with that, he may exile himself to where there is no civilization, and even there his descendants will necessarily grow up into a State.

Observe further, that the public welfare means more than the welfare of all the living individuals composing it. Since the State is an organism, it is more than all of us collectively.

It would be absurd to say that a man is nothing but an aggregation of his cells. Burke said rightly of the State that it includes the dead, the living, and the coming generations. We are what we are far more by the accumulated influence of past generations than by our own efforts, and our labor will principally benefit those who are to follow us. The public welfare thus includes the welfare of the generations to come. This comprehensive conception places the pettiness and impotency of our "individualism" in the most glaring light. For how can it ever be the private interest of mortal individuals to make immediate sacrifices for the distant future?

"But if the State's sphere is to be extended to everything that may affect the public welfare, why! then there is no stopping to what the State will attempt."

We let Professor Huxley[1] reply ("Administrative Nihilism.")

"Surely the answer is obvious, that, on similar grounds, the right of a man to eat when he is hungry, might be disputed, because if you once allow that he may eat at all there is no stopping, until he gorges himself and suffers all the ills of a surfeit."

Does it not now seem more profitable, especially to our dispossessed classes, to lay stress on *duty* rather than on *rights?*

Does our conception of the State not furnish a very firm foundation, firm enough to build a new social order on ?

Let us then give due credit to Herbert Spencer for his profound

---

[1]Thomas Henry Huxley (1825–1895) was an English natural scientist and champion of Darwin's view of evolution through natural selection. He nevertheless firmly resisted the Social Darwinists' application of a "struggle for survival" ethic to human society. Ed.

speculations on the social organism. He has, indeed, in them laid the foundation for constructive socialism, as far as the Anglo-Saxon peoples are concerned, just as Ricardo[2] by his speculations on value did it for critical socialism. True, Spencer is still the apostle of "individualism"; he exhibits still a morbid aversion to all State activity, but we have a right to call his present utterances on that point mere crotchets, since they do not receive the least. support from his splendid arguments in favor of the organic character of society.

That is also Professor Huxley's opinion. He says: "I cannot but think, that the real force of the analogy is totally opposed to the negative (individualistic) view of the State function.

"Suppose that in accordance with this view, each muscle were to maintain that the nervous system had no right to interfere with its contraction except to prevent it from hindering the contraction of another muscle; or each gland, that it had a right to secrete, as long as its secretion interfered with no other; suppose every separate cell left free to follow its own interests and be 'let alone.' Lord of all! what would become of the body physiological?"

This negative view of the State function is a very modern one. No thinker or philosophic statesmen up to the eighteenth century anywhere dreamt of it. Not until the exaggerated form of the Protestant doctrine of the independence of the individual had taken possession of men's minds; not until the great delusion had become prevalent, that we have been brought into this world, each for the sake of himself, did it come into vogue. Then it was that Wilhelm von Humboldt[3] (who may be said to be the father of the doctrine) deliberately degraded the State below a peace officer or a watchdog.

But even ultra-Protestant nations that adopted this view in theory have constantly been impelled by an inward necessity to repudiate it in practice. It forbids the State, as we have seen, to concern itself about the poor, and yet the poor law of Elizabeth (still in force in Great Britain and our country) confers upon every man a *legal* claim to relief from funds obtained by enforcing a contribution from the general community. It forbids the State to concern itself about schools, libraries, universities, asylums, and hospitals, and yet it concerns itself more and more with them. England is to this day proud of having spent a hundred million of dollars in abolishing slavery in her colonies, and in these latter days she is spreading her activity over

[2]David Ricardo (1772–1823) was one of the chief English expositors of classical, laissez-faire economic theories. Ed.

[3]Wilhelm von Humboldt (1767–1835) was a German philologist, statesman, educationalist—and was the author of *On the Limits of State Action*. Ed.

railroads and telegraphs, without the least apparent compunction of conscience. And our country (especially under democratic control the champion of this "let-alone" abomination) finds today her chief glory in having torn slavery up by the roots with its strong national arm.

But let it, in the *third* place, be emphatically understood that when we insist that the State ought to extend its sphere over all social activities, we do not mean the *present* State at all.

Our Republic is a State. Parliamentary Great Britain is a State. Imperial Germany, autocratic Russia and bureaucratic China are all social organisms. But not one of them is a *full grown* State, a fully developed organism. In all of them, our own country included, classes *exercise the authority* and direct all social activity.

Do not here bring forward the insipid commonplace that, properly speaking, we have no "classes" in our country and that the "people" govern here! No classes? Indeed!

Roam around in New York, Boston, Philadelphia, or any of our towns above a country village, for that matter, and you will find them all mapped out into districts strictly according to the poverty or wealth of the inhabitants. Those who live in the poorer districts along neglected dirty streets in badly arranged and badly furnished houses constitute a lower *caste* in fact, since nine-tenths of them cannot *by any possibility*, under our social system, get out of it. They and their children after them *must* remain in their poverty, squalor and degradation as long as this system endures. In the healthy, beautiful and comfortable quarters we find those who arrogate to themselves the name of "society," our "best people," "prominent citizens."

Which of these two classes govern—the majority living in tenement houses, back alleys and ill-smelling neighborhoods or the minority in the aristocratic districts?

It is frequently remarked that "our best people" have withdrawn themselves from politics. Suppose that is so—though it is also noticed that men of wealth lately have secured seats in Congress to such an extent that our national Senate, to a great extent, consists of very rich people—still that is very little to the point. For, since the State is the organized society, "politics" constitute but a trifle of the social activities, compared with the various forms of industry. We have seen that it is our "prominent citizens" who control our manufactures, transportation and commerce, who indeed exercise an *autocratic* control over these, and that they are destined to do the like in agriculture within a short time. Their control over the transporting interests of the country—interests so dominant that it has been justly said: "He who controls the highways of a nation, controls the nation itself"—is indeed so supreme that Vanderbilt is reported to have observed with refreshing candor: the roads are not run for the benefit of "the dear public." No matter, whether he has been so candid or not, they certainly are not.

Politics then form but a very small part of our social activities. The people are said to govern these; their "government," in fact, consists in choosing on election day between two sets of men presented for their suffrages. What that amounts to we shall see in another chapter, and shall here simply remark that as soon as the one or the other set of men have been elected they pass entirely out of the control of the voters. Who then control the actions of those thus chosen?

We shall entirely pass by the ever-recurring charges of bribery of legislators and whole legislatures; we shall pass by another reported candid admission by Vanderbilt: "When I want to buy up any politician I always find—the most purchasable"; we shall pass by the solemn declaration of a committee of the legislature of the state of New York, that no bill could pass the Senate without Vanderbilt's consent. We let all these things pass as perhaps *non proven*.

But one thing is so evident that no one will dream of disputing it, as soon as its meaning is fairly understood: these *autocrats* of our industrial affairs *dictate the policy of the government* to legislatures and Congress, to presidents, governors, and judges, and have dictated it since the establishment of our government. What we mean is simply what we have all along insisted upon, that both our national and local governments throughout profess allegiance to the "let-alone" policy; that all executive, legislative, and judicial officers are trained from the day they enter school or college to look on public affairs through capitalistic spectacles. We simply mean to say that not one so-called statesman of any influence in either of the two great political parties ever dreams of interfering with the "business"–interests of our plutocrats, if he can help it. They all echo the sentiment of Judge Foraker, the Republican candidate for governor of Ohio: "*Capital is sensitive; it shrinks from the very appearance of danger.*"

What need then for them "to go into politics" when they already have their devoted retainers in every place of authority?

They need have no fear ever to be interfered with as long as they retain their preeminent position in industrial affairs. The ruling class industrially will always be the ruling class politically.

Therefore we say it is Utopian to hope to have a legal normal working day of eight hours, much more so one of six hours, as Moody[4] proposes in his *Land and Labor*, as long as the established order lasts.

[4]William Godwin Moody's *Land and Labor in the United States* (New York, 1883) was an early attempt to explore the degrading impact of machine technology on the labor force. Ed.

Therefore it is Utopian to hope to have land nationalized as George advocates, as long as we have the wage system.

Therefore capitalists will very likely succeed in their strenuous opposition to the proposition made by a late postmaster general, that the nation shall take possession of the telegraphs of the country. But if they should at last be compelled to yield—because the necessities of the social organism command it—they are sure to demand and receive extravagant compensation for their "property," for the "vested rights" of capitalists have always been appreciated, while as we already have noted the working classes have never been thought entitled to compensation when new machinery drove them out of old employments.

While now our autocrats generally are satisfied, and well may be satisfied, with their *veto* on all proposed public measures, prejudicial to their sinister interests, and with interdicting all legislation in favor of the masses, they never have objected to any State action that would put money into their pockets. They have been, and still are to a great extent, beneficiaries of the nation, another proof that *they* really govern, even politically.

We all know that the national government has presented six railroad companies with an empire of land as large as Great Britain and Ireland and half as much more, and in addition has guaranteed bonds of theirs, which with accrued interest at the maturity of these bonds will amount to more than 180 million dollars.

We have already seen how the whole machinery of government has been set and kept in motion to acquire foreign markets for our autocrats and to prepare our working classes for the requisite reduction in wages, simply that this wage system might secure a new lease of life, however short and precarious and however injurious the effect which this policy would have on the condition of the workers.

We see today, as our forefathers have often seen, how agitated the two great political parties of our country are on the questions of free trade or protection. This issue makes it so very plain how paramount the influence of our autocrats is in political affairs. It is our *manufacturers* who want protection; it is our *commercial* men who want free trade. The former undoubtedly pretend that protection benefits the laboring classes; but that this claim is a mere sham is evident from the fact that they never have proposed to discourage the immigration of foreign laborers; that they would violently oppose a proposal to that effect; that they, on the contrary, always have done all they could to encourage foreign laborers to come here, that they even send agents over to Europe to coax them by false pretenses over here. Our protectionist fleecers want *protection for the results of labor, but free trade in labor.* The commercial men, on the other hand, whose interest it is to have free trade in all things, never have objected to handsome gifts from government for their ships in the guise of subsidies for the performance of mail services.

Class rule is always detrimental to the welfare of the whole social organism, because classes, when in power, cannot help considering themselves preeminently the State. They, furthermore, cannot help being biased in favor of their special interests and therefore are necessarily hostile to the rest of the nation, and as we daily see in our free-traders and protectionists, hostile to each other. Matthew Arnold speaks truly when he says that State action by a hostile class ought to be deprecated.

Our Republic, therefore, just as all other modern States, may properly be compared to some imaginable animal organism, where the blood, proceeding from the collective digestion, is principally diverted to the stomach or the brain, while the arms and legs are stinted as much as possible.

This *class* State will develop into a *commonwealth*—bless the Puritans for that splendid English word! It will develop into a State that will know of no "classes" either in theory or practice; in other words into a State *where the whole population is incorporated into society.* In the place of the present partially evolved organism in which the arms and legs, and to a great extent the brain, are stinted in blood as much as possible, we shall have an organism "whose every organ shall receive blood in proportion to the work it does" in the language of Spencer.

That is to say: *the commonwealth will be a State of equality.*

It is said that "we already have equality," and when we ask the meaning of the phrase we are told that all are "equal before the law." If that were really the case—what it is not—it would be but a poor kind of equality. The cells of the root and of the flower in a plant are "equal"; the cells of the foot and of the heart in an animal are "equal," for they are all properly cared for; the organism knows of no "higher" and "lower" organs or cells. And so it will be in the future commonwealth; there "equality" will mean that every unit of society can truly say to any other unit: "I am not less than a man, and thou art not more than a man."

Again, our commonwealth will put *interdependence* in the place of the phrases of our Declaration of Independence, which claims for every citizen the "right" to life, liberty, and the pursuit of "happiness." This declaration was evidently adopted by "individualists," as the French Revolution was a revolution of "individualism," for of what use is it to possess the "right" to do something, when you have not the power, the means, the opportunity to do it? Is this "right to the pursuit of happiness" not a mocking irony to the masses who *cannot* pursue "happiness"? We saw how the millionaire and beggar would be equally miserable outside of the State, and behold, how much this rights-of-man doctrine has done for the former and how very little for the latter!

The future commonwealth will *help* every individual to attain the highest development he or she has capacity for. It will lay a cover for every one at nature's table. "State" and "State *help*" will be as inseparable as a piano and music.

Do not now object, as *young* Spencer did in "Social Statics," that this means "transforming every citizen into a grown-up baby"; for the objection is not to the point at all.

State help is not to do away with a man's own efforts. I do not do away with a man's own efforts when I hand him a ladder. I do not set aside his own exertions in cultivating a field, because I give him a plow. Our State does not render useless the powers of a boy when it furnishes him schools, teachers, and libraries. Our commonwealth will relieve none of self-help, but make self-help possible to all. *It will help everybody to help himself.*

That is to say: this commonwealth will be a society all of whose units have a sense of belonging together, of being responsible for one another; a society, pervaded by a feeling of what we, using a foreign word, call *solidarity*, but what we not inaptly may in English term *corporate responsibility*.

It is worth noting that our modern insurance companies, particularly those of life insurance, are teaching us that responsibility, for do they not make the strong and temperate of us use their prolonged lives to pay up premiums which go to the progeny of the weak and reckless?

"But what about *liberty?*" the reader may ask.

Many worthy persons, as we said commencing this chapter, entertain the fear which shines forth in Mill's famous essay on "liberty"; the fear lest freedom should be drilled and disciplined out of human life, in order that the great mill of the commonwealth should grind smoothly. To ascertain whether this fear is well grounded or not we must first know what we are to understand by the words: "freedom" and "liberty."

Everybody calls the not being oppressed: "liberty." That is, undoubtedly, an indispensable and yet, as has been said, a most insignificant fractional part of human freedom. Then, again, we mean by "liberty" the not being restrained, being "at liberty" to do this or that. Now, that may be a good thing or otherwise. Whether it is the one or the other depends entirely upon the answer to the question: to do *what?*

To be "at liberty" to be a tramp, or to die of starvation, or to steal, or to be lodged in a jail are not good things. We sometimes find a great lout in a railroad car who thinks he is "at liberty" to spread himself over four seats, but occasionally he finds out that he is not; that he must take his feet down and sit along. The liberty of this lout is the "liberty" which our shrewd, grasping, vulgar autocrats glorify, for it means the predominance of their interests over everybody else's interests, over the general welfare. It is in the name of that "liberty" that all fleecing is done.

Of that kind of liberty there always has been too much in the world—somewhere. That kind of liberty means slavery to somebody; means as the Yankee defined it "to do what he liked and make everybody else."

Every struggle for real liberty has been a struggle against that sort of "liberty," entrenched in classes. Progress demands the curbing of that kind of "liberty," and our commonwealth will use no gloves in handling it.

The fact is there is a radical difference between liberty to do the right thing and liberty to do the wrong thing. That is why young Spencer could not draw any sound conclusion from his so-called principle: "that every man has freedom to do all that he wills provided he does not infringe on the like freedom of any other man," because no one can do any wrong act, without doing harm to other men; or as Professor Huxley puts it: "The higher the state of civilization, the more completely do the actions of one member of the social body influence all the rest, and the less possible is it for one man to do a wrong thing without interfering, more or less, with the freedom of all his fellow citizens."

As liberty is such a hazy term, why use it at all, when we have such a glorious word in the English language as *freedom?* There is the same difference between "liberty" and "freedom" as between "right" and "might," between "fiction" and "fact," between "shadow" and "substance."

"Freedom" is something substantial. A man who is ignorant is not free. A man who is a tramp is not free. A man who sees his wife and children starving is not free. A man who must toil twelve hours a day, in order to vegetate, is not free. A man who is full of cares is not free. A wage-worker, whether laborer or clerk, who every day for certain hours must be at the beck and call of a "master" is not free. As Shelley says in the Apostrophe to Freedom,

"For the laborer thou art bread."

Right so far. But freedom is not alone bread, but leisure, absence of cares, self-determination, ability and means to do the right thing. Restraint very often is just requisite to develop that ability; indeed, restraint is the very life of freedom.

Freedom is something the individual unaided can never achieve. He is as driftwood in a flood. It is something to be conferred on him by a well organized body politic.

Now certain people have altogether too much "liberty." Our Commonwealth will evolve that priceless good: *freedom*.

This is by no means a finished humanity, but there is a constant unfolding, a steady advance towards completeness and perfection. True, this or that nation may decay, but some other nation then comes to the rescue. All that socialists undertake to do is to ascertain the several stages so far reached by humanity on its onward march, therefrom to infer the next advance that will be made by some one of the social organisms in the van of progress, and then they reverently propose to help humanity in taking the next step. They full well know that all that individuals can do is to aid or check that onward movement, but that to stop it is even beyond a czar's control.

We have observed that it is round the working classes that the battle of progress has been waged; their condition has determined the stage of civilization, though history has given but scant account of them. During the two great periods that lie behind us, slavery and serfdom, they were in fact and in law subject to their lords who took the lion's share without disguise, as a matter of right. Based on that subjection, however, there was an intense feeling of *unity* which pervaded the whole of society; a unity that made these systems so strong and so lasting, and without which unity no social system can be enduring. But men rebelled against the subjection. Luther was fortunate enough to start that rebellion in the religious sphere, for it is always at the top that all radical changes commence.

Then was inaugurated the era in which we are living, which really is nothing but a *transition period* between the two great systems of the past and another great system of the future, *for it possesses no unity*. It corresponds exactly to the transition-period between slavery and serfdom, when Christianity was striving for mastery. It is an era of anarchy, of criticism, of negations, of opposition, of hypocrisy, as this was one. Instead of slavery or serfdom and *subjection* we now have the wage system and *contracts*. That is to say, while formerly the lords appropriated the results of labor openly, they now do it underhandedly. The wage-worker, if he will live, must *agree* to relinquish one-half of what he produces. There is, in fact, fully as much subjection now as formerly, but it has taken on a softer, a more hypocritic form. That is why the rebellion not only continues, but has reached down into the material sphere and is shaking the very foundation of society. It will not cease before all slavish subjection is done away with.

Then this "individualism," this reaction against unquestioned submission, will find its compensation in *another unity.* Everybody will again feel a dread of living for himself only. We shall have *corporate responsibility, equality, freedom,* all three combined in *interdependence, social cooperation.* It is with the social organism as with a harmoniously developed man, who has three stages of growth: implicit obedience, then restless self-assertion, at last intelligent, loyal cooperation with what has a rightful claim to his allegiance.

This interdependence will find its practical expression in *The Cooperative Commonwealth.*

4

THE AFFLUENT COMMONWEALTH

Edward Bellamy
LOOKING BACKWARD 2000–1887

Edward Bellamy's (1850–1898) Looking Backward enjoyed a greater vogue, however brief, than the work of any other author in this collection. The hero of the novel, Julian West, awoke from a mesmeric trance to find himself in a Boston of the year 2000 that resembled in many ways the cooperative commonwealth described by Gronlund. Gronlund in fact welcomed the work as a vivid popularization of his ideas, although he did object strenuously to Bellamy's emphasis on leisure and comfort in his imaginary republic. Socialism represented for Gronlund a triumph of principles of brotherly love and mutual sharing, but the regime depicted by Bellamy, Gronlund feared, would likely exert its greatest charm over materialists and idle aristocrats. Bellamy's appeal in fact proved to be a very complex thing. Bellamy himself had always wanted to be a soldier, and many readers to their alarm found in his pages an appeal to martial sentiment. The following description of the "industrial army" by Dr. Leete, who in the novel was West's host and principal teacher, gives the student a good opportunity to judge Bellamy's handling of the problem of coercion in his Utopian republic.

The questions which I needed to ask before I could acquire even an outline acquaintance with the institutions of the twentieth century being endless, and Dr. Leete's good nature appearing equally so, we sat up talking for several hours after the ladies left us. Reminding my host of the point at which our talk had broken off that morning, I expressed my curiosity to learn how the organization of the industrial army was made to afford a sufficient stimulus to diligence in the lack of any anxiety on the worker's part as to his livelihood.

"You must understand in the first place," replied the doctor, "that the supply of incentives to effort is but one of the objects sought in the

SOURCE. Edward Bellamy, *Looking Backward 2000–1887* (Boston, 1888), pp. 170–189.

organization we have adopted for the army. The other, and equally important, is to secure for the file leaders and captains of the force, and the great officers of the nation, men of proven abilities, who are pledged by their own careers to hold their followers up to their highest standard of performance and permit no lagging. With a view to these two ends the industrial army is organized. First comes the unclassified grade of common laborers, men of all work, to which all recruits during their first three years belong. This grade is a sort of school, and a very strict one, in which the young men are taught habits of obedience, subordination, and devotion to duty. While the miscellaneous nature of the work done by this force prevents the systematic grading of the workers which is afterwards possible, yet individual records are kept, and excellence receives distinction corresponding with the penalties that negligence incurs. It is not, however, policy with us to permit youthful recklessness or indiscretion, when not deeply culpable, to handicap the future careers of young men, and all who have passed through the unclassified grade without serious disgrace have an equal opportunity to choose the life employment they have most liking for. Having selected this, they enter upon it as apprentices. The length of the apprenticeship naturally differs in different occupations. At the end of it the apprentice becomes a full workman, and a member of his trade or guild. Now not only are the individual records of the apprentices for ability and industry strictly kept, and excellence distinguished by suitable distinctions, but upon the average of his record during apprenticeship the standing given the apprentice among the full workmen depends.

"While the internal organizations of different industries, mechanical and agricultural, differ according to their peculiar conditions, they agree in a general division of their workers into first, second, and third grades, according to ability, and these grades are in many cases subdivided into first and second classes. According to his standing as an apprentice a young man is assigned his place as a first, second, or third grade worker. Of course only young men of unusual ability pass directly from apprenticeship into the first grade of the workers. The most fall into the lower grades, working up as they grow more experienced, at the periodical regradings. These regradings take place in each industry at intervals corresponding with the length of the apprenticeship to that industry, so that merit never need wait long to rise, nor can any rest on past achievements unless they would drop into a lower rank. One of the notable advantages of a high grading is the privilege it gives the worker in electing which of the various branches or processes of his industry he will follow as his specialty. Of course it is not intended that any of these processes shall be disproportionately arduous, but there is often much difference between them, and the privilege of election is accordingly highly prized. So far as possible, indeed, the preferences even of the poorest workmen are considered in assigning them their line of work, because not only their happiness but their usefulness is thus enhanced. While, however, the wish of the lower grade man is consulted so far as the exigencies of the service permit, he is considered only after the upper grade men have been provided for, and often he has to put up with second or third choice, or even with an arbitrary assignment when help is needed. This privilege of election attends every regrading, and when a man loses his grade he also risks having to exchange the sort of work he likes for some other less to his taste. The results of each regrading, giving the standing of every man in his industry, are gazetted in the public prints, and those who have won promotion since the last regrading receive the nation's thanks and are publicly invested with the badge of their new rank."

"What may this badge be?" I asked.

"Every industry has its emblematic device," replied Dr. Leete, "and this, in the shape of a metallic badge so small that you might not see it unless you knew where to look, is all the insignia which the men of the army wear, except where public convenience demands a distinctive uniform. This badge is the same in form for all grades of industry, but while the badge of the third grade is iron, that of the second grade is silver, and that of the first is gilt.

"Apart from the grand incentive to endeavor afforded by the fact that the high places in the nation are open only to the highest class men, and that rank in the army constitutes the only mode of social distinction for the vast majority who are not aspirants in art, literature, and the professions, various incitements of a minor, but perhaps equally effective, sort are provided in the form of special privileges and immunities in the way of discipline, which the superior class men enjoy. These, while intended to be as little as possible invidious to the less successful, have the effect of keeping constantly before every man's mind the great desirability of attaining the grade next above his own.

"It is obviously important that not only the good but also the indifferent and poor workmen should be able to cherish the ambition of rising. Indeed, the number of the latter being so much greater, it is even more essential that the ranking system should not operate to discourage them than that it should stimulate the others. It is to this end that the grades are divided into classes. The grades as well as the classes being made numerically equal at each regrading, there is not at any time, counting out the officers and the unclassified and apprentice grades, over one-ninth of the industrial army in the lowest class, and most of this number are recent apprentices, all of whom expect to rise. Those who remain during the entire term of service in the lowest class are but a trifling fraction of the industrial army, and likely to be as deficient in sensibility to their position as in ability to better it.

"It is not even necessary that a worker should win promotion to a higher grade to have at least a taste of glory. While promotion requires a general excellence of record as a worker, honorable mention and various sorts of prizes are awarded for excellence less than sufficient for promotion, and also for special feats and single performances in the various industries. There are many minor distinctions of standing, not only within the grades but within the classes, each of which acts as a spur to the efforts of a group. It is intended that no form of merit shall wholly fail of recognition.

"As for actual neglect of work, positively bad work, or other overt remissness on the part of men incapable of generous motives, the discipline of the industrial army is far too strict to allow anything whatever of the sort. A man able to do duty, and persistently refusing, is sentenced to solitary imprisonment on bread and water till he consents.

"The lowest grade of the officers of the industrial army, that of assistant foremen or lieutenants, is appointed out of men who have held their place for two years in the first class of the first grade. Where this leaves too large a range of choice, only the first group of this class are eligible. No one thus comes to the point of commanding men until he is about thirty years old. After a man becomes an officer, his rating of course no longer depends on the efficiency of his own work, but on that of his men. The foremen are appointed from among the assistant foremen, by the same exercise of discretion limited to a small eligible class. In the appointments to the still higher grades another principle is introduced, which it would take too much time to explain now.

"Of course such a system of grading as I have described would have been impracticable applied to the small industrial concerns of your day, in some of which there were hardly enough employees to have left one apiece for the classes. You must remember that, under the national organization of labor, all industries are carried on by great bodies of men, many of your farms or shops being combined as one. It is also owing solely to the vast scale on which each industry is organized, with coordinate establishments in every part of the country, that we are able by exchanges and transfers to fit every man so nearly with the sort of work he can do best.

"And now, Mr. West, I will leave it to you, on the bare outline of its features which I have given, if those who need special incentives to do their best are likely to lack them under our system. Does it not seem to you that men who found themselves obliged, whether they wished or not, to work, would under such a system be strongly impelled to do their best?"

I replied that it seemed to me the incentives offered were, if any objection were to be made, too strong; that the pace set for the young men was too hot; and such, indeed, I would add with deference, still remains my opinion, now that by longer residence among you I have become better acquainted with the whole subject.

Dr. Leete, however, desired me to reflect, and I am ready to say that it is perhaps a sufficient reply to my objection, that the worker's livelihood is in no way dependent on his ranking, and anxiety for that never embitters his disappointments; that the working hours are short, the vacations regular, and that all emulation ceases at forty-five, with the attainment of middle life.

"There are two or three other points I ought to refer to," he added, "to prevent your getting mistaken impressions. In the first place, you must understand that this system of preferment given the more efficient workers over the less so, in no way contravenes the fundamental idea of our social system, that all who do their best are equally deserving, whether that best be great or small. I have shown that the system is arranged to encourage the weaker as well as the stronger with the hope of rising, while the fact that the stronger are selected for the leaders is in no way a reflection upon the weaker, but in the interest of the common weal.

"Do not imagine, either, because emulation is given free play as an incentive under our system, that we deem it a motive likely to appeal to the nobler sort of men, or worthy of them. Such as these find their motives within, not without, and measure their duty by their own endowments, not by those of others. So long as their achievement is proportioned to their powers, they would consider it preposterous to expect praise or blame because it chanced to be great or small. To such natures emulation appears philosophically absurd, and despicable in a moral aspect by its substitution of envy for admiration, and exultation for regret, in one's attitude toward the successes and the failures of others.

"But all men, even in the last year of the twentieth century, are not of this high order, and the incentives to endeavor requisite for those who are not must be of a sort adapted to their inferior natures. For these, then, emulation of the keenest edge is provided as a constant spur. Those who need this motive will feel it. Those who are above its influence do not need it.

"I should not fail to mention," resumed the doctor, "that for those too deficient in mental or bodily strength to be fairly graded with the main body of workers, we have a separate grade, unconnected with the others—a sort of invalid corps, the members of which are provided with a light class of tasks fitted to their strength. All our sick in mind and body, all our deaf and dumb, and lame and blind and crippled, and even our insane, belong to this invalid corps, and bear its insignia. The strongest often do nearly a man's work, the feeblest, of course, nothing; but none who can do anything are willing quite to give up. In their lucid intervals, even our insane are eager to do what they can."

"That is a pretty idea of the invalid corps," I said. "Even a barbarian from the nineteenth century can appreciate that. It is a very graceful way of disguising charity, and must be grateful to the feelings of its recipients."

"Charity!" repeated Dr. Leete. "Did you suppose that we consider the incapable class we are talking of objects of charity?"

"Why, naturally," I said, "inasmuch as they are incapable of self-support."

But here the doctor took me up quickly.

"Who is capable of self-support?" he demanded. "There is no such thing in a civilized society as self-support. In a state of society so barbarous as not even to know family cooperation, each individual may possibly support himself, though even then for a part of his life only; but from the moment that men begin to live together, and constitute even the rudest sort of society, self-support becomes impossible. As men grow more civilized, and the subdivision of occupations and services is carried out, a complex mutual dependence becomes the universal rule. Every man, however solitary may seem his occupation, is a member of a vast industrial partnership, as large as the nation, as large as humanity. The necessity of mutual dependence should imply the duty and guarantee of mutual support; and that it did not in your day constituted the essential cruelty and unreason of your system."

"That may all be so," I replied, "but it does not touch the case of those who are unable to contribute anything to the product of industry."

"Surely I told you this morning, at least I thought I did," replied Dr. Leete, "that the right of a man to maintenance at the nation's table depends on the fact that he is a man, and not on the amount of health and strength he may have, so long as he does his best."

"You said so," I answered, "but I supposed the rule applied only to the workers of different ability. Does it also hold of those who can do nothing at all?"

"Are they not also men?"

"I am to understand, then, that the lame, the blind, the sick, and the impotent are as well off as the most efficient and have the same income?"

"Certainly," was the reply.

"The idea of charity on such a scale," I answered, "would have made our most enthusiastic philanthropists gasp."

"If you had a sick brother at home," replied Dr. Leete, "unable to work, would you feed him on less dainty food, and lodge and clothe him more poorly, than yourself? More likely far, you would give him the preference; nor would you think of calling it charity. Would not the word, in that connection, fill you with indignation?"

"Of course," I replied; "but the cases are not parallel. There is a sense, no doubt, in which all men are brothers; but this general sort of brotherhood is not to be compared, except for rhetorical purposes, to the brotherhood of blood, either as to its sentiment or its obligations."

"There speaks the nineteenth century!" exclaimed Dr. Leete. "Ah, Mr. West, there is no doubt as to the length of time that you slept. If I were to give you, in one sentence, a key to what may seem the mysteries of our civilization as compared with that of your age, I should say that it is the fact that the solidarity of the race and the brotherhood of man, which to you were but fine phrases, are, to our thinking and feeling, ties as real and as vital as physical fraternity.

"But even setting that consideration aside, I do not see why it so surprises you that those who cannot work are conceded the full right to live on the produce of those who can. Even in your day, the duty of military service for the protection of the nation, to which our industrial service corresponds, while obligatory on those able to discharge it, did not operate to deprive of the privileges of citizenship those who were unable. They stayed at home, and were protected by those who fought, and nobody questioned their right to be, or thought less of them. So, now, the requirement of industrial service from those able to render it does not operate to deprive of the privileges of citizenship, which now implies the citizen's maintenance, him who cannot work.

The worker is not a citizen because he works, but works because he is a citizen. As you recognize the duty of the strong to fight for the weak, we, now that fighting is gone by, recognize his duty to work for him.

"A solution which leaves an unaccounted-for residuum is no solution at all; and our solution of the problem of human society would have been none at all had it left the lame, the sick, and the blind outside with the beasts, to fare as they might. Better far have left the strong and well unprovided for than these burdened ones, toward whom every heart must yearn, and for whom ease of mind and body should be provided, if for no others. Therefore it is, as I told you this morning, that the title of every man, woman, and child to the means of existence rests on no basis less plain, broad, and simple than the fact that they are fellows of one race—members of one human family. The only coin current is the image of God, and that is good for all we have.

"I think there is no feature of the civilization of your epoch so repugnant to modern ideas as the neglect with which you treated your dependent classes. Even if you had no pity, no feeling of brotherhood, how was it that you did not see that you were robbing the incapable class of their plain right in leaving them unprovided for?"

"I don't quite follow you there," I said. "I admit the claim of this class to our pity, but how could they who produced nothing claim a share of the product as a right?"

"How happened it," was Dr. Leete's reply, "that your workers were able to produce more than so many savages would have done? Was it not wholly on account of the heritage of the past knowledge and achievements of the race, the machinery of society, thousands of years in contriving, found by you ready-made to your hand? How did you come to be possessors of this knowledge and this machinery, which represent nine parts to one contributed by yourself in the value of your product? You inherited it, did you not? And were not these others, these unfortunate and crippled brothers whom you cast out, joint inheritors, co-heirs with you? What did you do with their share? Did you not rob them when you put them off with crusts, who were entitled to sit with the heirs, and did you not add insult to robbery when you called the crusts charity?

"Ah, Mr. West," Dr. Leete continued, as I did not respond, "what I do not understand is, setting aside all considerations either of justice or brotherly feeling toward the crippled and defective, how the workers of your day could have had any heart for their work, knowing that their children, or grandchildren, if unfortunate, would be deprived of the comforts and even necessities of life. It is a mystery how men with children could favor a system under which they were rewarded beyond those less endowed with bodily strength or mental power. For, by the same discrimination by which the father profited, the son, for whom he would give his life, being perchance weaker than others, might be reduced to crusts and beggary. How men dared leave children behind them, I have never been able to understand."

NOTE. Although in his talk on the previous evening Dr. Leete had emphasized the pains taken to enable every man to ascertain and follow his natural bent in choosing an occupation, it was not till I learned that the worker's income is the same in all occupations that I realized how absolutely he may be counted on to do so, and thus, by selecting the harness which sets most lightly on himself, find that in which he can pull best. The failure of my age in any systematic or effective way to develop and utilize the natural aptitudes of men for the industries and intellectual avocations was one of the great wastes, as well as one of the most common causes of unhappiness in that time. The vast majority of my contemporaries, though nominally free to do so, never really chose their occupations at all, but were forced by circumstances into work for which they were relatively inefficient, because not naturally fitted for it. The rich, in this respect, had little advantage over the poor. The latter, indeed, being generally deprived of education, had no opportunity even to ascertain the natural aptitudes they might have, and on account of their poverty were unable to develop them by cultivation even when ascertained. The liberal and technical professions, except by favorable accident, were shut to them, to their own great loss and that of the nation. On the other hand, the well-to-do, although they could command education and opportunity, were scarcely less hampered by social prejudice, which forbade them to pursue manual avocations, even when adapted to them, and destined them, whether fit or unfit, to the professions, thus wasting many an excellent handicraftsman. Mercenary considerations, tempting men to pursue money-making occupations for which they were unfit, instead of less remunerative employments for which they were fit, were responsible for another vast perversion of talent. All these things now are changed. Equal education and opportunity must needs bring to light whatever aptitudes a man has, and neither social prejudices nor mercenary considerations hamper him in the choice of his life work.

Part Three

TACTICS FOR A RADICAL MOVEMENT IN THE TWENTIETH CENTURY

1

THE MARXIST AS SECTARIAN

Daniel DeLeon
WHAT MEANS THIS STRIKE?

Daniel DeLeon (1852–1914) called himself a Marxist, but few Marxists in America or Europe acknowledged his right to speak for the master. It would be hard to find a more stubbornly sectarian character in the whole history of the Second International. Born in Curaçao, educated in Europe, he came to the United States in 1872. He practiced law in Texas and taught at Columbia University, but at the end of the 1880s he turned toward radical activities. In the middle of the 1890s, as leader of the Socialist Labor party, DeLeon decided that the major obstacle to socialism lay not in the power of the great capitalists, but in the conservatism of American labor leaders. His uncompromising nature revealed itself not only in his divisive decision to launch a socialist trade union to challenge the "pure and simple" economic goals of existing unions, but also in his political program. He refused to commit his party, which quickly declined after 1900, to any reformist measures and in his platform called exclusively for the abolition of capitalism. His speech to striking New Bedford, Massachusetts, workers illustrates DeLeon at his intransigent best.

You have seen that the wages you live on and the profits the capitalist riots in are the two parts into which is divided the wealth that you produce. The workingman wants a larger and larger share, so does the capitalist. A thing cannot be divided into two shares so as to increase the share of each. If the workingman produces, say, $4 worth of wealth a day, and the capitalist keeps 2, there are only 2 left for the workingman; if the capitalist keeps 3, there is only 1 left for the workingman; if the capitalist keeps 3 1/2 there is only 1/2 left for the workingman. Inversely, if the workingman pushes up his share from

SOURCE. Daniel DeLeon, *What Means This Strike? An Address by Daniel DeLeon at New Bedford, Massachusetts, February 11, 1898* (New York, 1898), pp. 11–27.

1/2 to 1, there are only 3 left to the capitalist; if the workingman secures 2, the capitalist will be reduced to 2; if the workingman push still onward and keep 3, the capitalist will have to put up with 1—and if the workingman makes up his mind to enjoy all that he produces, and keep all the 4, THE CAPITALIST WILL HAVE TO GO TO WORK. These plain figures upset the theory about the workingman and the capitalist being brothers. . . .

The pregnant point that underlies these pregnant facts is that, between the working class and the capitalist class, there is an irrespressible conflict, a class struggle for life. No glib-tongued politician can vault over it; no capitalist professor or official statistician can argue it away; no capitalist parson can veil it; no labor fakir can straddle it; no "reform" architect can bridge it over. It crops up in all manner of ways, like in this strike, in ways that disconcert all the plans and all the schemes of those who would deny or ignore it. It is a struggle that will not down, and must be ended only by either the total subjugation of the working class, or the abolition of the capitalist class.

Thus you perceive that the theory on which your "pure and simple" trade organizations are grounded, and on which you went into this strike, is false. There being no "common interests," but only hostile interests, between the capitalist class and the working class, the battle you are waging to establish "safe relations" between the two is a hopeless one.

Put to the touchstone of these undeniable principles the theory upon which your "pure and simple" trade organizations are built, and you will find it to be false; examined by the light of these undeniable principles the road that your false theory makes you travel and the failures that have marked your career must strike you as its inevitable result. How are we to organize and proceed? you may ask. . . .

Let us take a condensed page of the country's history. For the sake of plainness, and forced to it by the exigency of condensation, I shall assume small figures. Place yourselves back a sufficient number of years with but ten competing weaving concerns in the community. How the individual ten owners came by the "original accumulations" that enabled them to start as capitalists you now know. Say that each of the ten capitalists employs ten men; that each man receives $2 a day, and that the product of each of the ten sets of men in each of the ten establishments is worth $40 a day. You know now also that it is out of these $40 worth of wealth, produced by the men, that each of the ten competing capitalists takes the $20 that he pays the ten men in wages, and that of that same $40 worth of wealth he takes the $20 that he pockets as profits. Each of these ten capitalists makes, accordingly, $120 a week.

This amount of profits, one should think, should satisfy our ten capitalists. It is a goodly sum to pocket without work. Indeed, it may satisfy some, say most of them. But if for any of many reasons it does not satisfy any one of them, the whole string of them is set in commotion. "Individuality" is a deity at whose shrine the capitalist worships, or affects to worship. In point of fact, capitalism robs of individuality , not only the working class, but capitalists themselves. The action of any one of the lot compels action by all; like a row of bricks, the dropping of one makes all the others drop successively. Let us take No. 1. He is not satisfied with $120 a week. Of the many reasons he may have for that, let's take this: he has a little daughter; eventually, she will be of marriageable age; whom is he planning to marry her to? Before the public, particularly before the workers, he will declaim on the "sovereignty" of our citizens, and declare the country is stocked with nothing but "peers." In his heart, though, he feels otherwise. He looks even upon his fellow capitalists as plebeians; he aspires at a prince, a duke, or at least a count for a son-in-law; and in visions truly reflecting the vulgarity of his mind, he beholds himself the grandfather of prince, duke or count grandbrats. To realize this dream he must have money; princes, etc., are expensive luxuries. His present income, $120 a week, will not buy the luxury. He must have some more. To his employees he will recommend reliance on heaven; he himself knows that if he wants more money it will not come from heaven, but must come from the sweat of his employees' brows. As all the wealth produced in his shop is $40 a day, he knows that, if he increases his share of $20 to $30, there will be only $10 left for wages. He tries this. He announces a wage reduction of 50 percent. His men spontaneously draw themselves together and refuse to work; they go on strike. What is the situation?

In those days it needed skill, acquired by long training, to do the work; there may have been corner loafers out of work, but not weavers; possibly at some great distance there may have been weavers actually obtainable, but in those days there was neither telegraph nor railroad to communicate with them; finally, the nine competitors of No. 1, having no strike on hand, continued to produce, and thus threatened to crowd No. 1 out of the market. Thus circumstanced, No. 1 caves in. He withdraws his order of wage reduction. "Come in," he says to his striking workmen, "let's make up; labor and capital are brothers; the most loving of brothers sometimes fall out; we have had such a falling out; it was a slip; you have organized yourselves in a union with a $2 day wage scale; I shall never fight the union; I love it, come back to work." And the men did.

Thus ended the first strike. The victory won by the men made many of them feel bold. At their next meeting they argued: "The employer wanted to reduce our wages and got left; why may not we take the hint and reduce his profits by demanding higher wages; we licked him in his attempt to lower our wages, why should we not lick him in an attempt to resist our demand for more pay?" But the labor movement is democratic. No one man can run things. At that union meeting the motion to demand higher pay is made by one member, another must second it; amendments and amendments to the amendments are put with the requisite seconders; debate follows; points of order are raised, ruled on, appealed from and settled; in the meantime it grows late, the men must be at work early the next morning, the hour to adjourn arrives, and the whole matter is left pending. Thus much for the men.

Now for the employer. He locks himself up in his closet. With clenched fists and scowl on brow, he gnashes his teeth at the victory of his "brother" labor, its union, and its union regulations. And he ponders. More money he must have and is determined to have. This resolution is arrived at with the swiftness and directness which capitalists are able to. Differently from his men, he is not many , but one. He makes the motion, seconds it himself, puts it, and carries it unanimously. More profits he shall have. But how? Aid comes to him through the mail. The letter-carrier brings him a circular from a machine shop. Such circulars are frequent even today. It reads like this: "Mr. No. 1, you are employing ten men; I have in my machine shop a beautiful machine with which you can produce, with 5 men, twice as much as now with 10; this machine does not chew tobacco; it does not smoke (some of these circulars are cruel and add:) this machine has no wife who gets sick and keeps it home to attend to her; it has no children who die, and whom to bury it must stay away from work; it never goes on strike; it works and grumbles not; come and see it." . . .

No. 1 goes and sees the machine; finds it to be as represented; buys it; puts it up in his shop; picks out of his 10 men the 5 least active in the late strike; sets them to work at $2 a day as before; and full of bows and smirks, addresses the other 5 thus: "I am sorry I have no places for you; I believe in union principles and am paying the union scale to the 5 men I need; I don't need you now; good-bye. I hope I'll see you again." And he means this last as you will presently perceive.

What is the situation now? No. 1 pays, as before, $2 a day, but to only 5 men; these, with the aid of the machine, now produce twice as much as the 10 did before; their product is now $80 worth of wealth; as only $10 of this goes in wages, the capitalist has a profit of $70 a day, or 250 percent more. He is moving fast towards his prince, duke, or count son-in-law.

Now watch the men whom his machine displaced; their career throws quite some light on the whole question. Are they not "American citizens"? Is not this a "Republic with a Constitution"? Is anything else wanted to get a living? Watch them! They go to No. 2 for a job; before they quite reach the place, the doors open and 5 of that concern are likewise thrown out upon the street.—What happened there? The "individuality" of No. 2 yielded to the pressure of capitalist development. The purchase of the machine by No. 1 enabled him to produce so much more plentifully and cheaply; if No. 2 did not do likewise, he would be crowded out of the market by No. 1; No. 2, accordingly, also invested in a machine, with the result that 5 of his men are also thrown out.

These 10 unemployed proceed to No. 3, hoping for better luck there. But what sight is that that meets their astonished eyes? Not 5 men, as walked out of Nos. 1 and 2, but all No. 3's 10 have landed on the street; and, what is more surprising yet to them, No. 3 himself is on the street, now reduced to the condition of a workingman along with his former employees.—What is it that happened there? In this instance the "individuality" of No. 3 was crushed by capitalist development. The same reason that drove No. 2 to procure the machine, rendered the machine indispensable to No. 3. But having, differently from his competitors Nos. 1 and 2, spent all his stealings from the workingmen instead of saving up some, he is now unable to make the purchase; is, consequently, unable to produce as cheaply as they; is, consequently, driven into bankruptcy, and lands in the class of the proletariat, whose ranks are thus increased.

The now 21 unemployed proceed in their hunt for work, and make the round of the other mills. The previous experiences are repeated. Not only are there no jobs to be had, but everywhere workers are thrown out, if the employer got the machine; and if he did not, workers with their former employers, now ruined, join the army of the unemployed.

What happened in that industry happened in all others. Thus the ranks of the capitalist class are thinned out, and the class is made more powerful, while the ranks of the working class are swelled, and the class is made weaker. This is the process that explains how, on the one hand, your New Bedford mills become the property of ever fewer men; how, according to the census, their aggregate capital runs up to over $14,000,000; how, despite "bad times," their profits run up to upwards of $1,300,000; how, on the other hand, your position becomes steadily more precarious.

No. 1's men return to where they started from. Scabbing they will not. Uninformed upon the mechanism of capitalism, they know not what struck them; and they expect "better times"—just as so many equally uninformed workingmen are expecting today; in the meantime, thinking thereby to hasten the advent of the good times, No. 1's men turn out the Republican party and turn in the Democratic, turn out the Democratic and turn in the Republican—just as our misled workingmen are now doing, not understanding that, whether they put in or out Republicans or Democrats, Protectionists or Free Traders, Goldbugs or Silverbugs, they are every time putting in the capitalist platform, upholding the social principle that throws them out of work or reduces their wages.

But endurance has its limits. The superintendent of the Pennsylvania Railroad for the Indiana Division, speaking, of course, from the capitalist standpoint, recently said: "Many solutions are being offered for the labor question; but there is just one and no more. It is this: lay a silver dollar on the shelf, and at the end of a year you have a silver dollar left; lay a workingman on the shelf, and at the end of a month you have a skeleton left. This," said he, "is the solution of the labor problem." In short, starve out the workers. No. 1's men finally reached that point. Finally that happens that few if any can resist. A man may stand starvation and resist the sight of starving wife and children; but if he has not wherewith to buy medicine to save the life of a sick wife or child, all control is lost over him. On the heels of starvation, sickness follows, and No. 1's men throw to the wind all union principles; they are now ready to do anything to save their dear ones. Cap in hand, they appear before No. 1, the starch taken clean out of them during the period they "lay on the shelf." They ask for work; they themselves offer to work for $1 a day. And No. 1, the brother of labor, who but recently expressed devotion to the union, what of him? His eyes sparkle at "seeing again" the men he had thrown out; at their offer to work for less than the men now employed, his chest expands, and, grabbing them by the hand in a delirium of patriotic ecstasy, he says: "Welcome, my noble American citizens; I am proud to see you ready to work and earn an honest penny for your dear wives and darling children; I am delighted to notice that you are not, like so many others, too lazy to work; let the American eagle screech in honor of your emancipation from the slavery of a rascally union; let the American eagle wag his tail an extra wag in honor of your freedom from a dictatorial walking delegate; you are my long lost brothers; go in my $1-a-day brothers!" and he throws his former $2-a-day brothers heels over head upon the sidewalk.

When the late $2-a-day men have recovered from their surprise, they determine on war. But what sort of war? Watch them closely, and you may detect many a feature of your own in that mirror. "Have we not struck," argue they, "and beaten this employer once before? If we strike again, we shall again beat him." But the conditions have wholly changed.

In the first place, there were no unemployed skilled workers during that first strike; now there are; plenty of them, dumped upon the country, not out of the steerage of vessels from Europe, but by native-born machine.

In the second place, that very machine has to such an extent eliminated skill that, while formerly only the unemployed in a certain trade could endanger the jobs of those at work in that trade, now the unemployed of all trades (virtually the whole army of the unemployed) bear down upon the employed in each; we know of quondam shoemakers taking the jobs of hatters; quondam hatters taking the jobs of weavers; quondam weavers taking the jobs of cigarmakers; quondam cigarmakers taking the jobs of "machinists"; quondam farm hands taking the jobs of factory hands, etc., etc., so easy has it become to learn what is now needed to be known of a trade.

In the third place, telegraph and railroads have made all of the unemployed easily accessible to the employer.

Finally, differently from former days, the competitors have to a great extent consolidated; here in New Bedford, for instance, the false appearance of competition between the mill owners is punctured by the fact that to a great extent seemingly "independent" mills are owned by one family, as is the case with the Pierce family.

Not, as at the first strike, with their flanks protected, but now wholly exposed through the existence of a vast army of hungry unemployed; not, as before, facing a divided enemy, but now faced by a consolidated mass of capitalist concerns; how different is now the situation of the strikers! The changed conditions brought about changed results; instead of victory, there was defeat; and we have had a long series of them. Either hunger drove the men back to work; or the unemployed took their places; or, if the capitalist was in a hurry, he fetched in the help of the strong arm of the government, now his government.

We now have a sufficient survey of the field to enable us to answer the question, How shall we organize so as not to fight the same old hopeless battle?

Proceeding from the knowledge that labor alone produces all wealth; that less and less of this wealth comes to the working class, and more and more of it is plundered by the idle class or capitalist; that this is the result of the working class being stripped of the tool (machine), without which it cannot earn a living; and, finally, that the machine or tool has reached such a state of development that it can no longer be operated by the individual but needs the collective effort of many—proceeding from this knowledge, it is clear that the aim of all intelligent class-conscious workingmen must be the overthrow of the system of private ownership in the tools of production because that system keeps them in wage slavery.

Proceeding from the further knowledge of the use made of the government by the capitalist class, and of the necessity that class is under to own the government, so as to enable it to uphold and prop up the capitalist system—proceeding from that knowledge, it is clear that the aim of all intelligent, class-conscious workingmen must be to bring the government under the control of their own class by joining and electing the American wing of the International Socialist party—- the Socialist Labor party of America, and thus establishing the Socialist Cooperative Republic.

But in the meantime, while moving toward that ideal, though necessary, goal, what to do? The thing cannot be accomplished in a day, nor does election come around every twenty-four hours. Is there nothing that we can do for ourselves between election and election?

Yes; plenty.

When crowded, in argument, to the wall by us New Trade Unionists, by us of the Socialist Trade & Labor Alliance, your present, or old and "pure and simple" organizations, yield the point of ultimate aims; they grant the ultimate necessity of establishing socialism; but they claim "the times are not yet ripe" for that; and, not yet being ripe, they lay emphasis upon the claim that the "pure and simple" union does the workers some good *now* by getting something *now* from the employers and from the capitalist parties. We are not "practical" they tell us; they are. Let us test this theory on the spot. Here in New Bedford there is not yet a single New Trade Unionist organization in existence. The "pure and simple" trade union has had the field all to itself. All of you, whose wages are *now* higher than they were five years ago, kindly raise a hand. (No hand is raised.) All of you whose wages are now lower than five years ago, please raise a hand. (The hands of the large audience go up.) The proof of the pudding lies in the eating. Not only does "pure and simpledom" shut off your hope of emancipation by affecting to think such a state of things is unreachable now, but in the meantime and right now, the "good" it does to you, the "something" it secures for you "from the employers and from the politicians" is lower wages. . . .

The New Trade Unionist knows that no one or two or even half a dozen elections will place in the hands of the working class the government of the land; and New Trade Unionism, not only wishes to do something now for the workers, but it knows that the thing can be done, and how to do it.

"Pure and simple" or British trade unionism has done a double mischief to the workers: besides leaving them in their present pitiable plight, it has caused many to fly off the handle and lose all trust in the power of trade organization. The best of these, those who have not become pessimistic and have not been wholly demoralized, see nothing to be done but voting right on election day—casting their vote straight for the S. L. P. This is a serious error. By thus giving over all participation in the industrial movement, they wholly disconnect themselves from the class struggle that is going on every day; and by putting off their whole activity to a single day in the year—election day, they become floaters in the air, I know several such. Without exception they are dreamy and flighty and unbalanced in their methods.

The utter impotence of "pure and simple" unionism today is born of causes that may be divided under two main heads.

One is the contempt in which the capitalist and ruling class holds the working people. In 1886, when instinct was, unconsciously to myself, leading me to look into the social problem, when as yet it was to me a confused and blurred interrogation mark, I associated wholly with capitalists. Expressions of contempt for the workers were common. One day I asked a set of them why they treated their men so hard, and had so poor an opinion of them. "They are ignorant, stupid and corrupt," was the answer, almost in chorus.

"What makes you think so?" I asked. "Have you met them all?"

"No," was the reply, "we have not met them all individually, but we have had to deal with their leaders, and they are ignorant, stupid, and corrupt. Surely these leaders must be the best among them, or they would not choose them."

Now, let me illustrate. I understand that two days ago, in this city, Mr. [Samuel] Gompers went off at a tangent and shot off his mouth about me. What he said was too ridiculous for me to answer. You will have noticed that he simply gave what he wishes you to consider as his opinion; he furnished you no facts from which he drew it, so that you could judge for yourselves. He expected you to take him on faith. I shall not insult you by treating you likewise. Here are the facts on which my conclusion is based:

In the State of New York we have a labor law forbidding the working of railroad men more than ten hours. The railroad companies disregarded the law; in Buffalo, the switchmen struck in 1892 to enforce the law; thereupon the Democratic governor, Mr. Flower, who had himself signed the law, sent the whole militia of the state into

Buffalo to help the railroad capitalists break the law, incidentally to commit assault and battery with intent to kill, as they actually did, upon the workingmen. Among our state senators is one Jacob Cantor. This gentleman hastened to applaud Governor Flower's brutal violation of his oath of office to uphold the constitution and the laws; Cantor applauded the act as a patriotic one in the defense of "law and order." At a subsequent campaign, this Cantor being a candidate for reelection, the New York *Daily News,* a capitalist paper of Cantor's political complexion, published an autographed letter addressed to him and intended to be an indorsement of him by labor. This letter contained this passage among others: "If any one says you are not a friend of labor, he says what is not true." By whom was this letter written and by whom signed?—by Mr. Samuel Gompers, "President of the American Federation of Labor." . . .

Again: the Republican party, likewise the Democratic, is a party of the capitalist class; every man who is posted knows that; the conduct of its presidents, governors, judges, congresses and legislatures can leave no doubt upon the subject. Likewise the free coinage of silver, or Populist party, was, while it lived, well known to be a party of capital; the conduct of its runners, the silver mine barons, who skin and then shoot down their miners, leaves no doubt upon that subject. But the two were deadly opposed: one wanted gold, the other silver. Notwithstanding these facts, a "labor leader" in New York City appeared at a recent campaign standing, not upon the Republican capitalist party platform only, not upon the Free-Silver capitalist party platform only, but—*on both;* he performed the acrobatic feat of being simultaneously for gold and against silver, for silver against gold. Who was that "labor leader"?—Mr. Samuel Gompers, "President of the American Federation of Labor." . . .

The ignorance, stupidity and corruption of the "pure and simple" labor leaders is such that the capitalist class despises you. The first prerequisite for success in a struggle is the respect of the enemy.

The other main cause of the present impotence of "pure and simple" unionism is that, through its ignoring the existing class distinctions, and its ignoring the class connection there is between wages and politics, it splits up at the ballot box among the parties of capital, and thus unites in upholding the system of capitalist exploitation. Look at the recent miners' strike: the men are shot down and the strike was lost; this happened in the very midst of a political campaign; and these miners, who could at any election capture the government, or at least, by polling a big vote against capitalism announce their advance towards freedom, are seen to turn right around and vote back into power the very class that had just trampled upon them. What prospect is there, in sight of such conduct, of the capitalists becoming gentler? or of the union gaining for the men anything *now* except more wage reductions, enforced by bullets? None! The prospect of the miners and other workers doing the same thing over again, a prospect that is made all the surer if they allow themselves to be further led by the labor fakirs whom the capitalists keep in pay, renders sure that capitalist outrages will be repeated and further capitalist encroachments will follow. Otherwise were it if the union, identifying politics and wages, voted against capitalism; if it struck at the ballot box against the wage system with the same solidarity that it demands for the strike in the shop. Protected once a year by the guns of an increasing class-conscious party of labor, the union could be a valuable fortification behind which to conduct the daily class struggle in the shops. The increasing Socialist Labor party vote alone would not quite give that temporary protection in the shop that such an increasing vote would afford if in the shop also the workers are intelligently organized, and honestly, because intelligently, led. Without organization in the shop, the capitalist could outrage at least individuals. Shop organization alone, unbacked by that political force that threatens the capitalist class with extinction, the working class being the overwhelming majority, leaves the workers wholly unprotected. But the shop organization that combines in its warfare the annually recurring class-conscious ballot, can stem capitalist encroachment from day to day. The trade organization *is* impotent if built and conducted upon the impotent lines of ignorance and corruption. The trade organization *is not* impotent if built and conducted upon the lines of knowledge and honesty; if it understands the issue and steps into the arena fully equipped, not with the shield of the trade union only, but also with the sword of the socialist ballot.

The essential principles of sound organization are, accordingly, these:

1. A trade organization must be clear upon the fact that, not until it has overthrown the capitalist system of private ownership in the machinery of production, and made this the joint property of the people, thereby compelling everyone to work if he wants to live, is it at all possible for the workers to be safe.

2. A labor organization must be perfectly clear upon the fact that it cannot reach safety until it has wrenched the government from the clutches of the capitalist class; and that it cannot do that unless it votes, not for *men* but for *principle,* unless it votes into power its own class platform and program: *the abolition of the wages system of slavery.*

3. A labor organization must be perfectly clear upon the fact that

politics are not, like religion, a private concern, any more than the wages and the hours of a workingman are his private concern. For the same reason that his wages and hours are the concern of his class, so is his politics. Politics is not separable from wages. For the same reason that the organization of labor dictates wages, hours, etc., in the interest of the working class, for that same reason must it dictate politics also; and for the same reason that it execrates the scab in the shop, it must execrate the scab at the hustings.

Long did the Socialist Labor party and New Trade Unionists seek to deliver this important message to the broad masses of the American proletariat, the rank and file of our working class. But we could not reach, we could not get at them. Between us and them there stood a solid wall of ignorant, stupid, and corrupt labor fakirs. Like men groping in a dark room for an exit, we moved along that wall, bumping our heads, feeling ever onwards for a door; we made the circuit and no passage was found. The wall was solid. This discovery once made, there was no way other than to batter a breach through that wall. With the battering ram of the Socialist Trade & Labor Alliance we effected a passage; the wall now crumbles; at last we stand face to face with the rank and file of the American proletariat; *and we are delivering our message*—as you may judge from the howl that goes up from that fakirs' wall that we have broken through.

I shall not consider my time well spent with you if I see no fruit of my labors; if I leave not behind me in New Bedford Local Alliances of your trades organized in the Socialist Trade & Labor Alliance. That will be my best contribution toward your strike, as they will serve as centers of enlightenment to strengthen you in your conflict, to the extent that it may now be possible.

In conclusion, my best advice to you for immediate action, is to step out boldly upon the street, as soon as you can; organize a monster parade of the strikers and of all the other working people in the town; and let the parade be headed by a banner bearing the announcement to your employers:

"We will fight you in this strike to the bitter end; your money bag may beat us now; but whether it does or not, that is not the end, it is only the beginning of the song; in November we will meet again at Philippi, and the strike shall not end until, with the falchion of the Socialist Labor party ballot, we shall have laid you low for all time!"

2

SOCIALISM AND CITY MANAGEMENT

Victor Berger
BERGER BROADSIDES

If DeLeon represented the American socialist politician at his most revolutionary, Victor Berger (1860–1929) represented him at his most reformist. However, while socialists split into right and left wings, all of them, including Berger, considered themselves revolutionaries who aimed at the quickest possible destruction of capitalism. Believing that a victory for the proletariat could only be won by the ballot, Berger did everything in his power to broaden the base of socialist support, even to the point of playing to white labor's prejudices against black and yellow workers. Unlike DeLeon he wanted to keep activity on the political and trade union fronts distinct. Berger engineered some impressive electoral successes in Milwaukee and was himself elected to the United States Congress. He included in his socialist platform support for many reformist measures, but in doing so, no matter how much it evoked the wrath of DeLeon, Berger followed the general practice of his party as well as that of social democratic parties in Europe. Walter Lippmann remarked after working for a socialist mayor in Schenectady that he discerned no difference in practice between socialist water commissioners and Republican water commissioners. Despite the hopes expressed in this selection, Berger never found a way around state legislatures that enabled him to build even one solid step toward socialism.

As I have often said, whether with or without social reform we cannot escape social-democracy. The cooperative commonwealth is the aim towards which, from a law of nature, the entire political and economical development of modern times is moving.

A social-democracy is the goal of the evolution. And not by any means a far distant goal. Nor is it the *last station* on the road which humanity will have to follow. Progress will never stop.

SOURCE. Victor Berger, *Berger Broadsides* (Milwaukee, 1912), pp. 3–7, 159–165.

The social-democracy is the *next* station. We are speeding toward it with the accelerating velocity of a locomotive on the road.

It is only a convincing confirmation of this view, that the *"social question"* now stands everywhere in the *foreground of public discussion.*

We all know from history that an old order of society was always doomed, when its appointed guardians and supporters felt called upon to make the demands of the adherents of the new order their own— when they tried to steal the revolutionist thunder, as the saying is.

Of course, LaFollette, Bryan, Hearst, etc., want to "steal our thunder" for exactly opposite purposes from ours. They want to *preserve the system.*

But we *are revolutionists.*

We are *revolutionary* not in the vulgar meaning of the word, which is entirely wrong, but in the sense illustrated by history, the only logical sense. For it is foolish to expect any result from riots and dynamite, from murderous attacks and conspiracies, in a country where we have the ballot, as long as the ballot has not been given a full and fair trial.

We want to *convince* the *majority* of the people. As long as we are in the minority, we of course have *no right to force our opinions upon an unwilling majority.*

Besides, as modern men and true democrats, we have a somewhat less romantic and boyish idea of the development of human things and social systems. And we know that one can kill tyrants and scare individuals with dynamite and bullets, but one cannot develop a system in that way.

Therefore no true social-democrat ever dreams of a sudden change of society. Such fanatic dreamers nowhere find more determined opponents than in the ranks of the true social-democrats.

We know perfectly well that force serves only those who have it, that a sudden overthrow will breed dictators, that it can promote only subjection, never liberty.

We even propose a *general arming* of the *people* as the *safest* means of *preventing sudden upheavals* and of preserving democracy.

The social-democrats do not expect success from a *so-called* revolution—that is, a smaller or bigger riot—but from a *real* revolution, from *the revolutionizing of minds,* the only true revolution there is.

Yet we do not deny that *after* we have *convinced the majority* of the people, we are going to use force *if* the *minority* should *resist.* But in every democracy the majority rules, and *must* rule.

It is clear that this revolution of the minds cannot be brought about in a day or two, nor can it be arranged according to the pleasure of a few. It can only be attained by patient work and intelligent organization.

Therefore the social-democrats concentrate their whole force on agitation and organization. The social-democratic leaders in every country as a general rule are matter-of-fact, cool-headed persons. The social-democratic troops are known to be the best disciplined in existence.

Up to a certain point, therefore,the tactics of the social-democrats and the social reformers are *exactly the same*. Both build upon the past historical development and take into consideration the present conditions.

The social-democrats absolutely refuse to break off the thread of history at any one place. No social-democrat ever dreams of introducing a year I and beginning a new era with it, as did the fathers of the great French Revolution—which was indeed entirely in harmony with *their* "a priori" and doctrinaire methods.

The social-democrats leave the making of the calendars to *other people*.

But the tactics and the aims of the social-democrats do indeed *differ* from those of the social reformers in one *essential* point. The social-democrats never fail to declare that with all the social reforms, good and worthy of support as they may be, conditions cannot be radically and permanently improved.

We social-democrats say we are willing to accept and help on every social reform. But we also say that social reforms are but installments by which we must not allow ourselves to be bribed; that full economic freedom will only be achieved by social-democracy.

Yet as a *stepping stone*, as a *transition*—and even as a *necessary stepping stone and as an indispensable transition*—*social reforms* of all kinds are fully and wholly recognized by the social-democracy

We recognize their usefulness and necessity even when we do not agree with the motives of the promoters and leaders of social reform. We are willing to accept these reforms, even when we disagree about their speed and the methods to be employed.

On the other hand, while the social reformers and the social-democrats therefore have many points of contact, they *always will form and must form two entirely different parties*. And it is not arbitrary or willful that the social-democrats all over the world constitute a distinct, separate party. It is absolutely necessary. And it does not in any way exclude the possibility of making common cause with social reform in legislatures and city councils for this or any other good measure. But to keep our party organically *separate and intact* is a demand of *clearness* and *truth*, which after all have great importance in political life as everywhere else.

The social-democrats do *not* in the least expect to "make history," as certain ignorant and fanatical impossibilists dream of doing. What we aspire to is much more modest, more matter-of-fact, and therefore more reliable and more substantial.

We want to observe closely the course of things, the development of economic and political conditions. We want to find out, if possible, where this development leads. Then, supported by this knowledge, we want to put ourselves in line with the march of civilization, so that civilization will carry us, instead of crushing us, which it would do, if—knowingly or not—we should stand opposed to it.

Thinking workmen and thinking men of any class become social-democrats not because we like to be "different" from other people. Not because a man by the name of Karl Marx has " invented the cooperative commonwealth" and painted it as gorgeously as possible—which by the way he did *not* do. We are social-democrats because we have recognized that the economical development of the present capitalist system leads toward socialistic production. Not that we wish to urge upon humanity "our" socialist republic, but that the *socialist republic* has urged itself upon us as the *next stage of civilization* and will urge itself some day upon *all civilized* humanity.

And once *granted* that the socialist republic is the *necessary* product of our economical development, the question of the *possibility* of carrying out the demands of the social-democracy appears very *naive* and indeed absurd. That which *must* come by *necessity* is for that very reason *possible without further question.*

England is the home of modern trade unionism. There the trades unions developed directly from the old guilds and journeymen's societies of the Middle Ages. It is natural that in England every skilled workman should belong to a union, and under the influence of socialist thought and socialist agitation, a good many unions of non-skilled laborers have been formed, as for instance, the dockmen's union through John Burns, and the gasworkers' union through Will Thorne.

Yet although over a million and a half of organized workmen belong to the trade unions in England—which are a giant army of themselves—the trade union movement of England has failed to emancipate the wage-workers or even to alleviate the condition of the masses. Just now the telegraph every day reports the tremendous demonstrations of starving workingmen in London, Birmingham, and other towns. The English trade unionists begin to understand, that without a political class movement, their economic struggle is hopeless. Our American fraternal delegates to Europe reported in Pittsburgh that what most struck them at the last British Trade Union Congress as different from our American conventions, was the fact that almost all the time was taken up with politics, and with the discussion of the political labor movement.

So the workingmen in England have finally come to the same conclusion which the workingmen in Germany, France, Belgium, Italy, Austria, Holland, Sweden, Norway, etc., reached long ago—that the economic movement alone is absolutely insufficient even to materially and permanently improve the condition of the working class, let alone the abolition of wage slavery. They find now in England also that it is absolutely necessary for the workers to get hold of the latch of legislation if they intend to accomplish anything worth while and anything lasting.

In Germany, as we all know, the development of the labor movement was from exactly the opposite direction. There Ferdinand Lassalle started the modern labor movement absolutely upon a political basis. The Allgemeine Deutsche Arbeiter-Verein demanded before all things the universal electoral franchise for the workers, and then a hundred million dollars from the Prussian State, in order to start a cooperative workshop system. These demands, as all the others which Lassalle formulated, were purely political in their character. Lassalle and the iron-clad Lassalleans had nothing but derision for the trade unions which had been held up as one of the main panaceas for the working people by Lassalle's bourgeois opponent, Schultze-Delitsch. In the heat of the fight, Lassalle naturally went too far in his opposition to the trade unions. But even Lassalle's friend and successor in the dictatorship of the Allgemeine Deutsche Arbeiter-Verein and the young Socialist party of the time, Johann v. Schweitzer, by the mere force of conditions, found himself compelled to start trade unions of his own, which have grown to a membership of about 1,400,000, that is, they have now about as many members as the English trade union movement.

Thus while in England the tendency for a long time was to regard the political side of the labor question as something secondary—the labor representatives usually voted with the Liberal party—in Germany, on the other hand, the trade union movement was considered of less account until of late. For even the early Marxian socialists in Germany had little or no use for the trade unions. As a matter of fact, since the Lassallean wing had started the trade union movement, the Gewerkschaften, the early Marxians thought it their duty to fight them as much as possible—until 1875, when the union of the Lassalleans and the Eisenachers was affected. And similar conditions to those which forced upon the attention of the English working class the necessity of a strong political class movement, forced also upon the German working class the necessity of developing a strong economic movement of the laboring class.

So the political struggle, as an equally powerful factor with the economic struggle, is now becoming the watchword in England, and the strongest possible trade union movement, as a necessary help and adjunct to the political movement, is now the central idea of the social-democracy of Germany. At the last convention of the party, Bernstein and Bebel went so far as to strongly endorse and advocate the idea of a general political strike—an idea which in former years has been repeatedly rejected as anarchistic. Bebel even now would only use it in case of an attempt to disfranchise the workers in Germany—which the Junker party, the nobility and the emperor would very much like to try—and this would be a case of answering with anarchy from below the anarchy from above. Bernstein, however, would like to go very much further in the use of the strike weapon for political purposes.

So, at any rate, the trade unionists pure and simple, as well as the socialist politicians pure and simple, have pretty nearly disappeared in the labor movement of the world. The American labor movement derived its roots from England on the one side and Germany on the other. From England it received the idea of the trade union pure and simple, which was in vogue in England years ago, but is now being discarded. From Germany, the American labor movement received its socialism, an idea which originally was purely political, but now takes in the trade union movement.

But thanks to the fervor of the socialists in the eighties of the last century, we see from the beginning of the trade union movement in America a constant fight. The socialists at first tried to run the trade unions simply as an appendix to the socialist party, and fought and villified the labor leaders who resisted; while on the other hand, these labor leaders—some of whom were capitalist politicians—made use of these attacks to make the trades unionists of the country believe that the socialists were the *enemies* of the trade unions. This war went on relentlessly for years and found its first natural expression, when Daniel DeLeon (who made his entrance into the Socialist movement in 1892) started the Socialist Trade and Labor Alliance in 1896 in opposition to the American Federation of Labor, for the purpose of creating a purely political trade union movement. DeLeon was logical from the old socialist standpoint, but that standpoint was wrong and the attempt necessarily failed.

Since then, even the most fanatic Lassallean socialists in America could not help but learn from the example of the socialist parties in Europe and also from the failure of their own tactics in this country. The trouble is only that they went to the *opposite* extreme. And while they formerly tried to inject socialist politics into the trades unions, examples of which were the Socialist Trade and Labor Alliance and later the American Labor Union, they now try to inject trade unionism into socialist politics and to solve political questions by the trade union. The trade union is now the fetish before which we must bow down. And *"industrialism"*—a term which simply signifies *one* form of an organization for trades unions and per se has nothing to do with socialism—is in future to be considered by socialists as the magic *key* which will open the gate of freedom for the American proletariat. The result of this other extreme was the formation last June of the Industrial Workers of the World in Chicago, which in its platform demands that the trade union should also do the work of a political party. That is its sense, if any sense can be made out of its contradictions.

As usual, both extremes are wrong. The truth lies in the middle.

The trade union and the social-democratic party are both a part of the labor movement, but they have different and separate functions.

The trade union seeks the raising of wages in accordance with the conditions of the labor market, the abolition of overtime and better pay for it when it is absolutely necessary. Every trade union strives to secure more human working conditions. Every trade union opposes the reduction of wages. Every trade union strengthens the feeling of solidarity. Every trade union is a promise of a better standard of living for the working class.

So much for the trade union.

On the other hand, every lost strike—and every strike won—teaches the trades union man that his economic struggle alone is entirely inadequate. Wage scales adopted are incapable of overbridging the chasm between labor and capital. The fight will break out again, and must break out again. And the interference of the capitalist states and municipal governments—the police, the court, the military—constantly reminds the wage-workers that the economic rule of the capitalist class culminates in its political rule.

It also reminds the workers that the only adequate weapon is the ballot.

The concentration of wealth, the formation of trusts, the industrial crisis, do the rest.

Result? Every thinking trades union man is bound to join the social-democratic party, sooner or later.

And this is what we mean when we say that we must have a

two-armed labor movement—a labor movement with a political arm and with an economic arm. Each arm has its own work to do, and one arm ought not to interfere with the other, although they are parts of the same body. That is the "Milwaukee idea." In the personal union of the workers of both, that is, in having the same persons take an active interest in both the trade union and the political labor movement, we find the strongest connecting link between the social-democratic party and the trade union organization. This idea works successfully not only in Milwaukee, but everywhere wherever the true relationship between trades unionism and socialism is rightly understood. Then we find the same men, with the same thoughts, aims, and ideals, working in the economic and the political field, thus forming a grand army moving on *two roads* for the abolition of the capitalist system.

3

ORGANIZER OF THE "LUMPENPROLETARIAT"

William D. Haywood
SOCIALISM, THE HOPE OF THE WORKING CLASS

In the annals of American radicalism the Industrial Workers of the World has a special place. The radical labor movement has adopted the Wobblie bard and martyr Joe Hill as a folk hero. Yet socialists eventually decided against association with an organization whose leader reputedly advocated the kind of violence that had condemned the Haymarket anarchists in the minds of the American electorate. The speech of William Haywood (1869–1928) which follows makes clear his reservations about political activity and summarizes his own strategy for victory, usually associated with the European syndicalist movement, based on the organization of unskilled workers into a giant industrial union. What he says about sabotage and direct action is harder to interpret. His ideas differed a great deal from DeLeon's, not just in his denigration of political action, but in his refusal to worry about the Marxist purity of working class rhetoric. From Haywood's point of view DeLeon was just another intellectual who knew nothing about the problems faced by working people. Arrested for sedition in 1917, "Big Bill" Haywood gave up his struggles in the United States and died an exile in the Soviet Union.

Comrades and fellow workers: I am indeed gratified with this splendid reception. In fact, I am always pleased with a New York audience, and I hope this will be no different from the many audiences that I have addressed in this city.

I am here tonight, as the chairman has stated, to speak on "Socialism, the Hope of the Working Class." And there are some differences between socialists. If we are to judge socialism by the opinions that have recently been expressed in the present controversy going on in our socialist papers, and if our judgment were based on those ingredients, I am sure that we would have a mental chop suey, the mysticism of which would baffle the ingenuity of the brain of a Chinese

SOURCE. William D. Haywood, "Socialism, the Hope of the Working Class," *International Socialist Review*, XII, February 1912, pp. 461–471.

mandarin. But not all the things that you have read from the pens of our very learned brothers are socialism. Socialism is so plain, so clear, so simple that when a person becomes intellectual he doesn't understand socialism.

In speaking to you of socialism tonight I would urge that you do not turn your minds to the legislative halls at Albany or the halls of Congress in Washington or the council chambers of the city hall in New York. I would prefer that you turn your minds inward and think of the machines where you are employed every day. I would like you to think of the relation that you hold to society, which occurs in three distinct phases: first, the individual relation, the relation to your home and family, the conditions that present themselves there; then the group relation, the industrial relation, without any regard to craft or trade divisions—not thinking that you are a particular craft man, but that you are working in some particular line of industry which is absolutely interdependent with all other industries; and then, having left your shop, your group or industrial relation, I would like your mind to turn home again, and you will not find that home isolated. It is a group of many homes. And there you assume another relation. There you become, not an individual of your family group, nor an individual of your social or industrial group, but you become a unit in the fabric of society. You become one then of the entire working class. And my definition of socialism here tonight will be clear enough indeed to the working class and also to the enemy of the working class; but to the go-between, to the opportunist, it will not be clear, and in all probability they would ask me to define my definition. I am not here to waste time on the "immediate demanders" or the step-at-a-time people whose every step is just a little shorter than the preceding step. I am here to speak to the working class, and the working class will understand what I mean when I say that under socialism you will need no passports or citizenship papers to take a part in the affairs in which you are directly interested. The working class will understand me when I say that socialism is an industrial democracy and that industrialism is a social democracy.

And in this democracy we know no divisions. There will be no divisions of race, creed, sex or color. Every person who is a factor in industrial activity will take a part in this industrial democracy. Under socialism we workers will not be subjects of any state or nation, but we will be citizens, free citizens in the industries in which we are employed. Therefore, I want you at all times while I am speaking to keep your mind closely riveted on your own personal interests. You don't have to go outside of your own shop, the place where you are doing productive work, to establish socialism. Socialism is not a thing remote, and it is not necessary for you to follow our brothers who are standing on the heights of Utopia beckoning you to come up and enjoy the elysian fields, where you will receive $4 a week after you become 60 years of age, and where the conditions have arrived at such a perfect stage of security that no trust can do business if it holds more than 40 percent monopoly of any particular line of industry. In this place that is being mapped out for you you will find that it is very much more desirable to be exploited by three 33 1/3 percent trusts than it is to be exploited by one 100 percent trust.

And now we will keep distinctly in mind the shop. I want to say at this point, and emphatically, that with the success of socialism practically all of the political offices now in existence will be put out of business. I want to say also, and with as much emphasis, that while a member of the Socialist party and believing firmly in political action, it is decidedly better in my opinion to be able to elect the superintendent in some branch of industry than to elect a congressman to the United States congress. More than that: under socialism we will have no congresses, such as exist today, nor legislatures, nor parliaments, nor councils of municipalities. Our councils will not be filled with aspiring lawyers and ministers, but they will be the conventions of the working class, composed of men and women who will go there for purposes of education, to exchange ideas, and by their expert knowledge to improve the machinery so that we can use it for the advantage of the working class. We will then have made machinery the slave of the working class, rather than now when the working class is the slave of the man who owns the machinery.

Having established these facts, we will now begin to understand why the conditions are so much more violent in this stage of the world's history than at any previous period. There was never a time in all the history of the world but what the working class were dominated by tyrants. There never was a period so tyrannical as now. We have heard of the democracy of Athens and of that ancient civilization. All the beauties of that wonderful city of free men, with its marvelous sculptures of marble, rested upon the shoulders of the 300,000 slaves in the valley. There has never been a period in the world's history that the working class were free. They have been slaves, serfs, chattel slaves and today wage slaves. And more than that, they are being devoured today by the Frankenstein that they themselves created. The energy, genius and ambition of the working class have brought about this marvelous age of machinery and invention, until today a machine will do the work of ten, one hundred, aye, a thousand times as much work as a man could do 50 years ago. This then is what intensifies the struggle for existence on the part of the working class. The unemployed army is rapidly increasing, due largely to the fact that labor-saving machinery has been introduced in nearly all branches of industry. We find then that the very thing that should improve the condition of the working class has contrived to make the condition of the working class deplorable indeed.

If you would travel and visit the various industries, as I have, you could speak of these things at first hand; the changes that are going on. Even here in a city like New York you can see a period of 100 years ago still hanging on. For instance, passing this street will be a street car drawn by horses; not far distant, an eighteen or twenty story building with a platform on the top arranged for the aeroplanes that are coming as a means of transportation from one part of the city to the other. In all lines of industry the same changes have been going on. Fifty years ago the plowing on the farms was done by a yoke of cattle or a span of horses. Today it is neatly done by traction engines and steam plows. The picking of the cotton was formerly done by chattel slaves, then by wage slaves, white women—in Texas it is no unusual thing, or was no unusual thing, to see a white woman dragging an 8-foot cotton sack up and down the field all day long. In a corner of the field was something wrapped up in a bundle or a piece of blanket. As that woman approached the bundle you would see her stop quickly, pick it up and nurse it—her baby! She would nurse the little one and start again her round of weary toil. The day of the white woman and the day of the colored children in the cotton field has passed with the introduction of a great machine that goes down the field, and with a system of suction takes up all the ripe cotton, and the next day the thing is done all over again. The mining industry has been transformed in just such a manner. The steel industry likewise. Every branch of industry. Indeed, there are few, if any, lines of trade where the workingman today controls the tools with which he lives. In the manufacture of shoes, where a man used to make a pair of shoes, or a pair of boots, he was called a shoemaker. Now in the process of manufacturing a pair of shoes it goes through at least 100 different pairs of hands, and the machinery that makes the shoe doesn't belong to the shoe manufacturer, but to the United States Shoe Machinery Company, which is an entirely different concern, and one of at least as great proportions now as the Standard Oil trust.

So we find that while the worker has gone steadily on with his toil and his inventive genius, creating all this wonderful machinery by his labor power alone, he has with every step of progress exaggerated his own struggle for existence and he has brought about a keener struggle between himself and the capitalist class. And if it were not for this struggle between the owning, employing class and the working class, the philosophy of socialism would never have been written. And here tonight, I believe, while I am speaking on the hope of the worker, that the necessity of emphasizing the class struggle is more apparent than anything else, because if the working class, if the workers will recognize this class struggle and become a part of it, there is absolutely no question as to the speedy and early results if we can ever get up against the capitalist class with our bare hands. We then will be in a position to absolutely control the situation.

And here tonight I am going to speak on the class struggle, and I am going to make it so plain that even a lawyer can understand it. I am going to present the class struggle so clearly here tonight that even a preacher will know its meaning. And this, friends, is rather more difficult than you appreciate. The lawyer and the preacher have never fought with the under-dog. For the ages agone they have been the mouthpieces of the capitalist class. They are not entirely to blame. We socialists recognize that it is largely the result of environment. You can't see the class struggle through the stained-glass windows of a cathedral. You can't see the class struggle through the spectacles of capitalist law, written by capitalist representatives in the interest of the capitalist class. To understand the class struggle you must go into the factory and you must ride on top of the boxcars or underneath the boxcars. You must go into the mills. You must look through the dirty windows of the working shop. You must go with me down into the bowels of the earth 1,000, 2,000, 3,000, 5,000 feet: there by the uncertain flicker of a safety lamp, there by the rays of a tallow candle you will understand something about the class struggle.

You must know that there are two classes in society. There are no half-way measures. Just two classes. On the one side the capitalist class. On the other side the working class. On the one side those who produce all and have little or none. On the other side those who produce none and have all. This struggle is between capitalism and socialism. Socialists are not responsible for it. We say that it exists. We know the conditions that have brought it about and we know the only remedy for it. We say that it will continue just so long as a favored few are given the special privilege of exploiting the many. This class struggle will continue just so long as one man eats bread in the sweat of another man's face.

And now the workers are involved in this class struggle, and we will see what they are going to do. The men in the Los Angeles jail, 100 or more—they understand this class struggle, and so do the men who were taken from that jail to San Quentin. They know what the class struggle means. Let me say to you that while the capitalist class is writing the criminal record of the Bridge and Structural Iron Workers'

Union it is no part of the duty of the socialists to be assisting them in their work, but it is our duty to compile the category of crimes perpetrated by the capitalist class. As for me, I am a defendant in every case where the working class or its representatives are on trial and the capitalist class is the plaintiff. Therefore my heart is with the MacNamara boys as long as they are fighting in the interests of the working class. Let the capitalist class bury its own dead. There are 21 dead in Los Angeles. We are too busy to go there, because tonight we have 207 dead in Bryceville, Tennessee. A federal grand jury has been selected to ferret out the men responsible for Jim MacNamara's crime in Los Angeles; there has been no grand jury selected to investigate the crime at Bryceville. And let me say that that explosion in Bryceville was just as premeditated, just as much a cold-blooded murder as though they had set the fuse or timed the clock. Every day in the year in this country there are 100 men and women killed; 35,000 every year. Seven hundred thousand killed and wounded in preventable accidents in the industries of this country. Let me say to you that when you hear of an explosion in a mine, you can mark it down that murder has been committed; been committed with the connivance, or at least through the deliberate negligence of the capitalist class. Every miner and every mine owner knows that if the mines are properly ventilated, if they are properly equipped with either air shafts or suction fans there will be no accumulation of gas or firedamp. If the coal dust is wetted down or removed there will be no explosions from this source. But it requires money, and it reduces the profit in mining coal. Human life is cheaper. Therefore, they continue to murder us by the thousands every year. And until we have brought about that condition whereby we can protect ourselves, I can't find it in my heart to condemn one of my own class.

So I say to you that the men in the Los Angeles jail, the men who were doing picket duty while the Llewellyn Iron Foundry workers were on strike, thrown into jail for no other reason than because they were on the picket line, because they had violated an injunction —those men understand the class struggle. In Fresno, California, not far removed from Los Angeles, 116 members of the Socialist party and the Industrial Workers of the World were thrown into a prison intended to "accommodate" 24 persons. As the jail doors swung behind them they said with all the spirit and more of the earnestness of Patrick Henry, "Give us liberty or give us death." The sheriff of the county called out the fire department, turned three strong streams of water into that jail; the men were compelled to hold mattresses against the doors to keep their eyes and nostrils from being torn out by the water. One man had his eye torn from his head. They left them all night long standing up to their knees in water. They understand the class struggle.

The men who fought the terrible battle for free speech in Spokane, where there were 1,800 hospital cases and only 500 prisoners—they understand the class struggle. They were competent to do that. Their jaws were broken by the minions of the capitalist class.

But most of us out west understand the class struggle, and I don't know how I can better portray what the class struggle means than to give you here tonight a brief history of the Western Federation of Miners. I don't think I have ever told this story in the city of New York. At least it will bear repetition.

The Western Federation of Miners is a fighting organization of the working class. It was born in jail, and we are proud of our birth. We were the child of an injunction. It was the first injunction ever issued in a labor controversy. President Taft is credited with being the father of injunctions, but that doubtful honor rests with Judge Beattie of the federal district court in Idaho, and Bill Taft is only the stepdad. That injunction was issued during a strike in the Coeur d'Alenes in the panhandle of Idaho in 1892. The miners went on strike to prevent a reduction of wages, and the mine owners, violating all laws, brought in thugs and hired gun men from foreign territory, and there was a pitched battle between union men and non-union men. A few were killed on each side, and during the fight a mill was blown up and the soldiers were sent in and 1,200 union men were arrested. They were placed in what the authorities were pleased to call a "bullpen." That particular bullpen was a hurriedly erected two-story structure built out of rough lumber, where those 1,200 men were crowded in much closer than you are here tonight. They were held, most of them, for a period of seven months. During the early weeks of their incarceration they were not permitted to leave that building, not even to answer the calls of nature. They became diseased and vermin infested, and many, many of them died as a result of that cruel imprisonment. Among the number were 14 who were arrested for violating the injunction that I referred to. They were sent to Ada county jail, and by the merest coincidence they occupied the same cells that Moyer, Pettibone and myself lived in for so many weary months, commencing some 14 years later. And it was while those 14 men were within the gloomy walls of that prison that they conceived the idea and formulated the plan of federating all the miners of the west, or amalgamating all the miners of the west into one general organization.

As soon as they were released they called a convention. It was held in Butte, Montana. And on the 15th of May, 1893, the Western Federation of Miners was born. Quick on the heels of its inception came the Cripple Creek strike of 1894, when the miners went out to establish an eight-hour day and a minimum wage of $3.50 to protect the members of their organization from discrimination. The mine owners at once called on the governor for the soldiers, but at this time we had a governor in the chair who was a member of the organization himself. He refused to become an ally of the operators. But they had a tool in the person of the sheriff of what was then called El Paso county, and this sheriff organized an army of deputies. Those deputies were composed, as deputy sheriffs usually are, of the dregs of society. Society, you know, is in three layers. There is the dregs on the bottom and the great working-class paystreak in the center, and the scum on the top. You can usually tell the female of the species: she is more deadly than the male. Those on the bottom begin cutting off their clothes at the bottom, and those on the top begin cutting them off at the top. The same species, scum and dregs. This army of deputies were instructed to go up and kill or capture the miners who had built a fort. I don't like to admit all these things—you will think they were not law abiding out west. When I speak to you about building a fort it puts me in mind of a story that I heard about "fighting like tigers on the barricades." But this was really and truly a barricade, and there were miners behind it that had never read or written a brief in their lives. They had guns, and they were prepared to meet their enemies.

But remember! We also believed in political action, and had elected one of our own class as governor of the state. And he called out the militia to protect the miners and put them in between the warring factions and told the deputy sheriffs that if they didn't disband he would fire on them as insurrectos. You understand, then, why I believe in political action. We will have control then of whatever forces government can give us, but we will not use them to continue to uphold and advance this present system, but we will use the forces of the police power to overthrow this present system. And instead of using the powers of the police to protect the strikebreakers, we will use the powers of the police to protect the strikers. That's about as far as I go on political action. But that's a long way. And the reason that I don't go into the halls of parliament to make laws to govern the working class is because the working class is working with machines, and every time some fellow has a thought, inspiration, the machine changes, and I don't know that laws can be made quick enough to keep up with the changing machinery. And I know this: that laws, under socialism, will not be made to govern individuals. We have got too much of that kind of law, and we want a little freedom from now on. The only kind of government that we will have then will be that kind that will administer industry. That's all. No other kind of government. And that will apply not only in the machine shop, but in every municipality. The municipality itself will become a part of the industrial life.

But now, to get back to that fight on Bull Hill. There, when these soldiers dispersed the deputies, the miners went into session in their union hall and passed an eight-hour law. Just think of the impudence of those miners! And that law has proved to be court-decision proof. It's never been declared unconstitutional by any supreme court.

And now, perhaps you would consider that "direct action." I believe in direct action. If I wanted something done and could do it myself I wouldn't delegate that job to anybody. That's the reason I believe in direct action. You are certain of it, and it isn't nearly so expensive.

We won the strike on Bull Hill then because we were organized industrially and because we were in control of the situation politically. But we lost the strike in Leadville in 1896. You see, the women voted in 1894 in Colorado. They had started a campaign, and the slogan of the campaign was "Save the State!" It was the first time that the women voted. And they proceeded to defeat one of the best men in the state and elected a man for governor that they wouldn't invite into their homes. I wanted to mention this fact because of the strong campaign that is being made for woman suffrage. Now, while I believe in women having everything that men have, I believe that they are entitled—well, they're just a part of the human race, that's all, and I don't know of any reason why I should have something and deprive them of it. Give them equal rights in everything. And that's what we say in Colorado now, "Here's to the women, God bless them. Once our superiors, but now our equals." We have brought them down to our same level. That strike in 1896 was in the lead mines. It was lost. In 1897 and 1898 we had the same difficulty. In Leadville we had 900 men in the bullpen for eight months. Then came the second strike in the Coeur d'Alenes in 1899.

As before, the question involved was reduction of wages. And let me say to you, friends, so that you will understand the position of the Western Federation of Miners: we have never been involved in a controversy of any kind, except for the man underneath. We have always fought the battle of the under dog. We have never tried to establish an apprentice system or to do anything especially for the skilled men. As before, the mine owners brought in deputies, and there was another mill blown up, and this time it was the Bunker Hill and Frisco. It is said that there were 3,000 pounds of powder put under that mill. Naturally, when that powder went off the mill went up, and some of it probably hasn't come down yet.

Then the troops came, which was not the militia. The militia had

gone to fight in the Spanish war. It was the regular troops, sent in by
President McKinley, and they were black soldiers. Another bullpen
was erected, this time a low rambling one-story structure; the bare
earth, no floor, rough boards to sleep on, a wisp of hay for bedding;
food unfit for animals; the whole thing fenced in with barbed wire 18
and 20 strands high. On the inside of that enclosure, over a thousand
union men, just as good as any of you are. And on the outside, a
thousand black soldiers. And while those young miners were fighting
for the flag, for the freedom, the honor of this country—I don't mean
the red flag—the black soldiers were at home insulting, outraging,
ravishing their wives, mothers, sisters and sweethearts.

And that brings us down then to the Colorado strike, with which
you are all well acquainted. Sixteen hundred men under arrest and in
the bullpen at one time; 400 deported, thrown out on the prairie
without food and without water; hundreds of homes demolished. Our
stores, four of them, robbed. Many of our members murdered. Many of
our wives outraged.

So you understand that we know the class struggle in the west. And
realizing, having contended with all the bitter things that we have
been called upon to drink to the dregs, do you blame me when I say
that *I despise the law* and I am not a law-abiding citizen. And more
than that, no socialist can be a law-abiding citizen. When we come
together and are of a common mind, and the purpose of our minds is
to overthrow the capitalist system, we become conspirators then
against the United States government. And certainly it is our purpose
to abolish this government and establish in its place an industrial
democracy. . . .

They say that it's wrong for me to speak to you this way; that it
would be inciting the workers to riot. That's the reason that I didn't
speak to the garbage workers here one night. Just as though I would
try to get an unarmed garbage worker to go up against one of these
murderous brutes of policemen here in New York! It isn't likely. But I
would like to have tried to have all the working class of New York to
stand by the garbage workers, even to the extent of a general strike.
There in Wales, when they whipped the police the managers of the
mines called upon the king for the soldiers. The soldiers came. Some
of them had been permeated with the spirit of class consciousness.
They took out and threw away part of the locks of their guns, making
them useless.

I know that some of you members here will think that this is not
patriotic; that really you ought to fight for the flag; that you ought to
live up to your obligations and fulfill your duties. But let me say to
you that that isn't being a traitor. If it is, it's better to be a traitor to

your country than it is to be a traitor to your class. Not only that, but there are no foreigners in the working class. The only foreigner that the working class should know is the capitalist. . . .

I don't want to leave you without the constructive policy of this meeting. There are many ways to describe how the socialists will get control of the industries. There are those who say that we will confiscate them. "Confiscate!" That's good. I like that word. It suggests stripping the capitalist, taking something away from him. But there has got to be a good deal of force to this thing of taking. You might have a majority of voters, but some of them might be crippled; they wouldn't be fighters. Remember that the capitalists have standing tonight their whole well-disciplined army of capitalism—bayonets, Maxim guns, long Toms, the navy, the army, the militia, the secret service, the detectives, the police are all there to protect the property of capital. I have got a better way, so I am temporarily going to pass up that confiscation idea.

Another one will say, "Well, competition. We could accomplish these things by competition." They look at the shop, it isn't a very big shop and they know that it was built by workers. "Well, why can't we build another shop and go into competition; build another railroad?" All these things can be done. But you can't build another Niagara Falls, can you, where the power is generated to run the shops? You can't build another coal bed, can you, nor another forest, nor other wheat fields? So we will have to pass up the idea of competition.

But another socialist comes along with the idea of compensation, and that is the worst of the three C's. Really, we have already purchased these things, and haven't they been compensated enough? They have been riding on our backs all these years. They have enjoyed life and luxury. Compensation means, then, that we are to take control of the industries and relieve them of the responsibilities and pay them interest-bearing bonds, gold bonds, and that these capitalists, whom we have always regarded as exploiters, will have no harder work than to hire some one to clip coupons for them; that we will have a bond-holding aristocracy in this country that will ride us harder than the aristocracy of any country in the world. No, I say, pass up this compensation.

Well, there is another fellow, the Christian socialist. He has an idea of "conversion." And I want to say to you that a Christian socialist is one who is drunk on religious fanaticism and is trying to sober up on economic truth, and when he gets about half-sober he thinks that he can convert the capitalist to Christianity and that the capitalist will be willing to turn over all these things to the brotherhood of man. He overlooks the fact that the capitalist is a child of the devil, and that's a poor place for a Christian socialist to proselyte. We will pass up the Christian socialist with the "conversion."

Here is another man—they all follow in the line of C's. I use the C's so that you can—I was speaking down in Missouri where I had to show them—confiscation, compensation, competition, conversion. Now, the trade unionist believes in coercion. I like that. I believe in the strike. I believe in the boycott. I believe in coercion. But I believe that it ought to be by two million men instead of by a handful of men. If they are going to play a game of coercion, let that game be strong so that the capitalist class will know that the trade unionists will mean every word they say. But they don't. Never did. Because they no sooner have the capitalists in a position where they recognize that this coercion means something, than some of their representatives will step in with a compromise—there is another C—and then tie them up with a contract, and that contract for an indefinite period, one, two, or three years. And let me say to you that the trade unionist who becomes a party to a contract takes his organization out of the columns of fighting organizations; he removes it from the class struggle and he binds it up and makes it absolutely useless. For instance, let me give you a humble illustration. A labor organization is a fighting machine of the working class, or ought to be. If it is not, it isn't fulfilling its mission. . . .

Now we come to the constructive program, the program which every Industrialist understands. Remember that there isn't an Industrialist but what is a socialist, and knows why. There are many socialists who are trade unionists, but they couldn't tell you why in a hundred years. They couldn't justify it in a hundred years, except that they have to be to hold their jobs. Then we have the constructive program of socialism, which means that the working class can be organized in a constructive and a defensive organization at the same time. Let me show you what I mean. Now, I want to present it to you so clearly that you will take it home with you. Suppose that the United Mine Workers of America, organized as they are industrially—but let me say they are hampered with all the tools of trade unionism—suppose that they would join hands with the Western Federation of Miners and we would cut loose entirely from the capitalist class, recognizing them on the economic as well as the political field as our enemies, having absolutely nothing to do with them. We would start a program then of organization, having for its purpose the taking in of every man employed in the mining industry throughout the United States. This work having been accomplished, or nearly perfected, is there a man or woman in this hall who believes that with such an organization we could not protect our lives? Don't you believe that if we had a class-conscious organization of the miners we could compel the mine owners to properly ventilate the mine, to remove the coal dust, to equip them with safety appliances for the protection of life and limb and to furnish a sufficient amount of timber to work them?

Can we do this? You know that we could if we had this power behind us; this organization. We then could protect our lives. We would have the mines in better shape. We could produce more coal. But first having protected our lives we would think about our families and we would improve their conditions around the mines. We would see that there were better company houses for our families to live in; that the young men had first-class up-to-date apartment houses to dwell in; that the schools were first-class. Any reason why we couldn't? Not at all.

Having preserved our lives, improved the conditions of our homes, we would become better men physically and mentally. We can produce more coal. But—you garment workers have got all the power you need; don't need any more coal. We wouldn't produce coal just for fun, nor would we let each other ever deprive us of the luxuries and necessities of life. Not at all. How then could we reduce the output of coal? We would reduce the hours of labor. If we can produce enough coal in eight hours or six or four, you wouldn't want us to work any longer, would you?

Having preserved our lives, improved our home conditions, reduced our hours of labor, what does that suggest? Well, we would look around and see that the rest of the working class had kept pace with us, every one marching in rhythm, and we would say to you, "We will cut out the capitalist class now. We will lock them out. Every man that quits his job now is a scab. We want every man to work and we in turn will contribute for your labor everything that you need." This is the understanding that we would have. There would be no capitalist class in this game. There would be nothing but the working class. And this being an accomplished fact, we would say then that the socialists despise covering up their aims and purposes. We would say that it is our purpose to overthrow the capitalist system by forcible means if necessary.

And I urge you workers tonight: determine upon this program. Workers of the world, unite! You have nothing to lose but your chains. You have a world to gain.

4

THE SPIRIT OF RADICALISM

Eugene V. Debs
SOUND SOCIALIST TACTICS

It is not easy to locate Eugene Debs along the spectrum of socialist thought. Running many times as the presidential candidate of the Socialist party, he more than anyone embodied the force of unity within the party. Its most widely known spokesman, he did his best to remain aloof from squabbles that rocked the party's national executive committee. The letter of socialist doctrine was not nearly as important to him as the dream of a unified working class striving in a common cause. He wrote this article in answer to Haywood, but he bent over backward to keep Haywood's views within the bounds of permissible party doctrine. Debs strongly believed in political action, if only because it served educational purposes, but he extended his heart to the sort of downtrodden laborer whom Haywood represented. When Debs was jailed in 1918 under provisions of the Espionage Act, he declared to the court: "Your Honor, years ago I recognized my kinship with all living things, and I made up my mind that I was not one bit better than the meanest on earth. I said then, and I say now, that while there is a lower class, I am in it, while there is a criminal element I am of it, and while there is a soul in prison, I am not free." No one ever captured the moving force behind American radicalism better than Debs in those words.

Socialists are practically all agreed as to the fundamental principles of their movement. But as to tactics there is wide variance among them. The matter of sound tactics, equally with the matter of sound principles, is of supreme importance. The disagreements and dissensions among socialists relate almost wholly to tactics. The party splits which have occurred in the past have been due to the same cause, and if the party should ever divide again, which it is to be hoped it will not, it will be on the rock of tactics.

Revolutionary tactics must harmonize with revolutionary princi-

SOURCE. Eugene V. Debs, "Sound Socialist Tactics," *International Socialist Review*, XII, February 1912, pp. 481–486.

ples. We could better hope to succeed with reactionary principles and revolutionary tactics than with revolutionary principles and reactionary tactics.

The matter of tactical differences should be approached with open mind and in the spirit of tolerance. The freest discussion should be allowed. We have every element and every shade of capitalist society in our party, and we are in for a lively time at the very best before we work out these differences and settle down to a policy of united and constructive work for socialism instead of spending so much time and energy lampooning one another.

In the matter of tactics we cannot be guided by the precedents of other countries. We have to develop our own and they must be adapted to the American people and to American conditions. I am not sure that I have the right idea about tactics; I am sure only that I appreciate their importance, that I am open to correction, and that I am ready to change whenever I find myself wrong.

It seems to me there is too much rancor and too little toleration among us in the discussion of our differences. Too often the spirit of criticism is acrid and hypercritical. Personal animosities are engendered, but opinions remain unchanged. Let us waste as little as possible of our militant spirit upon one another. We shall need it all for our capitalist friends.

There has recently been some rather spirited discussion about a paragraph which appears in the pamphlet on "Industrial Socialism," by William D. Haywood and Frank Bohn. The paragraph follows:

"When the worker, either through experience or study of socialism, comes to know this truth, he acts accordingly. *He retains absolutely no respect for the property 'rights' of the profit-takers. He will use any weapon which will win his fight.* He knows that the present laws of property are made by and for the capitalists. *Therefore he does not hesitate to break them.*"

The sentences which I have italicized provoked the controversy.

We have here a matter of tactics upon which a number of comrades of ability and prominence have sharply disagreed. For my own part I believe the paragraph to be entirely sound.

Certainly all socialists, knowing how and to what end capitalist property "rights" are established, must hold such "rights" in contempt. In the Manifesto Marx says: "The communist (socialist) revolution is the most radical rupture with traditional property relations; no wonder that its development involves the most radical rupture with traditional ideas."

As a revolutionist I can have no respect for capitalist property laws, nor the least scruple about violating them. I hold all such laws to have been enacted through chicanery, fraud and corruption, with the sole end in view of dispossessing, robbing and enslaving the working class. But this does not imply that I propose making an individual lawbreaker of myself and butting my head against the stone wall of existing property laws. That might be called force, but it would not be that. It would be mere weakness and folly.

If I had the force to overthrow these despotic laws I would use it without an instant's hesitation or delay, but I haven't got it, and so I am law-abiding under protest—not from scruple—and bide my time.

Here let me say that for the same reason I am opposed to sabotage and to "direct action." I have not a bit of use for the "propaganda of the deed." These are the tactics of anarchist individualists and not of socialist collectivists. They were developed by and belong exclusively to our anarchist friends and accord perfectly with their philosophy. These and similar measures are reactionary, not revolutionary, and they invariably have a demoralizing effect upon the following of those who practice them. If I believed in the doctrine of violence and destruction as party policy; if I regarded the class struggle as guerilla warfare, I would join the anarchists and practice as well as preach such tactics.

It is not because these tactics involve the use of force that I am opposed to them, but because they do not. The physical forcist is the victim of his own boomerang. The blow he strikes reacts upon himself and his followers. The force that implies power is utterly lacking, and it can never be developed by such tactics.

The foolish and misguided, zealots and fanatics, are quick to applaud and eager to employ such tactics, and the result is usually hurtful to themselves and to the cause they seek to advance.

There have been times in the past, and there are countries today where the frenzied deed of a glorious fanatic like old John Brown seems to have been inspired by Jehovah himself, but I am now dealing with the twentieth century and with the United States.

There may be, too, acute situations arise and grave emergencies occur, with perhaps life at stake, when recourse to violence might be justified, but a great body of organized workers, such as the socialist movement, cannot predicate its tactical procedure upon such exceptional instances.

But my chief objection to all these measures is that they do violence to the class psychology of the workers and cannot be successfully inculcated as mass doctrine. The very nature of these tactics adapts them to guerilla warfare, to the bomb planter, the midnight assassin; and such warfare, in this country at least, plays directly into the hands of the enemy.

Such tactics appeal to stealth and suspicion, and cannot make for solidarity. The very teaching of sneaking and surreptitious practices has a demoralizing effect and a tendency to place those who engage in them in the category of "Black Hand" agents, dynamiters, safe-blowers, hold-up men, burglars, thieves and pickpockets.

If sabotage and direct action, as I interpret them , were incorporated in the tactics of the Socialist party, it would at once be the signal for all the agents provocateur and police spies in the country to join the party and get busy. Every solitary one of them would be a rabid "direct actionist," and every one would safely make his "get-away" and secure his reward, a la McPartland, when anything was "pulled off' by their dupes, leaving them with their necks in the nooses.

With the sanctioning of sabotage and similar practices the Socialist party would stand responsible for the deed of every spy or madman, the seeds of strife would be subtly sown in the ranks, mutual suspicion would be aroused, and the party would soon be torn into warring factions to the despair of the betrayed workers and the delight of their triumphant masters.

If sabotage or any other artifice of direct action could be successfully employed, it would be wholly unnecessary, as better results could be accomplished without it. To the extent that the working class has power based upon class-consciousness, force is unnecessary; to the extent that power is lacking, force can only result in harm.

I am opposed to any tactics which involve stealth, secrecy, intrigue, and necessitate acts of individual violence for their execution.

The work of the socialist movement must all be done out in the broad open light of day. Nothing can be done by stealth that can be of any advantage to it in this country.

The workers can be emancipated only by their own collective will, the power inherent in themselves as a class, and this collective will and conquering power can only be the result of education, enlightenment and self-imposed discipline.

Sound tactics are constructive, not destructive. The collective reason of the workers repels the idea of individual violence where they are free to assert themselves by lawful and peaceable means.

The American workers are law-abiding and no amount of sneering or derision will alter that fact. Direct action will never appeal to any considerable number of them while they have the ballot and the right of industrial and political organization.

Its tactics alone have prevented the growth of the Industrial Workers of the World. Its principles of industrial unionism are sound, but its tactics are not. Sabotage repels the American worker. He is ready for the industrial union, but he is opposed to the "propaganda of the deed," and as long as the I.W.W. adheres to its present tactics and ignores political action, or treats it with contempt by advising the workers to "strike at the ballot box with an ax," they will regard it as an anarchist organization, and it will never be more than a small fraction of the labor movement.

The sound education of the workers and their thorough organization, both economic and political, on the basis of the class struggle, must precede their emancipation. Without such education and organization they can make no substantial progress, and they will be robbed of the fruits of any temporary victory they may achieve, as they have been through all the centuries of the past.

For one, I hope to see the Socialist party place itself squarely on record at the coming national convention against sabotage and every other form of violence and destructiveness suggested by what is known as "direct action."

It occurs to me that the Socialist party ought to have a standing committee on tactics. The art or science of proletarian party tactics might well enlist the serious consideration of our clearest thinkers and most practical propagandists.

To return for a moment to the paragraph above quoted from the pamphlet of Haywood and Bohn. I agree with them that in their fight against capitalism the workers have a right to use any weapon that will help them to win. It should not be necessary to say that this does not mean the black-jack, the dirk, the lead-pipe or the sawed-off shotgun. The use of these weapons does not help the workers to win, but to lose, and it would be ridiculous to assume that they were in the minds of the authors when they penned that paragraph.

The sentence as it reads is sound. It speaks for itself and requires no apology. The workers will use any weapon which will help them win their fight.

The most powerful and the all-sufficient weapons are the industrial union and the Socialist party, and they are not going to commit suicide by discarding these and resorting to the slung-shot, the dagger and the dynamite bomb.

Another matter of party concern is the treatment of so-called intellectuals in the socialist movement. Why the term "intellectual" should be one of reproach in the Socialist party is hard to understand, and yet there are many socialists who sneer at a man of intellect as if he were an interloper and out of place among socialists. For myself I am always glad to see a man of brains, of intellect, join the movement. If he comes to us in good faith he is a distinct acquisition and is entitled to all the consideration due to any other comrade.

To punish a man for having brains is rather an anomalous attitude for an educational movement. The Socialist party, above every other, should offer a premium on brains, intellectual capacity, and attract to itself all the mental forces that can be employed to build up the socialist movement, that it may fulfill its emancipating mission.

Of course the socialist movement is essentially a working class movement, and I believe that as a rule party officials and representatives, and candidates for public office, should be chosen from the ranks of the workers. The intellectuals in office should be the exceptions, as they are in the rank and file.

There is sufficient ability among the workers for all official demands, and if there is not, it should be developed without further delay. It is their party, and why should it not be officered and represented by themselves?

An organization of intellectuals would not be officered and represented by wage-earners; neither should an organization of wage-earners be officered and represented by intellectuals.

There is plenty of useful work for the intellectuals to do without holding office, and the more intellectual they are the greater can their service be to the movement. Lecturers, debaters, authors, writers, artists, cartoonists, statisticians, etc., are in demand without number, and the intellectuals can serve to far better advantage in those capacities than in official positions.

I believe, too, in rotation in office. I confess to a prejudice against officialism and a dread of bureaucracy. I am a thorough believer in the rank and file, and in ruling from the bottom up instead of being ruled from the top down. The natural tendency of officials is to become bosses. They come to imagine that they are indispensable and unconsciously shape their acts to keep themselves in office .

The officials of the Socialist party should be its servants, and all temptation to yield to the baleful influence of officialism should be removed by constitutional limitation of tenure.

There is a tendency in some states to keep the list of locals a solemn secret. The sheep have got to be protected against the wolves. No one must know what locals there are, or who its officials, for fear they may be corrupted by outside influences. This is an effective method for herding sheep, but not a good way to raise men. If the locals must be guarded against the wolves on the outside, then someone is required to guard them, and that someone is a boss, and it is the nature of the boss to be jealous of outside influences.

If our locals and the members who compose them need the protection of secrecy, they are lacking in the essential revolutionary fiber which can be developed only in the play of the elements surrounding them, and with all the avenues of education and information, and even of miseducation and misinformation, wide open for their reception. They have got to learn to distinguish between their friends and their enemies and between what is wise and what is otherwise and until the rank and file are so educated and enlightened their weakness will sooner or later deliver them as the prey of their enemies. . . .

I cannot close without appealing for both the industrial and political solidarity of the workers.

I thoroughly believe in economic as well as political organization, in the industrial union and in the Socialist party.

I am an industrial unionist because I am a socialist and a socialist because I am an industrial unionist.

I believe in making every effort within our power to promote industrial unionism among the workers and to have them all united in one economic organization. To accomplish this I would encourage industrial independent organization, especially among the millions who have not yet been organized at all, and I would also encourage the "boring from within" for all that can be accomplished by the industrial unionists in the craft unions.

I would have the Socialist party recognize the historic necessity and inevitability of industrial unionism, and the industrial union reciprocally recognize the Socialist party, and so declare in the respective preambles to their constitutions.

The Socialist party cannot be neutral on the union question. It is compelled to declare itself by the logic of evolution, and as a revolutionary party it cannot commit itself to the principles of reactionary unionism. Not only must the Socialist party declare itself in favor of economic unionism, but the kind of unionism which alone can complement the revolutionary action of the workers on the political field.

I am opposed under all circumstances to any party alliances or affiliations with reactionary trade unions and to compromising tactics of every kind and form, excepting alone in event of some extreme emergency. While the "game of politics," as it is understood and as it is played under capitalist rules, is as repugnant to me as it can possibly be to any one, I am a thorough believer in political organization and political action.

Political power is essential to the workers in their struggle, and they can never emancipate themselves without developing and exercising that power in the interests of their class.

It is not merely in a perfunctory way that I advocate political action, but as one who has faith in proletarian political power and in the efficacy of political propaganda as an educational force in the socialist movement. I believe in a constructive political program and in electing all the class-conscious workers we can, especially as mayors, judges, sheriffs and as members of the state legislatures and the national congress.

The party is now growing rapidly, and we are meeting with some of the trials which are in store for us and which will no doubt subject us to the severest tests. We need to have these trials, which are simply the fires in which we have to be tempered for the work before us.

There will be all kinds of extremists to deal with, but we have nothing to fear from them. Let them all have their day. The great body of the comrades, the rank and file, will not be misled by false teachings or deflected from the true course.

We must put forth all our efforts to control our swelling ranks by the use of wise tactics and to assimilate the accessions to our membership by means of sound education and party discipline.

The new year has opened auspiciously for us, and we have never been in such splendid condition on the eve of a national campaign.

Let us all buckle on our armor and go forth determined to make this year mark an epoch in the social revolution of the United States.

Part Four

RADICAL CRITIQUES OF PROGRESSIVE AMERICA

1

THE CONCENTRATION OF POWER

William J. Ghent
THE NEXT STEP: A BENEVOLENT FEUDALISM

*In some cases a fine line existed between socialists and social reformers.
Charles Edward Russell, Robert Hunter, and William English Walling were
for varying lengths of time members of the Socialist party. They are remembered however as "muckrakers" and enjoyed cordial relations with a number
of Progressive politicians. In the 1890s William Ghent (1866–1942) was an
independent socialist and worked for a variety of reform causes. Although he
did join the Socialist party, he remained only marginally involved in its
operations and resigned in protest of its opposition to American participation
in World War I. Later he gained a reputation as a historian of the West.
Despite his independence the point of view expressed in this article was
firmly socialist and went well beyond any analysis that could be placed
within a Progressive consensus. He gave no immediate hope of victory to
socialist politicians. Instead, Ghent delivered a frightening description of the
ability of big business and big government to anesthetize the voice of social
protest. His predictions proved to be effective propaganda, and inspired Jack
London, one of the most popular writers among socialists, to write* The Iron
Heel.

The next distinct stage in the socioeconomic evolution of America
may be something entirely different from any of the forms usually
predicted. Anarchist prophecies are, of course, futile; and the Tolstoyan utopia of a return to primitive production, with its prodigal waste
of effort and consequent impoverishment of the race, allures but few
minds. The Kropotkinian dream of a communistic union of shop
industry and agriculture is of a like type; and well-nigh as barren are
the Neo-Jeffersonian visions of a general revival of small-farm and
small-shop production and the dominance of a middle-class democra-

SOURCE. William J. Ghent, "The Next Step: A Benevolent Feudalism," *The
Independent*, LIV, April 3, 1902, pp. 781–788.

cy. The orthodox economists, with their notions of a slightly modified individualism, wherein each unit secures the just reward of his capacity and service, are but worshiping an image which they have created out of their books, and which has no real counterpart in life; and finally, the Marxists, who predict the establishment of a cooperative commonwealth, are, to say the least, too sanguine in foreshortening the time of its triumph. Whatever the more distant future may bring to pass, there is but little evidence to prove that collectivism will be the next status of society. Rather, that coming status, of which the contributing forces are now energetically at work and of which the first phases are already plainly observable, will be something in the nature of a benevolent feudalism.

That the concentration of capital and the increase of individual holdings of wealth will continue is almost unanimously conceded. Forty years ago Marx laid down the formula of capitalist accumulation which has ever since been a fixed article of creed with the orthodox socialists. "One capitalist always kills many" is its central maxim. And only recently Professor John B. Clark, doubtless our most distinguished representative of the orthodox economists, declared, in the pages of *The Independent*, that

"the world of the near future . . . will present a condition of vast and ever-growing inequality. . . . The rich will continually grow richer, and the multi-millionaires will approach the billion-dollar standard."

It is a view that needs no particular buttressing of authority, for it is held by most of those who seriously scan the outlook.

There are, it is not to be disputed, certain tendencies and data which apparently conflict with this view. There is a marked persistence, and in some cases a growth, of small-unit farming and of small-shop production and distribution. This tendency is strongly insisted upon by Prince Kropotkin and by the German socialist Bernstein, and is conceded, though cautiously, by a number of other radicals, among them the Belgian socialist Vandervelde. That it is a real tendency seems unquestioned on the face of the figures from Germany, France, England and Belgium; and it is not unlikely that further confirmation will be found in the detailed reports of the last United States census. Furthermore, the great commercial combinations are not necessarily a proof of individual increase of wealth. Often, perhaps generally, they result in this individual increase; but the two things are not inevitably related. These combinations are generally, as William Graham pointed out nearly twelve years ago, a massing together of separate portions of capital, small, great and moderate—a union of capitals for a common purpose while still separately owned. Lipton's great company, for instance, has over 62,000 shareholders; and many of America's most powerful combinations are built up out of a multitude of small and moderate holdings.

But though these facts and tendencies be admitted, they do not really affect the foregoing generalization. The drift toward small-unit production and distribution in certain lines argues no growth of economic independence. On the contrary, it is attended by a constant pressure and constraint. The more the great combinations increase their power, the greater is the subordination of the small concerns. They may, for one reason of another, find it possible, and even fairly profitable, to continue; but they will be more and more confined to particular activities, to particular territories, and in time to particular methods, all dictated and enforced by the pressure of the larger concerns. The petty tradesmen and producers are thus an economically dependent class; and their dependence increases with the years. In a like position, also, are the owners of small and moderate holdings in the trusts. The larger holdings—often the single largest holding—determines the rules of the game; the smaller ones are either acquiescent, or if recalcitrant, are powerless to enforce their will. Especially is this true in America, where the head of a corporation is often an absolute ruler, who determines not only the policy of the enterprise, but the *personnel* of the board of directors.

The tendencies thus make, on the one hand, toward the centralization of vast power in the hands of a few men—the morganization of industry, as it were—and on the other, toward a vast increase in the number of those who compose the economically dependent classes. The latter number is already stupendous. The laborers and mechanics were long ago brought under the yoke through their divorcement from the land and the application of steam to factory operation. They are economically unfree except in so far as their organizations make possible a collective bargaining for wages and hours. The growth of commerce raised up an enormous class of clerks and helpers, perhaps the most dependent class in the community. The growth and partial diffusion of wealth in America has in fifty years largely altered the character of domestic service and increased the number of servants many fold. Railroad pools and farm-implement trusts have drawn a tightening cordon about the farmers. The professions, too, have felt the change. Behind many of our important newspapers are private commercial interests which dictate their general policy, if not, as is frequently the case, their particular attitude upon every public question; while the race for endowments made by the greater number of the churches and by all colleges except a few state-supported ones, compels a cautious regard on the part of synod and faculty for the wishes, the views and prejudices of men of great wealth. To this growing deference of preacher, teacher and editor is added that of two yet more important classes—the makers and the interpreters of law. The record of legislation and judicial interpretation regarding slavery previous to the Civil War has been paralleled in recent years by the record of legislatures and courts in matters relating to the lives and health of manual workers, especially in such cases as employers' liability and factory inspection. Thus, with a great addition to the number of subordinate classes, with a tremendous increase of their individual components, and with a corresponding growth of power in the hands of a few score magnates, there is needed little further to make up a socio-economic status that contains all the essentials of a renascent feudalism.

It is, at least in its beginning, less a personal than a class feudalism. History may repeat itself, as the adage runs; but not by identical forms and events. The great spirals of evolutionary progress carry us for a time back to the general direction of older journeyings, but not to the well-worn pathways themselves. The old feudalism exacted faithful service, industrial and martial, from the underling; protection and justice from the overlord. It is not likely that personal fidelity, as once known, can ever be restored: the long period of dislodgment from the land, the diffusion of learning, the exercise of the franchise, and the training in individual effort have left a seemingly unbridgeable chasm between the past and the present forms. But the personal fidelity, in the old sense, is improbable, group fidelity, founded upon the conscious dependence of a class, is already observable, and it grows apace. Out of the sense of class dependence arises the extreme deference which we yield, the rapt homage which we pay—not as individuals, but as units of a class—to the men of wealth. We do not know them personally, and we have no sense of personal attachment. But in most things we grant them priority. We send them or their legates to the Senate to make our laws; we permit them to name our administrators and our judiciary; we listen with eager attention to their utterances and we abide by their judgment. Not always, indeed; for some of us grumble at times and ask angrily where it will all end. We talk threateningly of instituting referendums to curb excessive power; of levying income taxes, or of compelling the government to acquire the railroads and the telegraphs. We subscribe to newspapers and other publications which criticize the acts of the great corporations, and we hail as a new Gracchus the ardent reformer who occasionally comes forth for a season to do battle for the popular cause. But this revolt is, for the most part, sentimental; it is a mental attitude but rarely transmutable into terms of action. It is, moreover, sporadic and flickering; it dies out after a time, and we revert to our usual moods, concerning ourselves with our particular interests and letting the rest of the world wag as it will.

The new feudalism is thus characterized by a class dependence rather than by a personal dependence. But it differs in still other respects from the old. It is qualified and restricted, and by agencies hardly operative in medieval times. Democracy tends to restrain it, and ethics to moralize it. Though it has its birth and nurture out of the "rough and unsocialized barbarians of wealth," in Mr. Henry D. Lloyd's phrase, its youth and maturity promise a modification of character. More and more it tends to become a *benevolent* feudalism. On the ethical side it is qualified by a growing and diffusive sense of responsibility and of kinship. The principle of the "trusteeship of great wealth" having found lodgment, like a seed, in the erstwhile barren soil of mammonism, has become a flourishing growth. The enormous benefactions for social purposes, which have been common of late years, and which in 1901 reached a total of $107,000,000, could come only from men and women who have been taught to feel an ethical duty to society. It is a duty, true enough, which is but dimly seen and imperfectly fulfilled. The greater part of these benefactions is directed to purposes which have but a slight or indirect bearing upon the relief of social distress, the restraint of injustice, or the mitigation of remediable hardships. The giving is even often economically false, and if carried to an extreme would prove disastrous to the community; for in many cases it is a transmutation of wealth from a status of active capital, wherein it makes possible a greater diffusion of comfort, to a status of comparative sterility. But though often mistaken as is the conception and futile the fulfilment of this duty, the fact that it is apprehended at all is one of far-reaching importance.

The limitation which democracy puts upon the new feudalism is also important. For democracy will endure, in spite of the new order. "Like death," said Disraeli, "it gives back nothing." Something of its substance it gives back, it must be confessed; for it permits the most serious encroachments upon its rights; but of its outer forms it yields nothing, and thus it retains the potentiality of exerting its will in whatever direction it may see fit. And this fact though now but feebly recognized by the feudal barons, will be better understood by them as time runs on, and they will bear in mind the limit of popular patience. It is an elastic limit, of a truth; for the mass of mankind, as both Hamlet and Thomas Jefferson observed, are more ready to endure known ills than to fly to others that they know not. It is a limit which, to be heeded, needs only to be carefully studied. Macaulay's famous dictum, that the privileged classes, when their rule is threatened, always bring about their own ruin by making further exactions, is likely, in this case, to prove untrue. A wiser forethought begins to prevail among the autocrats of today—a forethought destined to grow and expand and to prove of inestimable value when bequeathed to their successors. Our nobility will thus temper their exactions to an endurable limit; and they will distribute benefits to a degree that makes a tolerant, if not a satisfied people. They may even make a working principle of Bentham's maxim, and after, of course, appropriating the first and choicest fruits of industry to themselves, may seek to promote the "greatest happiness of the greatest number." For therein will lie their greater security.

Of the particular forms which this new feudalism will take there are already numerous indications which furnish grounds for more or less confident prediction. All societies evolve naturally out of their predecessors. In sociology, as in biology, there is no cell without a parent cell. The society of each generation develops a multitude of spontaneous and acquired variations, and out of these, by a blending process of natural and conscious selection, the succeeding society is evolved. The new feudalism is but an orderly outgrowth of past and present tendencies and conditions.

Unlike the old feudalism it is not confined to the country. Qualified in certain respects though it be, it has yet a far wider province and scope of action. The great manorial estates now being created along the banks of the Hudson, along the shores of Long Island Sound and Lake Michigan, are but its pleasure places—its Sans Soucis, its Bagatelles. For from being the foundation of its revenues, as were the estates of the old feudalism, these are the prodigally expensive playthings of the new. The oil wells, the mines, the grain fields, the forests and the great thoroughfares of the land are its ultimate sources of revenue; but its strongholds are in the cities. It is in these centers of activity, with their warehouses, where the harvests are hoarded; their workshops, where the metals and woods are fashioned into articles of use; their great distributing houses; their exchanges; their enormously valuable franchises to be had for the asking or the seizing, and their pressure of population, which forces an hourly increase in the exorbitant value of land, that the new feudalism finds the field best adapted for its main operations.

Bondage to the land was the basis of villeinage in the old régime; bondage to the job will be the basis of villeinage in the new. The wage-system will endure, for it is an incomparably simpler means of determining the baron's volume of profits than were the "boon-works," the "week-works" and the corvées of old. But with increasing concentration on the one hand, and the fiercer competition for employment on the other, the secured job will become the laborer's fortress, which he will hardly dare to evacuate. The hope of bettering his condition by surrendering one place in the expectation of getting another will be qualified by a restraining prudence. He will no longer trust his individual strength, but will protest against ill conditions, or, in the last resort, strike, only in company with a formidable host of his fellows. And even the collective assertion of his demands will be restrained more and more as he considers recurring failures of his efforts such as that of the recent steel strike. Moreover, concentration gives opportunity for an almost indefinite extension of the blacklist: a person of offensive activity may be denied work in every feudal shop and on every feudal farm from one end of the country to the other. He will be a hardy and reckless industrial villein indeed who will dare incur the enmity of the duke of the Oil Trust when he knows that his actions will be promptly communicated to the banded autocracy of dukes, earls and marquises of the steel, coal, iron, window glass, lumber and traffic industries.

Of the three under classes of the old feudalism—sub-tenants, cotters and villeins—the first two are already on the ground, and the last is in process of restoration. But the vast complexity of modern society specializes functions, and for the new feudalism still other classes are required. It is a difficult task properly to differentiate these classes. They shade off almost imperceptibly into one another; and the dynamic processes of modern industry often hurl, in one mighty convulsion, great bodies of individuals from a higher to a lower class, blurring or obscuring the lines of demarcation. Nevertheless, to take a figure from geology, these convulsions become less and less frequent as the substratum of industrial processes becomes more fixed and regular; the classes become more stable and show more distinct differences, and they will tend, under the new *régime*, to the formal institution of graded caste. At the bottom are the wastrels, at the top the barons; and the gradation, when the new *régime* shall have become fully developed, whole and perfect in its parts, will be about as follows:

I. The barons, graded on the basis of possessions.

II. The courtiers and court-agents.

III. The workers in pure and applied science, artists and physicians. The new feudalism, like most autocracies, will foster not only the arts, but also certain kinds of learning—particularly the kinds which are unlikely to disturb the minds of the multitude. A future Marsh or Cope or Le Conte will be liberally patronized and left free to discover what he will; and so, too, an Edison or a Marconi. Only they must not meddle with anything relating to social science. For obvious reasons, also, physicians will occupy a position of honor and comparative freedom under the new *régime*.

IV. The *entrepreneurs*, the managers of the great industries, transformed into a salaried class.

V. The foremen and superintendents. This class has heretofore been recruited largely from the skilled workers, but with the growth of technical education in schools and colleges and the development of fixed caste, it is likely to become entirely differentiated.

VI. The villeins of the cities and towns, more or less regularly employed, who do skilled work and are partially protected by organization.

VII. The villeins of the cities and towns who do unskilled work and are unprotected by organization. They will comprise the laborers, domestics and clerks.

VIII. The villeins of the manorial estates, of the great farms, the mines and the forests.

IX. The small-unit farmers (land owning), the petty tradesmen and manufacturers.

X. The sub-tenants on the manorial estates and great farms (corresponding to the class of "free tenants" in the old feudalism).

XI. The cotters, living in isolated places and on the margin of cultivation.

XII. The tramps, the occasionally employed, the unemployed—the wastrels of city and country.

This, then, is the table of socio-industrial rank leading down from the feudatory barons. It is a classification open, of course, to amendment. The minor shareholders, it may be suggested, are not provided for; and certain other omissions might be named. But it is not possible to anticipate every detail; and, as for the small shareholders, who now occupy a wide range, from comparative poverty to comparative affluence, it seems likely that the complete development of the new *régime* will practically eliminate them. Other critics, furthermore, will object to the basis of gradation. The basis employed is not relative wealth, a test which nine out of ten persons would unhesitatingly apply in social classification; it is not comparative earning capacity, economic freedom, nor intellectual ability. Rather, it is the relative degree of comfort—material, moral and intellectual—which each class contributes to the nobility. The wastrels contribute least, and they are the lowest. The foremen, superintendents and *entrepreneurs* contribute most of the purely material comfort, and their place is correspondingly high. But higher yet is the rank of the courtiers and court agents, the legates and nuncios. This class will include the editors of "respectable" and "safe" newspapers, the pastors of "conservative" and "wealthy" churches, the professors and teachers in endowed colleges and schools, lawyers generally, and most judges and politicians. During the transition period there will be a gradual elimination of the more unserviceable of these persons, with the result that in the end this class will be largely transformed. The individual security of place and livelihood of its members will then depend on the harmony of their utterances and acts with the wishes of the great nobles: and so long as they rightly fulfil their functions their recompense will be generous. They will be at once the assuagers of popular suspicion and discontent and the providers of moral and intellectual anodynes for the barons. Such of them, however, as have not the tact or fidelity to do or say what is expected of them will be promptly forced into class XI or XII, or, in extreme cases, banished from all classes, to become the wretched pariahs of society.

Through all the various activities of these populous classes (except the last) our benevolent feudalism will carry on the nation's work. Its operations will begin with the land, whence it extracts the raw material of commerce. It is just at this stage of its workings that it will differ most from the customary forms of the old. The cotters will be pushed further back into isolation, and the sub-tenants will be confined to the grubbing away at their ill-recompensed labors. It is with the eighth class, the villeins of farm and wood and mine, that we have here to deal. The ancient ceremony of "homage," the swearing of personal fidelity to the lord, is transformed into that of the beseeching of the foreman for work. The wage system, with its mechanical simplicity, continuing in force, there is an absence of the old exactions of special work from the employed villein. A mere altering of the wage scale appropriates to the great noble whatever share of the product he feels he may safely demand for himself. Thus "week-work," the three or four days' toil in each week which the villein had to give unrecompensed to the lord, and "boon-work," the several days of extra toil three or four times a year, will never be revived. Even the company store, the modern form of feudal exaction, will in time be given up, for at best it is but a clumsy and offensive makeshift, and defter and less irritating means are at hand for reaching the same result. There will hardly be a restoration of "relief," the payment of a year's dues on inheriting an allotment of land, or of "heriot," the payment of a valuable gift from the possessions of a deceased relative. Indeed, these tithes may not be worth the bother of collecting; for the villein's inheritance will probably be but moderate, as befits his state and the place which God and the nobility have ordained for him.

The raw materials gathered, the scene of operations shifts from the country to the cities and great towns. But many of the latter will lose, during the transition period, a considerable part of their greatness, from the shutting up of needless factories and the concentration of production in the larger workshops. There will thus be large displacements of labor, and for a time a wide extension of suffering. Popular discontent will naturally follow, and it will be fomented, to some extent, by agitation; but the agitation will be guarded in expression and action, and it will be relatively barren of result. The possible danger therefrom will have been provided against, and a host of economists, preachers and editors will be ready to show indisputably that the evolution taking place is for the best interests of all; that it follows a "natural and inevitable law"; that those who have been thrown out of work have only their own incompetency to blame; that all who really want work can get it, and that any interference with the prevailing *régime* will be sure to bring on a panic, which will only make matters worse. Hearing this, the multitude will hesitatingly acquiesce and thereupon subside; and though occasionally a radical journal or a radical agitator will counsel revolt, the mass will remain quiescent. Gradually, too, by one method or another, sometimes by the direct action of the nobility, the greater part of the displaced workers will find some means of getting bread, while those who cannot will be eliminated from the struggle and cease to be a potential factor for trouble.

In its general aspects shop industry will be carried on much as now. Only the shops will be very much larger, the individual and total output will be greater, the unit cost of production will be lessened. Wages and hours will for a time continue on something like the present level; but, despite the persistence of the unions, no considerable gains in behalf of labor are to be expected. The owners of all industry worth owning, the barons will laugh at threats of striking and boycotting. No competitor can possibly make capital out of the labor disputes of another, for there will be no competitors, actual or potential. What the barons will most dread will be the collective assertion of the villeins at the polls; but this, from experience, they will know to be a thing of no immediate danger. By the putting forward of a hundred irrelevant issues they can hopelessly divide the voters at each election; or, that failing, there is always to be trusted as a last resort the cry of impending panic.

Practically all industry will be regulated in terms of wages, and the *entrepreneurs*, who will then have become the chief salaried officers of the nobles, will calculate to a hair the needful production for each year. Waste and other losses will thus be reduced to a minimum. A vast scheme of exact systematization will have taken the place of the old free competition, and industry will be carried on as by clockwork.

Gradually a change will take place in the aspirations and conduct of the younger generations. Heretofore there has been at least some degree of freedom of choice in determining one's occupation, however much that freedom has been curtailed by actual economic conditions. But with the settling of industrial processes comes more and more constraint. The dream of the children of the farms to escape from their drudgery by migrating to the city, and from the stepping stone of a clerkly place at $3 a week to rise to affluence, will be given over, and they will follow the footsteps of their fathers. A like fixity of condition will be observed in the cities, and the sons of clerks and of mechanics and of day laborers will tend to accept their environment of birth and training and abide by it. It is a phenomenon observable in all countries where the economic pressure is severe, and it is certain to obtain in feudal America.

The sub-tenants and the small-unit producers and distributers will be confined within smaller and smaller limits, while the foremen, the superintendents and the *entrepreneurs* of the workshops will attain to greater power and recompense. But the chief glory of the new *régime*, next to that of the nobles, will be that of the class of courtiers and court-agents. Theirs, in a sense, will be the most important function in the State—"to justify the ways of God [and the nobility] to man." Two divisions of the courtier class, however, will find life rather a burdensome travail. They are the judges and the politicians. Holding their places at once by popular election and by the grace of the barons, they will be fated to a constant see-saw of conflicting obligations. They must, in some measure, satisfy the demands of the multitude, and yet, on the other hand, they must obey the commands from above.

The outlines of the present State loom but feebly through the intricate network of the new system. The nobles will have attained to complete power, and the motive and operation of government will have become simply the registering and administering of their collective will. And yet the State will continue very much as now, just as the form and name of the Roman Republic continued under Augustus. The present State machinery is admirably adapted for the subtle and extra-legal exertion of power by an autocracy; and while improvements to that end might unquestionably be made, the barons will hesitate to take action which will needlessly arouse popular suspicions. From petty constable to Supreme Court Justice the officials will understand, or be made to understand, the golden mean of their duties; and except for an occasional rascally Jacobin, whom it may for a time be difficult to suppress, they will be faithful and obey.

The manorial courts, with powers exercised by the local lords, will not, as a rule, be restored. Probably the "court baron," for determining tenantry and wage questions, will be revived. It may even come as a natural outgrowth of the present conciliation boards, with a successor of the Committee of Thirty-six as a sort of general court baron for the nation. But the "court leet," the manorial institution for punishing misdemeanors, wherein the baron holds his powers by special grant from the central authority of the State, we shall never know again. It is far simpler and will be less disturbing to the popular mind to leave in existence the present courts so long as the baron can dictate the general policy of justice.

Armed force will, of course, be employed to overawe the discontented and to quiet unnecessary turbulence. Unlike the armed forces of the old feudalism, the nominal control will be that of the State; the soldiery will be regular and not irregular. Not again will the barons risk the general indignation arising from the employment of Pinkertons and other private armies. The worker has unmistakably shown his preference, when he is to be subdued, for the militia and the federal army. Broadly speaking, it is not an unreasonable attitude; and it goes without saying that it will be respected. The militia of our benevolent feudalism will be recruited, as now, mostly from the clerkly class; and it will be officered largely by the sons and nephews of the barons. But its actions will be tempered by a saner policy. Governed by those who have most to fear from popular exasperation, it will show a finer restraint.

A general view of the new society will present little of startling novelty. A person leaving this planet today and revisiting "the pale glimpses of the moon" when the new order is in full swing will from superficial observation see but few changes. *Alter et idem*—another, yet the same—he will say. Only by closer view will he mark the deepening and widening of channels along which the powerful currents of present tendencies are borne; only so will he note the effect of the more complete development of the mighty forces now at work.

So comprehensive and so exact will be the social and political control that it will be exercised in a constantly widening scope and over a growing multiplicity of details. The distribution of wages and dividends will be nicely balanced with a watchful regard for possible dissatisfaction. Old-age pensions to the more faithful employees, such as those granted by the Illinois Central, the Pennsylvania, the Colorado Fuel & Iron Company, the Metropolitan Traction Company, or the Lackawanna, will be generally distributed, for the hard work will be done only by the most vigorous, and a large class of destitute unemployed will be a needless menace to the *régime*. Peace will be the main desideratum, and its cultivation will be the most honored science of the age. A happy blending of generosity and firmness will characterize all dealings with open discontent; but the prevention of discontent will be the prior study, to which the intellect and the energies of the nobles and their legates will be ever bent. To that end the teachings of the schools and colleges, the sermons, the editorials, the stump orations, and even the plays at the theaters will be skillfully and persuasively molded; and the questioning heart of the poor, which perpetually seeks some answer to the painful riddle of the earth, will meet with a multitude of mollifying responses. These will be: from the churches, that discontent is the fruit of atheism, and that religion alone is a solace for earthly woe; from the colleges, that discontent is ignorant and irrational, since conditions have certainly bettered in the last one hundred years; from the newspapers, that discontent is anarchy; and from the stump orators that it is unpatriotic, since this nation is the greatest and most glorious that ever the sun shone upon. As of old, these reasons will for the time suffice; and against the possibility of recurrent questionings new apologetics will be skillfully formulated, to be put forth as occasion requires. On all sides will be observed a greater respect for power; and the former tendency toward rash and bitter criticism of the upper classes will decline.

The arts, too, will be modified. Literature will take on the hues and tones of the good-natured days of Charles II. Instead of poetry, however, the innocuous novel will flourish best; every flowery courtier will write romance, and the literary darling of the renascence will be an Edmund Waller of fiction. A lineal descendant of the famous Lely, who

> ". . . on animated canvas stole
> The sleepy eye that spoke the melting soul,"

will be the laureled chief of our painters; and sculpture, architecture and the lesser arts, under the spell of changed influences, will undergo a like transformation.

This, then, in the rough, is our benevolent feudalism to-be. It is not precisely a utopia, not an "island valley of Avilion"; and yet it has its commendable, even its fascinating features. "The empire is peace," shouted the partisans of Louis Napoleon; and a like cry, with an equal ardency of enthusiasm, will be uttered by the supporters of the new *régime*. Peace and stability will be its defensive arguments, and peace and stability it will probably bring. But tranquil or unquiet, whatever it may be, its triumph is assured; and existent forces are carrying us toward it with an ever accelerating speed. One power alone might prevent it—the collective popular will that it shall not be. But of this there is no fear on the part of the barons, and but little expectation on the part of the underlings.

2

THE DISCOVERY OF POVERTY

John Spargo
THE BITTER CRY OF THE CHILDREN

John Spargo (1876–1966) became a socialist in his native England, and nothing in his initial American experience changed his mind about the need for a sweeping social revolution. In some ways he found the system of capitalism even crueler in its operation in America than anywhere in Europe, for here there was such a shocking discrepancy between promise and reality. As this selection reveals, "scientific" socialists were not above appealing to the emotions of their readers, but Spargo's research on child labor called public attention to many facts about the operation of the factory system that were virtually unknown at the turn of the century. Uncovering abuse did not produce an immediate remedy, but Spargo later became sufficiently impressed by the ability of the American system to correct injustice that he left socialist politics altogether. Marx had warned earlier socialist immigrants about the corrupting influence of "American conditions." Life in rural Vermont eroded Spargo's socialist viewpoint, and by the time of the election of Franklin Roosevelt, whom Spargo vehemently opposed, there was no crustier conservative anywhere in the Union.

Children have always worked, but it is only since the reign of the machine that their work has been synonymous with slavery. Under the old form of simple, domestic industry even the very young children were assigned their share of the work in the family. But this form of child labor was a good and wholesome thing. There may have been abuses; children may have suffered from the ignorance, cupidity, and brutality of fathers and mothers, but in the main the child's share in the work of the family was a good thing. In the first place, the child was associated in its work with one or both of its parents, and thus kept under all those influences which we deem of most worth, the

SOURCE. John Spargo, *The Bitter Cry of the Children* (New York, 1906), pp. 127–129, 175–184, 195–200, 216–217.

171

influences of home and parental care. Secondly, the work of the child constituted a major part of its education. And it was no mean education, either, which gave the world generation after generation of glorious craftsmen. The seventeenth-century glass-blower of Venice or Murano, for instance, learned his craft from his father in this manner, and in turn taught it to his son. There was a bond of interest between them; a parental pride and interest on the part of the father infinitely greater and more potent for good than any commercial relation would have allowed. On the part of the child, too, there was a filial pride and devotion which found its expression in a spirit of emulation, the spirit out of which all the rich glory of that wonderfully rich craft was born. So, too, it was with the potters of ancient Greece, and with the tapestry weavers of fourteenth-century France. In the golden age of the craftsman, child labor was child training in the noblest and best sense. The training of hand and heart and brain was the end achieved, even where it was not the sole purpose of the child's labor.

But with the coming of the machine age all this was changed. The craftsman was supplanted by the tireless, soulless machine. The child still worked, but in a great factory throbbing with the vibration of swift, intricate machines. In place of parental interest and affection there was the harsh, pitiless authority of an employer or his agent, looking, not to the child's well-being and skill as an artificer, but to the supplying of a great, ever widening market for cash gain. . . .

There has been no extensive, systematic investigation in this country of the physical condition of working children. In 1893–1894 volunteer physicians examined and made measurements of some 200 children, taken from the factories and workshops of Chicago. These records show a startling proportion of undersized, rachitic, and consumptive children, but they are too limited to be of more than suggestive value. So far as they go, however, they bear out the results obtained in more extensive investigations in European countries. It is the consensus of opinion among those having the best opportunities for careful observation that physical deterioration quickly follows a child's employment in a factory or workshop.

It is a sorry but indisputable fact that where children are employed, the most unhealthful work is generally given them. In the spinning and carding rooms of cotton and woollen mills, where large numbers of children are employed, clouds of lint-dust fill the lungs and menace the health. The children have often a distressing cough, caused by the irritation of the throat, and many are hoarse from the same cause. In bottle factories and other branches of glass manufacture, the atmosphere is constantly charged with microscopic particles of glass. In the wood-working industries, such as the manufacture of cheap furniture and wooden boxes, and packing cases, the air is laden with fine sawdust. Children employed in soap and soap powder factories work, many of them, in clouds of alkaline dust which inflames the eyelids and nostrils. Boys employed in filling boxes of soap-powder work all day long with handkerchiefs tied over their mouths. In the coal mines the breaker boys breathe air that is heavy and thick with particles of coal, and their lungs become black in consequence. In the manufacture of felt hats, little girls are often employed at the machines which tear the fur from the skins of rabbits and other animals. Recently, I stood and watched a young girl working at such a machine; she wore a newspaper pinned over her head and a handkerchief tied over her mouth. She was white with dust from head to feet, and when she stooped to pick anything from the floor the dust would fall from her paper head-covering in little heaps. About seven feet from the mouth of the machine was a window through which poured thick volumes of dust as it was belched out from the machine. I placed a sheet of paper on the inner sill of the window and in twenty minutes it was covered with a layer of fine dust, half an inch deep. Yet that girl works midway between the window and the machine, in the very center of the volume of dust, sixty hours a week. These are a few of the occupations in which the dangers arise from the forced inhalation of dust.

In some occupations, such as silk-winding, flax-spinning, and various processes in the manufacture of felt hats, it is necessary, or believed to be necessary, to keep the atmosphere quite moist. The result of working in a close, heated factory, where the air is artificially moistened, in summer time, can be better imagined than described. So long as enough girls can be kept working, and only a few of them faint, the mills are kept going; but when faintings are so many and so frequent that it does not pay to keep going, the mills are closed. The children who work in the dye rooms and print-shops of textile factories, and the color rooms of factories where the materials for making artificial flowers are manufactured, are subject to contact with poisonous dyes, and the results are often terrible. Very frequently they are dyed in parts of their bodies as literally as the fabrics are dyed. One little fellow, who was employed in a Pennsylvania carpet factory, opened his shirt one day and showed me his chest and stomach dyed a deep, rich crimson. I mentioned the incident to a local physician, and was told that such cases were common. "They are simply saturated with the dye," he said. "The results are extremely severe, though very often slow and, for a long time, almost imperceptible. If they should cut or scratch themselves where they are so thoroughly dyed, it might mean death." In Yonkers, New York, are some of the largest carpet factories in the United States, and many children are employed in them. Some of the smallest children are employed in the "drum room," or print-shop, where the yarns are "printed" or dyed. Small boys, mostly Slavs and Hungarians, push the trucks containing boxes of liquid dye from place to place, and get it all over their clothing. They can be seen coming out of the mills at night literally soaked to the skin with dye of various colors. In the winter time, after a fall of snow, it is possible to track them to their homes, not only by their colored footprints, but by the drippings from their clothing. The snow becomes dotted with red, blue, and green, as though some one had sprinkled the colors for the sake of the variegated effect.

Children employed as varnishers in cheap furniture factories inhale poisonous fumes all day long and suffer from a variety of intestinal troubles in consequence. The gilding of picture frames produces a stiffening of the fingers. The children who are employed in the manufacture of wall papers and poisonous paints suffer from slow poisoning. The naphtha fumes in the manufacture of rubber goods produce paralysis and premature decay. Children employed in morocco leather works are often nauseated and fall easy victims to consumption. The little boys who make matches, and the little girls who pack them in boxes, suffer from phosphorous necrosis, or "phossy-jaw," a gangrene of the lower jaw due to phosphor poisoning. Boys employed in type foundries and stereotyping establishments are employed on the most dangerous part of the work, namely, rubbing the type and the plates, and lead poisoning is excessively prevalent among them as a result. Little girls who work in the hosiery mills and carry heavy baskets from one floor to another, and their sisters who run machines by foot-power, suffer all through their after life as a result of their employment. Girls who work in factories where caramels and other kinds of candies are made are constantly passing from the refrigerating department, where the temperature is perhaps 20 degrees Fahr., to other departments with temperatures as high as 80 or 90 degrees. As a result, they suffer from bronchial troubles.

These are only a few of the many occupations of children that are inherently unhealthful and should be prohibited entirely for children and all young persons under eighteen years of age. In a few instances it might be sufficient to fix the minimum age for employment at sixteen, if certain improvements in the conditions of employment were insisted upon. Other dangers to health, such as the quick transition from the heat of the factory to the cold outside air, have already been noted. They are highly important causes of disease, though not inherent in the occupation itself in most cases. A careful study of the child-labor problem from this largely neglected point of view would be most valuable. When to the many dangers to health are added the dangers to life and limb from accidents, far more numerous among child workers than adults, the price we pay for the altogether unnecessary and uneconomic service of children would, in the Boer patriot's phrase, "stagger humanity," if it could be comprehended.

No combination of figures can give any idea of that price. Statistics cannot express the withering of child lips in the poisoned air of factories; the tired, strained look of child eyes that never dance to the glad music of souls tuned to nature's symphonies; the binding to wheels of industry the little bodies and souls that should be free, as the stars are free to shine and the flowers are free to drink the evening dews. Statistics may be perfected to the extent of giving the number of child workers with accuracy, the number maimed by dangerous machines, and the number who die year by year, but they can never give the spiritual loss, if I may use that word in its secular, scientific sense. Who shall tally the deaths of childhood's hopes, ambitions, and dreams? How shall figures show the silent atrophy of potential genius, the brutalizing of potential love, the corruption of potential purity? In what arithmetical terms shall we state the loss of shame, and the development of that less than brute view of life, which enables us to watch with unconcern the toil of infants side by side with the idleness of men?

The moral ills resulting from child labor are numerous and far-reaching. When children become wage-earners and are thrown into constant association with adult workers, they develop prematurely an adult consciousness and view of life. About the first consequence of their employment is that they cease almost at once to be children. They lose their respect for parental authority, in many cases, and become arrogant, wayward, and defiant. There is always a tendency in their homes to regard them as men and women as soon as they become wage-earners. Discipline is at once relaxed, at the very time when it is most necessary. When children who have just entered upon that most critical period of life, adolescence, are associated with adults in factories, are driven to their tasks with curses, and hear continually the unrestrained conversation, often coarse and foul, of the adults, the psychological effect cannot be other than bad. The mothers and fathers who read this book need only to know that children, little boys and girls, in mills and factories where men and women are employed, must frequently see women at work in whom the signs of a developing life within are evident, and hear them made the butt of the coarsest taunts and jests, to realize how great the moral peril to the adolescent boy or girl must be.

No writer dare write, and no publisher dare publish, a truthful description of the moral atmosphere of hundreds of places where children are employed—a description truthful in the sense of telling the whole truth. No publisher would dare print the language current in an average factory. Our most "realistic" writers must exercise stern artistic reticence, and tone down or evade the truth. No normal boy or girl would think of repeating to father or mother the language heard in the mill—language which the children begin before long to use occasionally, to *think* oftener still. I have known a girl of thirteen or fourteen, just an average American girl, whose parents, intelligent and honest folk, had given her a moral training above rather than below the average, mock a pregnant woman worker and unblushingly attempt to caricature her condition by stuffing rags beneath her apron. I do not make any charge against the tens of thousands of women who have worked and are working in factories. Heaven forbid that I should seek to brand as impure these women of my own class! But I do say that for the plastic and impressionable mind of a child the moral atmosphere of the average factory is exceedingly bad, and I know that none will more readily agree with me than the men and women who work, or who have worked, in mills and factories.

I know a woman, and she is one of many, who has worked in textile factories for more than thirty years. She began to work as a child before she was ten years old, and is now past forty. She has never married, though many men have sought her in marriage. She is not an abnormal woman, indifferent to marriage, but just a normal, healthy, intelligent woman who has yearned hundreds of times for a man's affection and companionship. To her more intimate friends she confesses that she chose to remain lonely and unwed, chose to stifle her longings for affection, rather than to marry and bring children into the world and live to see them enter the mills for employment before they became men and women. When I say that the moral atmosphere of factory life is contaminated and bad, and that the employment of children in mills and factories subjects them to grave moral perils, I am confident that I shall be supported, not, perhaps, by the owners of the mills and factories, but by the vast majority of intelligent men and women employed in them.

In a report upon the physical conditions of child workers in Pennsylvania, the Reverend Peter Roberts has discussed at some length the moral dangers of factory employment for children. He quotes an Allentown physician as saying, "No vice was unknown to many of the girls of fifteen working in the factories of the city"; and another physician in the same city said, "There are more unhappy homes, ruined lives, blasted hopes, and diseased bodies in Allentown than any other city of its size, because of the factories there." Another physician in Lancaster is quoted as saying that he had "treated boys of ten years old and upwards for venereal affections which they had contracted." In upwards of a score of factory towns I have had very similar testimony given to me by physicians and others. The proprietor of a large drug store in a New England factory town told me that he had never known a place where the demand for cheap remedies for venereal diseases was so great, and *that many of those who bought them were boys under fifteen.* . . .

What are the reasons for the employment of children? It is almost needless to argue that child labor is socially unnecessary, that the labor of little boys and girls is not required in order that wealth sufficient for the needs of society may be produced. If such a claim were made, it would be an all-sufficing reply to point to the great army of unemployed men in our midst, and to say that the last man must be employed before the employment of the first child can be justified. When there is not an unemployed man, when there is not a man employed in useless, unproductive, and wasteful labor, if there is then a shortage of the things necessary for social maintenance, child labor may be necessary and justifiable. Under any other conditions than these it is unjustifiable and brutally wrong. In the primitive struggle with the hostile forces of nature, such struggles as pioneers have had in all lands before the deserts could be made to yield harvests of fruit and grain, the labor of wives and children has been necessary to supplement that of husbands and fathers. But what would be thought of the men, under such conditions, if they forced their wives and children to work while they idled, ate, and slept? Yet that is, essentially, the practice of modern industrial society. Here is a great country with natural resources unparalleled in human experience for their richness and variety; here labor is so productive, and inventive genius so highly developed, that wealth overflows our granaries and warehouses, and forces us to seek foreign markets for its disposal. The children employed in our factories are not employed because it would otherwise be impossible to produce the necessities of life for the nation. The little five-year-old girl seen by Miss [Jane] Addams working at night in a southern cotton mill was not so employed because it was necessary in order that the American people might have enough cotton goods to supply their needs. On the contrary, she was making sheeting for the Chinese Army! Not that she or those by whom she was employed had any interest in the Chinese Army, but because there was a prospective profit for the manufacturer in the making of sheeting for sale to China for the use of her soldiers. The manufacturer would just as readily have sacrificed little American girls in the manufacture of beads for Hottentots, or gilt idols for poor Hindu ryots, if the profit were equal.

That is the root of the child-labor evil; it has no social justification and exists only for the sordid gain of profit-seekers. It is not difficult, therefore, to understand the manufacturers' interest in child labor, or their opposition to all efforts to legislate against it. Cheap production is the maxim of success in industry, and a plentiful supply of cheap labor is a powerful contributor to that end. The principal items in productive cost are the raw material and the labor necessary, the relative importance of each depending upon the nature of the industry itself. Now, it is obviously to the interest of the manufacturer, as manufacturer, to get both raw material and labor-power as cheaply as possible, whether the industry in which he is interested is governed by competitive, or monopolistic, or any intermediate conditions. If competition rules, cheapness is vitally important to him, since if he can get an advantage over his competitors in that respect he can undersell them, while if he fails to get his supplies of labor and raw material as cheaply as his competitors, he will be undersold. If, on the other hand, monopoly conditions prevail, it is still an important interest to secure them as cheaply as possible, thereby increasing his profit.

It is an axiom of commercial economy that supply follows demand, and it is certain that the constant demand for the cheap, tractable labor of children has had much to do with the creation of the supply. At bottom the employers, or, rather, the system of production for profit, must be held responsible for child labor. There are evidences of this on every hand. We see manufacturers in New Jersey and Pennsylvania getting children from orphan asylums, regardless of their physical, mental, and moral ruin, merely because it *pays* them. When the glass-blowers of Minotola, New Jersey, went on strike, in 1902, the child-labor question was one of their most important issues. The exposures made of the frightful enslavement of little children attracted widespread attention. There is very little in the history of the English factory system which excels in horror the conditions which existed in that little South Jersey town at the beginning of the twentieth century. When the proprietor of the factory was asked about the employment of young boys ten and eleven years of age, many of whom often fell asleep and were awakened by the men pouring water over them, and at least two of whom died from overexhaustion, he said: "If two men apply to me for work and one has one or two or three children and the other has none, I take the man with children. I need the boys." In actual practice this meant that no man could get work as a glass-blower unless he was able to bring boys with him. A regular padrone system was developed in consequence of this: the glass-blowers, determined to keep their own boys out of the factories if possible, secured children from orphan asylums, or took the little boys of Italian immigrants, boarded them, and paid the parents a regular weekly sum.

In the mills of the south it is frequently made a condition of the employment of married men or women that all their children shall be bound to work in the same mills. The following is one of the rules posted in a South Carolina cotton mill:

"All children, members of a family, above twelve years of age, shall work regularly in the mill, and shall not be excused from service therein without the consent of the superintendent for good cause."

Many times I have heard fathers and mothers—in the north as well as in the south—say that they did not want their children to work, that they could have done without the children's wages and kept them at school a little longer, or apprenticed them to better employment, but that they were compelled to send them into the mills to work, or lose their own places. Even more eloquent as evidencing the keen demand of the manufacturers for child labor is the fact to which Mr. McKelway calls attention, that, in response to their demand, cotton-mill machinery is being made with adjustable legs to suit small child workers. Mr. McKelway rightly contrasts this with the experience in India when the first cotton mills were erected there. Then, for the first time, it was found necessary to manufacture spinning frames high enough from the floor to accommodate adult workers.

With such facts as these before us, it is easy to see that the urgency of the employers' demands for child labor is an important factor in the problem. Underlying all other causes is the fundamental fact that the exploitation of the children is in the interests of the employing class. It may be urged that it is necessary for children to begin work at an early age because the work they do cannot be done by men or women, but the contention is wholly unsupported by facts. There is no work done by boys in the glass factories which men could not do; no skill or training is required to enable one to do the work done by breaker boys in the coal mines; the work done by children in the textile mills could be done equally well by adults. The fact that in some cases adults are employed to do the work which in other cases is done by children, is sufficient proof that child labor is not resorted to because it is inevitable and necessary, but on account of its cheapness. . . .

It is a solemn responsibility which the presence of this menacing evil of child labor places upon the nation. It is not only the interests of the children themselves that are menaced; even more important and terrible is the thought that civilization itself is imperilled when children are dwarfed physically, mentally, and morally by hunger, heavy toil, and unwholesome surroundings. If one of the forts along our far-stretching coasts were attacked by an enemy, or if a single square mile of our immense territory were invaded, the nation would rise in patriotic unison, and there would be no lack either of men or money for the defence. Surely, it is not too much to hope that, before long, the nation will realize in the destruction of its future citizens by greed and ignorance a far more serious attack upon the republic than any that could be made by fleets or armed legions. To sap the strength and weaken the moral fibres of the children is to grind the seed corn, to wreck the future for today's fleeting gain.

A great Frenchman once said of the alphabet, "These twenty-six letters contain all the good things that ever were, or ever can be, said—only they need to be arranged." To complete the truth of this aphorism, he should have included all the bad things as well. And so it is with the children of a nation. Capable of expressing all the good or evil the world has known or may know, it is essentially a matter of arrangement, opportunity, environment. Whether the children of today become physical, mental, and moral cretins, or strong men and women, fathers and mothers of virile sons and daughters, depends upon the decision of the nation. If the responsibility of this is fully recognized, and the employment of children under fifteen years of age is forbidden throughout the length and breadth of this great country; if the nation realizes that the demand for the protection of the children is the highest patriotism, and enfolds every child within its strong, protecting arms, then and not till then will it be possible to look with confidence toward the future, unashamed and unafraid.

3

IMMIGRANT LABOR AND THE FACTORY SYSTEM

Upton Sinclair
THE JUNGLE

Upton Sinclair (1878–1968) published far too many books in his lifetime to need much of an introduction. The following selection is taken from The Jungle, which was originally printed in serial form in the socialist newspaper The Appeal to Reason. However one judges Sinclair's art, no book ever described with such unrelenting horror the crumbling of the American dream in the lives of a family of immigrant workers. The book helped gain passage of the Pure Food and Drug Act, but Sinclair claimed that in writing the novel he was far more concerned about the miserable plight of workers in the Chicago stockyards than he was about the stomachs of middle class Americans. Sinclair was eccentric in his socialist views, but then Sinclair was eccentric in all things. More than any other American he was linked in the public mind with the cause of socialism, and, inside or outside of the party, he championed the cause of men and women who had not received justice from the American system.

All summer long the family toiled, and in the fall they had money enough for Jurgis and Ona to be married according to home traditions of decency. In the latter part of November they hired a hall, and invited all their new acquaintances, who came and left them over a hundred dollars in debt.

It was a bitter and cruel experience, and it plunged them into an agony of despair. Such a time, of all times, for them to have it, when their hearts were made tender! Such a pitiful beginning it was for their married life; they loved each other so, and they could not have the briefest respite! It was a time when everything cried out to them that they ought to be happy; when wonder burned in their hearts, and leaped into flame at the slightest breath. They were shaken to the

SOURCE. Upton Sinclair, *The Jungle* (New York, 1906), pp. 86–98.

depths of them, with the awe of love realized—and was it so very weak of them that they cried out for a little peace? They had opened their hearts, like flowers to the springtime, and the merciless winter had fallen upon them. They wondered if ever any love that had blossomed in the world had been so crushed and trampled!

Over them, relentless and savage, there cracked the lash of want; the morning after the wedding it sought them as they slept, and drove them out before daybreak to work. Ona was scarcely able to stand with exhaustion; but if she were to lose her place they would be ruined, and she would surely lose it if she were not on time that day. They all had to go, even little Stanislovas, who was ill from over-indulgence in sausages and sarsaparilla. All that day he stood at his lard machine, rocking unsteadily, his eyes closing in spite of him; and he all but lost his place even so, for the foreman booted him twice to waken him.

It was fully a week before they were all normal again, and meantime, with whining children and cross adults, the house was not a pleasant place to live in. Jurgis lost his temper very little, however, all things considered. It was because of Ona; the least glance at her was always enough to make him control himself. She was so sensitive—she was not fitted for such a life as this, and a hundred times a day, when he thought of her, he would clench his hands and fling himself again at the task before him. She was too good for him, he told himself, and he was afraid, because she was his. So long he had hungered to possess her, but now that the time had come he knew that he had not earned the right; that she trusted him so was all her own simple goodness, and no virtue of his. But he was resolved that she should never find this out, and so was always on the watch to see that he did not betray any of his ugly self; he would take care even in little matters, such as his manners, and his habit of swearing when things went wrong. The tears came so easily into Ona's eyes, and she would look at him so appealingly—it kept Jurgis quite busy making resolutions, in addition to all the other things he had on his mind. It was true that more things were going on at this time in the mind of Jurgis than ever had in all his life before.

He had to protect her, to do battle for her against the horror he saw about them. He was all that she had to look to, and if he failed she would be lost; he would wrap his arms about her, and try to hide her from the world. He had learned the ways of things about him now. It was a war of each against all, and the devil take the hindmost. You did not give feasts to other people, you waited for them to give feasts to you. You went about with your soul full of suspicion and hatred; you understood that you were environed by hostile powers that were trying to get your money, and who used all the virtues to bait their traps with. The storekeepers plastered up their windows with all sorts of lies to entice you; the very fences by the wayside, the lampposts and telegraph poles, were pasted over with lies. The great corporation which employed you lied to you, and lied to the whole country—from top to bottom it was nothing but one gigantic lie.

So Jurgis said that he understood it; and yet it was really pitiful, for the struggle was so unfair—some had so much the advantage! Here he was, for instance, vowing upon his knees that he would save Ona from harm, and only a week later she was suffering atrociously, and from the blow of an enemy that he could not possibly have thwarted. There came a day when the rain fell in torrents, and it being December, to be wet with it and have to sit all day long in one of the cold cellars of Brown's was no laughing matter. Ona was a working girl, and did not own waterproofs and such things, and so Jurgis took her and put her on the streetcar. Now it chanced that this car line was owned by gentlemen who were trying to make money. And the city having passed an ordinance requiring them to give transfers, they had fallen into a rage; and first they had made a rule that transfers could be had only when the fare was paid; and later, growing still uglier, they had made another—that the passenger must ask for the transfer, the conductor was not allowed to offer it. Now Ona had been told that she was to get a transfer; but it was not her way to speak up, and so she merely waited, following the conductor about with her eyes, wondering when he would think of her. When at last the time came for her to get out, she asked for the transfer, and was refused. Not knowing what to make of this, she began to argue with the conductor, in a language of which he did not understand a word. After warning her several times, he pulled the bell and the car went on—at which Ona burst into tears. At the next corner she got out, of course, and as she had no more money, she had to walk the rest of the way to the yards in the pouring rain. And so all day long she sat shivering, and came home at night with her teeth chattering and pains in her head and back. For two weeks afterward she suffered cruelly—and yet every day she had to drag herself to her work. The forewoman was especially severe with Ona, because she believed that she was obstinate on account of having been refused a holiday the day after her wedding. Ona had an idea that her "forelady" did not like to have her girls marry—perhaps because she was old and ugly and unmarried herself.

There were many such dangers, in which the odds were all against them. Their children were not as well as they had been at home; but how could they know that there was no sewer to their house, and that the drainage of fifteen years was in a cesspool under it? How could they know that the pale-blue milk that they bought around the corner was watered, and doctored with formaldehyde besides? When the children were not well at home, Teta Elzbieta would gather herbs and cure them; now she was obliged to go to the drugstore and buy extracts—and how was she to know that they were all adulterated? How could they find out that their tea and coffee, their sugar and flour, had been doctored; that their canned peas had been colored with copper salts, and their fruit jams with aniline dyes? And even if they had known it, what good would it have done them, since there was no place within miles of them where any other sort was to be had? The bitter winter was coming, and they had to save money to get more clothing and bedding; but it would not matter in the least how much they saved, they could not get anything to keep them warm. All the clothing that was to be had in the stores was made of cotton and shoddy, which is made by tearing old clothes to pieces and weaving the fibre again. If they paid higher prices, they might get frills and fanciness, or be cheated; but genuine quality they could not obtain for love nor money. A young friend of Szedvilas', recently come from abroad, had become a clerk in a store on Ashland Avenue, and he narrated with glee a trick that had been played upon an unsuspecting countryman by his boss. The customer had desired to purchase an alarm clock, and the boss had shown him two exactly similar, telling him that the price of one was a dollar and of the other a dollar seventy-five. Upon being asked what the difference was, the man had wound up the first half-way and the second all the way, and showed the customer how the latter made twice as much noise; upon which the customer remarked that he was a sound sleeper, and had better take the more expensive clock!

There is a poet who sings that

"Deeper their heart grows and nobler their bearing,
Whose youth in the fires of anguish hath died."

But it is not likely that he had reference to the kind of anguish that comes with destitution, that is so endlessly bitter and cruel, and yet so sordid and petty, so ugly, so humiliating—unredeemed by the slightest touch of dignity or even of pathos. It is a kind of anguish that poets have not commonly dealt with; its very words are not admitted into the vocabulary of poets—the details of it cannot be told in polite society at all. How, for instance, could anyone expect to excite sympathy among lovers of good literature by telling how a family found their home alive with vermin, and of all the suffering and inconvenience and humiliation they were put to, and the hard-earned money they spent, in efforts to get rid of them? After long hesitation and uncertainty they paid twenty-five cents for a big package of insect-powder—a patent preparation which chanced to be ninety-five percent gypsum, a harmless earth which had cost about two cents to prepare. Of course it had not the least effect, except upon a few roaches which had the misfortune to drink water after eating it, and so got their inwards set in a coating of plaster of Paris. The family, having no idea of this, and no more money to throw away, had nothing to do but give up and submit to one more misery for the rest of their days.

Then there was old Antanas. The winter came, and the place where he worked was a dark, unheated cellar, where you could see your breath all day, and where your fingers sometimes tried to freeze. So the old man's cough grew every day worse, until there came a time when it hardly ever stopped, and he had become a nuisance about the place. Then, too, a still more dreadful thing happened to him; he worked in a place where his feet were soaked in chemicals, and it was not long before they had eaten through his new boots. Then sores began to break out on his feet, and grow worse and worse. Whether it was that his blood was bad, or there had been a cut, he could not say, but he asked the men about it, and learned that it was a regular thing—it was the saltpeter. Every one felt it, sooner or later, and then it was all up with him, at least for that sort of work. The sores would never heal—in the end his toes would drop off, if he did not quit. Yet old Antanas would not quit; he saw the suffering of his family, and he remembered what it had cost him to get a job. So he tied up his feet, and went on limping about and coughing, until at last he fell to pieces, all at once and in a heap, like the One-Horse Shay. They carried him to a dry place and laid him on the floor, and that night two of the men helped him home. The poor old man was put to bed, and though he tried it every morning until the end, he never could get up again. He would lie there and cough and cough, day and night, wasting away to a mere skeleton. There came a time when there was so little flesh on him that the bones began to poke through—which was a horrible thing to see or even to think of. And one night he had a choking fit, and a little river of blood came out of his mouth. The family, wild with terror, sent for a doctor, and paid half a dollar to be told that there was nothing to be done. Mercifully the doctor did not say this so that the old man could hear, for he was still clinging to the faith that tomorrow or next day he would be better, and could go back to his job. The company had sent word to him that they would keep it for him—or rather Jurgis had bribed one of the men to come one Sunday afternoon and say they had. Dede Antanas continued to believe it, while three more hemorrhages came, and then at last one morning they found him stiff and cold. Things were not going well with them then, and though it nearly broke Teta Elzbieta's heart, they were forced to dispense with nearly all the decencies of a funeral; they had only a hearse, and one hack for the women and children; and Jurgis, who was learning things fast, spent all Sunday making a bargain for these, and he made it in the presence of witnesses, so that when the man tried to charge him for all sorts of incidentals, he did not have to pay. For twenty-five years old Antanas Rudkus and his son had dwelt in the forest together, and it was hard to part in this way; perhaps it was just as well that Jurgis had to give all his attention to the task of having a funeral without being bankrupted, and so had no time to indulge in memories and grief.

Now the dreadful winter was come upon them. In the forests, all summer long, the branches of the trees do battle for light, and some of them lose and die; and then come the raging blasts, and the storms of snow and hail, and strew the ground with these weaker branches. Just so it was in Packingtown; the whole district braced itself for the struggle that was an agony, and those whose time was come died off in hordes. All the year round they had been serving as cogs in the great packing machine, and now was the time for the renovating of it, and the replacing of damaged parts. There came pneumonia and grippe, stalking among them, seeking for weakened constitutions; there was the annual harvest of those whom tuberculosis had been dragging down. There came cruel, cold, and biting winds, and blizzards of snow, all testing relentlessly for failing muscles and impoverished blood. Sooner or later came the day when the unfit one did not report for work; and then, with no time lost in waiting, and no inquiries or regrets, there was a chance for a new hand.

The new hands were here by the thousands. All day long the gates of the packing houses were besieged by starving and penniless men; they came, literally, by the thousands every single morning, fighting with each other for a chance for life. Blizzards and cold made no difference to them, they were always on hand; they were on hand two hours before the sun rose, an hour before the work began. Sometimes their faces froze, sometimes their feet and their hands; sometimes they froze all together—but still they came, for they had no other place to go. One day Durham advertised in the paper for two hundred men to cut ice; and all that day the homeless and starving of the city came trudging through the snow from all over its two hundred square miles. That night forty score of them crowded into the station house of the stockyards district—they filled the rooms, sleeping in each other's laps, toboggan-fashion, and they piled on top of each other in the corridors, till the police shut the doors and left some to freeze outside. On the morrow, before daybreak, there were three thousand at Durham's, and the police reserves had to be sent for to quell the riot. Then Durham's bosses picked out twenty of the biggest; the "two hundred" proved to have been a printer's error.

Four or five miles to the eastward lay the lake, and over this the bitter winds came raging. Sometimes the thermometer would fall to ten or twenty degrees below zero at night, and in the morning the streets would be piled with snowdrifts up to the first-floor windows. The streets through which our friends had to go to their work were all unpaved and full of deep holes and gullies; in summer, when it rained hard, a man might have to wade to his waist to get to his house, and now in winter it was no joke getting through these places, before light in the morning and after dark at night. They would wrap up in all they owned, but they could not wrap up against exhaustion, and many a man gave out in these battles with the snowdrifts, and lay down and fell asleep.

And if it was bad for the men, one may imagine how the women and children fared. Some would ride in the cars, if the cars were running, but when you are making only five cents an hour, as was little Stanislovas, you do not like to spend that much to ride two miles. The children would come to the yards with great shawls about their ears, and so tied up that you could hardly find them—and still there would be accidents. One bitter morning in February the little boy who worked at the lard machine with Stanislovas came about an hour late, and screaming with pain. They unwrapped him, and a man began vigorously rubbing his ears, and as they were frozen stiff, it took only two or three rubs to break them short off. As a result of this, little Stanislovas conceived a terror of the cold that was almost a mania. Every morning, when it came time to start for the yards, he would begin to cry and protest. Nobody knew quite how to manage him, for threats did no good—it seemed to be something that he could not control, and they feared sometimes that he would go into convulsions. In the end it had to be arranged that he always went with Jurgis, and came home with him again, and often, when the snow was deep, the man would carry him the whole way on his shoulders. Sometimes Jurgis would be working until late at night, and then it was pitiful, for there was no place for the little fellow to wait, save in the doorways or in a corner of the killing beds, and he would all but fall asleep there, and freeze to death.

There was no heat upon the killing beds; the men might exactly as well have worked out of doors all winter. For that matter, there was very little heat anywhere in the building, except in the cooking rooms and such places—and it was the men who worked in these who ran the most risk of all, because whenever they had to pass to another room they had to go through ice-cold corridors, and sometimes with nothing on above the waist except a sleeveless undershirt. On the killing beds you were apt to be covered with blood, and it would freeze solid; if you leaned against a pillar, you would freeze to that, and if you put your hand upon the blade of your knife, you would run a chance of leaving your skin on it. The men would tie up their feet in newspapers and old sacks, and these would be soaked in blood and frozen, and then soaked again, and so on, until by nighttime a man would be walking on great lumps the size of the feet of an elephant. Now and then, when the bosses were not looking, you would see them plunging their feet and ankles into the steaming hot carcass of the steer, or darting across the room to the hot-water jets. The cruelest thing of all was that nearly all of them—all of those who used knives—were unable to wear gloves, and their arms would be white with frost and their hands would grow numb, and then of course there would be accidents. Also the air would be full of steam, from the hot water and the hot blood, so that you could not see five feet before you; and then, with men rushing about at the speed they kept up on the killing beds, and all with butcher knives, like razors, in their hands—well, it was to be counted as a wonder that there were not more men slaughtered than cattle.

And yet all this inconvenience they might have put up with, if only it had not been for one thing—if only there had been some place where they might eat. Jurgis had either to eat his dinner amid the stench in which he had worked, or else to rush, as did all his companions, to any one of the hundreds of liquor stores which stretched out their arms to him. To the west of the yards ran Ashland Avenue, and here was an unbroken line of saloons—"Whiskey Row," they called it; to the north was Forty-seventh Street, where there were half a dozen to the block, and at the angle of the two was "Whiskey Point," a space of fifteen or twenty acres, and containing one glue factory and about two hundred saloons.

One might walk among these and take his choice: "Hot pea soup and boiled cabbage today." "Sauerkraut and hot frankfurters. Walk in." "Bean soup and stewed lamb. Welcome." All of these things were printed in many languages, as were also the names of the resorts, which were infinite in their variety and appeal. There was the "Home Circle" and the "Cosey Corner"; there were "Firesides" and "Hearthstones" and "Pleasure Palaces" and "Wonderlands" and "Dream Castles" and "Love's Delights." Whatever else they were called, they were sure to be called "Union Headquarters," and to hold out a welcome to workingmen; and there was always a warm stove, and a chair near it, and some friends to laugh and talk with. There was only one condition attached,—you must drink. If you went in not intending to drink, you would be put out in no time, and if you were slow about going, like as not you would get your head split open with a beer bottle in the bargain. But all of the men understood the convention and drank; they believed that by it they were getting something for nothing—for they did not need to take more than one drink, and upon the strength of it they might fill themselves up with a good hot dinner. This did not always work out in practice, however, for there was pretty sure to be a friend who would treat you, and then you would have to treat him. Then some one else would come in—and, anyhow, a few drinks were good for a man who worked hard. As he went back he did not shiver so, he had more courage for his task; the deadly brutalizing monotony of it did not afflict him so—he had ideas while he worked, and took a more cheerful view of his circumstances. On the way home, however, the shivering was apt to come on him again; and so he would have to stop once or twice to warm up against the cruel cold. As there were hot things to eat in this saloon too, he might get home late to his supper, or he might not get home at all. And then his wife might set out to look for him, and she too would feel the cold; and perhaps she would have some of the children with her—and so a whole family would drift into drinking, as the current of a river drifts downstream. As if to complete the chain, the packers all paid their men in checks, refusing all requests to pay in coin; and where in Packingtown could a man go to have his check cashed but to a saloon, where he could pay for the favor by spending a part of the money?

From all of these things Jurgis was saved because of Ona. He never would take but the one drink at noontime; and so he got the reputation of being a surly fellow, and was not quite welcome at the saloons, and had to drift about from one to another. Then at night he would go straight home, helping Ona and Stanislovas, or often putting the former on a car. And when he got home perhaps he would have to trudge several blocks, and come staggering back through the snow-drifts with a bag of coal upon his shoulder. Home was not a very attractive place—at least not this winter. They had only been able to buy one stove, and this was a small one, and proved not big enough to warm even the kitchen in the bitterest weather. This made it hard for Teta Elzbieta all day, and for the children when they could not get to school. At night they would sit huddled around this stove, while they ate their supper off their laps; and then Jurgis and Jonas would smoke a pipe, after which they would all crawl into their beds to get warm, after putting out the fire to save the coal. Then they would have some frightful experiences with the cold. They would sleep with all their clothes on, including their overcoats, and put over them all the bedding and spare clothing they owned; the children would sleep all crowded into one bed, and yet even so they could not keep warm. The outside ones would be shivering and sobbing, crawling over the others and trying to get down into the center, and causing a fight. This old house with the leaky weather boards was a very different thing from their cabins at home, with great thick walls plastered inside and outside with mud; and the cold which came upon them was a living thing, a demon-presence in the room. They would waken in the midnight hours, when everything was black; perhaps they would hear it yelling outside, or perhaps there would be deathlike stillness—and that would be worse yet. They could feel the cold as it crept in through the cracks, reaching out for them with its icy, death-dealing fingers, and they would crouch and cower, and try to hide from it, all in vain. It would come, and it would come; a grisly thing, a specter born in the black caverns of terror; a power primeval, cosmic, shadowing the tortures of the lost souls flung out to chaos and destruction. It was cruel, iron-hard; and hour after hour they would cringe in its grasp, alone, alone. There would be no one to hear them if they cried out; there would be no help, no mercy. And so on until morning—when they would go out to another day of toil, a little weaker, a little nearer to the time when it would be their turn to be shaken from the tree.

4
LIBERATING THE SEXES

Emma Goldman
THE TRAFFIC IN WOMEN

American radicalism has been fortunate in its women. The embarrassment Victoria Woodhull may have caused radical leaders was more than compensated for by the work of Mother Jones, Florence Kelly, Kate O'Hare, Elizabeth Gurley Flynn, and Rose Pastor Stokes. None, however, quite achieved the eminence, or notoriety, of Emma Goldman (1869–1940) who first came into American consciousness as the consort of Alexander Berkman, the man who unsuccessfully tried to kill Henry Frick during the Homestead strike. From the point of view of the American establishment Goldman was all the wrong things: she was an immigrant, Jewish, an anarchist, a free lover and, as this selection illustrates, a woman who wished to root out all vestiges of traditional arrangements between the sexes. As editor of Mother Earth *she attacked a wide variety of social ills that she felt grew out of the country's economic system. After exile from the United States in 1919 she lived in the Soviet Union. She found nothing there commensurate with her personal vision of human liberation, and she left in 1921 "desolate and denuded of dreams." Yet, in her seventies she roused herself to champion the losing cause of the anarchists in the Spanish Civil War. When she died, her body was shipped to America to be buried near the Haymarket anarchists in Chicago's Waldheim Cemetery.*

Our reformers have suddenly made a great discovery—the white slave traffic. The papers are full of these "unheard-of conditions," and lawmakers are already planning a new set of laws to check the horror.

It is significant that whenever the public mind is to be diverted from a great social wrong, a crusade is inaugurated against indecency, gambling, saloons, etc. And what is the result of such crusades? Gambling is increasing, saloons are doing a lively business through

SOURCE. Emma Goldman, "The Traffic in Women," *Anarchism and Other Essays* (New York, 1917), pp. 183–200.

back entrances, prostitution is at its height, and the system of pimps and cadets is but aggravated.

How is it that an institution, known almost to every child, should have been discovered so suddenly? How is it that this evil, known to all sociologists, should now be made such an important issue?

To assume that the recent investigation of the white slave traffic (and, by the way, a very superficial investigation) has discovered anything new, is, to say the least, very foolish. Prostitution has been, and is, a widespread evil, yet mankind goes on its business, perfectly indifferent to the sufferings and distress of the victims of prostitution. As indifferent, indeed, as mankind has remained to our industrial system, or to economic prostitution.

Only when human sorrows are turned into a toy with glaring colors will baby people become interested—for a while at least. The people are a very fickle baby that must have new toys every day. The "righteous" cry against the white slave traffic is such a toy. It serves to amuse the people for a little while, and it will help to create a few more fat political jobs—parasites who stalk about the world as inspectors, investigators, detectives, and so forth.

What is really the cause of the trade in women? Not merely white women, but yellow and black women as well. Exploitation, of course; the merciless Moloch of capitalism that fattens on underpaid labor, thus driving thousands of women and girls into prostitution. With Mrs. Warren[1] these girls feel, "Why waste your life working for a few shillings a week in a scullery, eighteen hours a day?"

Naturally our reformers say nothing about this cause. They know it well enough, but it doesn't pay to say anything about it. It is much more profitable to play the Pharisee, to pretend an outraged morality, than to go to the bottom of things.

However, there is one commendable exception among the young writers: Reginald Wright Kauffman, whose work *The House of Bondage* is the first earnest attempt to treat the social evil—not from a sentimental Philistine viewpoint. A journalist of wide experience, Mr. Kauffman proves that our industrial system leaves most women no alternative except prostitution. The women portrayed in *The House of Bondage* belong to the working class. Had the author portrayed the life of women in other spheres, he would have been confronted with the same state of affairs.

Nowhere is woman treated according to the merit of her work, but rather as a sex. It is therefore almost inevitable that she should pay for

[1]The title character, a prostitute, in George Bernard Shaw's play, *Mrs. Warren's Profession.* Ed.

her right to exist, to keep a position in whatever line, with sex favors. Thus it is merely a question of degree whether she sells herself to one man, in or out of marriage, or to many men. Whether our reformers admit it or not, the economic and social inferiority of woman is responsible for prostitution.

Just at present our good people are shocked by the disclosures that in New York City alone one out of every ten women works in a factory, that the average wage received by women is six dollars per week for forty-eight to sixty hours of work, and that the majority of female wage workers face many months of idleness which leaves the average wage about $280 a year. In view of these economic horrors, is it to be wondered at that prostitution and the white slave trade have become such dominant factors?

Lest the preceding figures be considered an exaggeration, it is well to examine what some authorities on prostitution have to say:

"A prolific cause of female depravity can be found in the several tables, showing the description of the employment pursued, and the wages received, by the women previous to their fall, and it will be a question for the political economist to decide how far mere business consideration should be an apology on the part of employers for a reduction in their rates of remuneration, and whether the savings of a small percentage on wages is not more than counterbalanced by the enormous amount of taxation enforced on the public at large to defray the expenses incurred on account of a system of vice, *which is the direct result, in many cases, of insufficient compensation of honest labor.*"

Our present-day reformers would do well to look into Dr. Sanger's book. There they will find that out of 2,000 cases under his observation, but few came from the middle classes, from well-ordered conditions, or pleasant homes. By far the largest majority were working girls and working women; some driven into prostitution through sheer want, others because of a cruel, wretched life at home, others again because of thwarted and crippled physical natures (of which I shall speak later on). Also it will do the maintainers of purity and morality good to learn that out of two thousand cases, 490 were married women, women who lived with their husbands. Evidently there was not much of a guaranty for their "safety and purity" in the sanctity of marriage.

Dr. Alfred Blaschko, in *Prostitution in the Nineteenth Century*, is even more emphatic in characterizing economic conditions as one of the most vital factors of prostitution:

"Although prostitution has existed in all ages, it was left to the nineteenth century to develop it into a gigantic social institution. The development of industry with vast masses of people in the competitive market, the growth and congestion of large cities, the insecurity and uncertainty of employment, has given prostitution an impetus never dreamed of at any period in human history."

And again Havelock Ellis, while not so absolute in dealing with the economic cause, is nevertheless compelled to admit that it is indirectly and directly the main cause. Thus he finds that a large percentage of prostitutes is recruited from the servant class, although the latter have less care and greater security. On the other hand, Mr. Ellis does not deny that the daily routine, the drudgery, the monotony of the servant girl's lot, and especially the fact that she may never partake of the companionship and joy of a home, are no mean factors in forcing her to seek recreation and forgetfulness in the gaiety and glimmer of prostitution. In other words, the servant girl, being treated as a drudge, never having the right to herself, and worn out by the caprices of her mistress, can find an outlet, like the factory or shopgirl, only in prostitution.

The most amusing side of the question now before the public is the indignation of our "good, respectable people," especially the various Christian gentlemen, who are always to be found in the front ranks of every crusade. Is it that they are absolutely ignorant of the history of religion, and especially of the Christian religion? Or is it that they hope to blind the present generation to the part played in the past by the Church in relation to prostitution? Whatever their reason, they should be the last to cry out against the unfortunate victims of today, since it is known to every intelligent student that prostitution is of religious origin, maintained and fostered for many centuries, not as a shame, but as a virtue, hailed as such by the Gods themselves.

"It would seem that the origin of prostitution is to be found primarily in a religious custom, religion, the great conserver of social tradition, preserving in a transformed shape a primitive freedom that was passing out of the general social life. The typical example is that recorded by Herodotus, in the fifth century before Christ, at the Temple of Mylitta, the Babylonian Venus, where every woman, once in her life, had to come and give herself to the first stranger, who threw a coin in her lap, to worship the goddess. Very similar customs existed in other parts of western Asia, in North Africa, in Cyprus, and other islands of the eastern Mediterreanean, and also in Greece, where the temple of Aphrodite on the fort at Corinth possessed over a thousand hierodules, dedicated to the service of the goddess.

"The theory that religious prostitution developed, as a general rule, out of the belief that the generative activity of human beings possessed a mysterious and sacred influence in promoting the fertility of Nature is maintained by all authoritative writers on the subject. Gradually, however, and when prostitution became an organized institution under priestly influence, religious prostitution developed utilitarian sides, thus helping to increase public revenue.

"The rise of Christianity to political power produced little change in policy. The leading fathers of the Church tolerated prostitution. Brothels under municipal protection are found in the thirteenth century. They constituted a sort of public service, the directors of them being considered almost as public servants."

To this must be added the following from Dr. Sanger's work:

"Pope Clement II issued a bull that prostitutes would be tolerated if they pay a certain amount of their earnings to the Church.

"Pope Sixtus IV was more practical; from one single brothel, which he himself had built, he received an income of 20,000 ducats."

In modern times the Church is a little more careful in that direction. At least she does not openly demand tribute from prostitutes. She finds it much more profitable to go in for real estate, like Trinity Church, for instance, to rent out death traps at an exorbitant price to those who live off and by prostitution.

Much as I should like to, my space will not admit speaking of prostitution in Egypt, Greece, Rome, and during the Middle Ages. The conditions in the latter period are particularly interesting, inasmuch as prostitution was organized into guilds, presided over by a brothel queen. These guilds employed strikes as a medium of improving their condition and keeping a standard price. Certainly that is more practical a method than the one used by the modern wage-slave in society.

It would be one-sided and extremely superficial to maintain that the economic factor is the only cause of prostitution. There are others no less important and vital. That, too, our reformers know, but dare discuss even less than the institution that saps the very life out of both men and women. I refer to the sex question, the very mention of which causes most people moral spasms.

It is a conceded fact that woman is being reared as a sex commodity, and yet she is kept in absolute ignorance of the meaning and importance of sex. Everything dealing with that subject is suppressed, and persons who attempt to bring light into this terrible darkness are persecuted and thrown into prison. Yet it is nevertheless true that so long as a girl is not to know how to take care of herself, not to know the function of the most important part of her life, we need not be surprised if she becomes an easy prey to prostitution, or to any other form of a relationship which degrades her to the position of an object for mere sex gratification.

It is due to this ignorance that the entire life and nature of the girl is thwarted and crippled. We have long ago taken it as a self-evident fact that the boy may follow the call of the wild; that is to say, that the boy may, as soon as his sex nature asserts itself, satisfy that nature; but our moralists are scandalized at the very thought that the nature of a girl should assert itself. To the moralist prostitution does not consist so much in the fact that the woman sells her body, but rather that she sells it out of wedlock. That this is no mere statement is proved by the fact that marriage for monetary considerations is perfectly legitimate, sanctified by law and public opinion, while any other union is condemned and repudiated. Yet a prostitute, if properly defined, means nothing else than "any person for whom sexual relationships are subordinated to gain."

"Those women are prostitutes who sell their bodies for the exercise of the sexual act and make of this a profession."

In fact, Banger goes further; he maintains that the act of prostitution is "intrinsically equal to that of a man or woman who contracts a marriage for economic reasons."

Of course, marriage is the goal of every girl, but as thousands of girls cannot marry, our stupid social customs condemn them either to a life of celibacy or prostitution. Human nature asserts itself regardless of all laws, nor is there any plausible reason why nature should adapt itself to a perverted conception of morality.

Society considers the sex experiences of a man as attributes of his general development, while similar experiences in the life of a woman are looked upon as a terrible calamity, a loss of honor and of all that is good and noble in a human being. This double standard of morality has played no little part in the creation and perpetuation of prostitution. It involves the keeping of the young in absolute ignorance on sex matters, which alleged "innocence," together with an overwrought and stifled sex nature, helps to bring about a state of affairs that our Puritans are so anxious to avoid or prevent.

Not that the gratification of sex must needs lead to prostitution; it is the cruel, heartless, criminal persecution of those who dare divert from the beaten track, which is responsible for it.

Girls, mere children, work in crowded, overheated rooms ten to twelve hours daily at a machine, which tends to keep them in a constant over-excited sex state. Many of these girls have no home or comforts of any kind; therefore the street or some place of cheap amusement is the only means of forgetting their daily routine. This naturally brings them into close proximity with the other sex. It is hard to say which of the two factors brings the girl's over-sexed condition to a climax, but it is certainly the most natural thing that a climax should result. That is the first step toward prostitution. Nor is the girl to be held responsible for it. On the contrary, it is altogether the fault of society, the fault of our lack of understanding, of our lack of appreciation of life in the making; especially is it the criminal fault of our moralists, who condemn a girl for all eternity, because she has gone from the "path of virtue"; that is, because her first sex experience has taken place without the sanction of the Church.

The girl feels herself a complete outcast, with the doors of home and society closed in her face. Her entire training and tradition is such that the girl herself feels depraved and fallen, and therefore has no ground to stand upon, or any hold that will lift her up, instead of dragging her down. Thus society creates the victims that it afterwards vainly attempts to get rid of. The meanest, most depraved and decrepit man still considers himself too good to take as his wife the woman whose grace he was quite willing to buy, even though he might thereby save her from a life of horror. Nor can she turn to her own sister for help. In her stupidity the latter deems herself too pure and chaste, not realizing that her own position is in many respects even more deplorable than her sister's of the street.

"The wife who married for money, compared with the prostitute," says Havelock Ellis, "is the true scab. She is paid less, gives much more in return in labor and care, and is absolutely bound to her master. The prostitute never signs away the right over her own person, she retains her freedom and personal rights, nor is she always compelled to submit to man's embrace."

Nor does the better-than-thou woman realize the apologist claim of Lecky that "though she may be the supreme type of vice, she is also the most efficient guardian of virtue. But for her, happy homes would be polluted, unnatural and harmful practice would abound."

Moralists are ever ready to sacrifice one-half of the human race for the sake of some miserable institution which they can not outgrow. As a matter of fact, prostitution is no more a safeguard for the purity of the home than rigid laws are a safeguard against prostitution. Fully fifty percent of married men are patrons of brothels. It is through this virtuous element that the married women—nay, even the children—are infected with venereal diseases. Yet society has not a word of condemnation for the man, while no law is too monstrous to be set in motion against the helpless victim. She is not only preyed upon by those who use her, but she is also absolutely at the mercy of every policeman and miserable detective on the beat, the officials at the station house, the authorities in every prison.

In a recent book by a woman who was for twelve years the mistress of a "house," are to be found the following figures: "The authorities compelled me to pay every month fines between $14.70 to $29.70, the girls would pay from $5.70 to $9.70 to the police." Considering that the writer did her business in a small city, that the amounts she gives do not include extra bribes and fines, one can readily see the tremendous revenue the police department derives from the blood money of its victims, whom it will not even protect. Woe to those who refuse to pay their toll; they would be rounded up like cattle, "if only to make a favorable impression upon the good citizens of the city, or if the powers needed extra money on the side. For the warped mind who believes that a fallen woman is incapable of human emotion it would be impossible to realize the grief, the disgrace, the tears, the wounded pride that was ours every time we were pulled in."

Strange, isn't it, that a woman who has kept a "house" should be able to feel that way? But stranger still that a good Christian world should bleed and fleece such women, and give them nothing in return except obloquy and persecution. Oh, for the charity of a Christian world!

Much stress is laid on white slaves being imported into America. How would America ever retain her virtue if Europe did not help her out? I will not deny that this may be the case in some instances, any more than I will deny that there are emissaries of Germany and other countries luring economic slaves into America; but I absolutely deny that prostitution is recruited to any appreciable extent from Europe. It may be true that the majority of prostitutes of New York City are foreigners, but that is because the majority of the population is foreign. The moment we go to any other American city, to Chicago or the Middle West, we shall find that the number of foreign prostitutes is by far a minority.

Equally exaggerated is the belief that the majority of street girls in this city were engaged in this business before they came to America. Most of the girls speak excellent English, are Americanized in habits and appearance—a thing absolutely impossible unless they had lived in this country many years. That is, they were driven into prostitution by American conditions, by the thoroughly American custom for excessive display of finery and clothes, which, of course, necessitates money—money that cannot be earned in shops or factories.

In other words, there is no reason to believe that any set of men would go to the risk and expense of getting foreign products, when American conditions are overflooding the market with thousands of girls. On the other hand, there is sufficient evidence to prove that the export of American girls for the purpose of prostitution is by no means a small factor.

Thus Clifford G. Roe, ex-Assistant State Attorney of Cook County, Illinois, makes the open charge that New England girls are shipped to Panama for the express use of men in the employ of Uncle Sam. Mr. Roe adds that "there seems to be an underground railroad between Boston and Washington which many girls travel." Is it not significant that the railroad should lead to the very seat of federal authority? That Mr. Roe said more than was desired in certain quarters is proved by the fact that he lost his position. It is not practical for men in office to tell tales from school.

The excuse given for the conditions in Panama is that there are no brothels in the Canal Zone. That is the usual avenue of escape for a hypocritical world that dares not face the truth. Not in the Canal Zone, not in the city limits—therefore prostitution does not exist.

Next to Mr. Roe, there is James Bronson Reynolds, who has made a thorough study of the white slave traffic in Asia. As a staunch American citizen and friend of the future Napoleon of America, Theodore Roosevelt, he is surely the last to discredit the virtue of his country. Yet we are informed by him that in Hong Kong, Shanghai, and Yokohama, the Augean stables of American vice are located. There American prostitutes have made themselves so conspicuous that in the Orient "American girl" is synonymous with prostitute. Mr. Reynolds reminds his countrymen that while Americans in China are under the protection of our consular representatives, the Chinese in America have no protection at all. Everyone who knows the brutal and barbarous persecution Chinese and Japanese endure on the Pacific Coast will agree with Mr. Reynolds.

In view of the above facts it is rather absurd to point to Europe as the swamp whence come all the social diseases of America. Just as absurd is it to proclaim the myth that the Jews furnish the largest contingent of willing prey. I am sure that no one will accuse me of nationalistic tendencies. I am glad to say that I have developed out of them, as out of many other prejudices. If, therefore, I resent the statement that Jewish prostitutes are imported, it is not because of any Judaistic sympathies, but because of the facts inherent in the lives of these people. No one but the most superficial will claim that Jewish girls migrate to strange lands, unless they have some tie or relation that brings them there. The Jewish girl is not adventurous. Until recent years she had never left home, not even so far as the next village or town, except it were to visit some relative. Is it then credible that Jewish girls would leave their parents or families, travel thousands of miles to strange lands, through the influence and promises of strange forces? Go to any of the large incoming steamers and see for yourself if these girls do not come either with their parents, brothers, aunts, or other kinsfolk. There may be exceptions, of course, but to state that large numbers of Jewish girls are imported for prostitution, or any other purpose, is simply not to know Jewish psychology.

Those who sit in a glass house do wrong to throw stones about them; besides, the American glass house is rather thin, it will break easily, and the interior is anything but a gainly sight.

To ascribe the increase of prostitution to alleged importation, to the growth of the cadet system, or similar causes, is highly superficial. I have already referred to the former. As to the cadet system, abhorrent as it is, we must not ignore the fact that it is essentially a phase of modern prostitution—a phase accentuated by suppression and graft, resulting from sporadic crusades against the social evil.

The procurer is no doubt a poor specimen of the human family, but in what manner is he more despicable than the policeman who takes the last cent from the street walker, and then locks her up in the station house? Why is the cadet more criminal, or a greater menace to society, than the owners of department stores and factories, who grow fat on the sweat of their victims, only to drive them to the streets? I make no plea for the cadet, but I fail to see why he should be merci- lessly hounded, while the real perpetrators of all social iniquity enjoy immunity and respect. Then, too, it is well to remember that it is not the cadet who makes the prostitute. It is our sham and hypocrisy that create both the prostitute and the cadet.

Until 1894 very little was known in America of the procurer. Then we were attacked by an epidemic of virtue. Vice was to be abolished, the country purified at all cost. The social cancer was therefore driven out of sight, but deeper into the body. Keepers of brothels, as well as their unfortunate victims, were turned over to the tender mercies of the police. The inevitable consequence of exorbitant bribes, and the penitentiary, followed.

While comparatively protected in the brothels, where they repre- sented a certain monetary value, the girls now found themselves on the street, absolutely at the mercy of the graft-greedy police. Desper- ate, needing protection and longing for affection, these girls naturally proved an easy prey for cadets, themselves the result of the spirit of our commercial age. Thus the cadet system was the direct outgrowth of police persecution, graft, and attempted suppression of prostitu- tion. It were sheer folly to confound this modern phase of the social evil with the causes of the latter.

Mere suppression and barbaric enactments can serve but to embitter, and further degrade, the unfortunate victims of ignorance and stupidity. The latter has reached its highest expression in the proposed law to make humane treatment of prostitutes a crime, punishing any one sheltering a prostitute with five years' imprisonment and $10,000 fine. Such an attitude merely exposes the terrible lack of understanding of the true causes of prostitution, as a social factor, as well as manifesting the puritanic spirit of the Scarlet Letter days.

There is not a single modern writer on the subject who does not refer to the utter futility of legislative methods in coping with the issue. Thus Dr. Blaschko finds that governmental suppression and moral crusades accomplish nothing save driving the evil into secret channels, multiplying its dangers to society. Havelock Ellis, the most thorough and humane student of prostitution, proves by a wealth of data that the more stringent the methods of persecution the worse the condition becomes. Among other data we learn that in France, "in 1560, Charles IX abolished brothels through an edict, but the numbers of prostitutes were only increased, while many new brothels appeared in unsuspected shapes, and were more dangerous. In spite of all such legislation, or *because of it*, there has been no country in which prostitution has played a more conspicuous part."

An educated public opinion, freed from the legal and moral hounding of the prostitute, can alone help to ameliorate present conditions. Wilful shutting of eyes and ignoring of the evil as a social factor of modern life can but aggravate matters. We must rise above our foolish notions of "better than thou," and learn to recognize in the prostitute a product of social conditions. Such a realization will sweep away the attitude of hypocrisy, and insure a great understanding and more humane treatment. As to a thorough eradication of prostitution, nothing can accomplish that save a complete transvaluation of all accepted values—especially the moral ones—coupled with the abolition of industrial slavery.

5
WAR AND THE INDIVIDUAL

Max Eastman
THE RELIGION OF PATRIOTISM

In his lifetime Max Eastman (1883-1969) ran the gamut of political opinion from radical to reactionary. There was a stable theme in all his work, however, which was voiced in this article written while Eastman edited the socialist periodical The Masses. *Eastman believed in the integrity of the individual, and he turned to socialism precisely because he blamed capitalism for fostering conformity. That fact became especially clear to Eastman when the United States entered World War I, and, under the guise of patriotism, coerced men and women to support the war effort. In later years Eastman attacked the repressive Soviet regime and eventually saw no alternative except to renounce his faith in socialism. But in the joyous younger years before World War I, he shared with many other radicals living in Greenwich Village a faith that any doctrine challenging the morality of American business must work toward the freedom of the individual. Not above fighting capitalism with a sense of humor, a weapon that radicals have usually neglected,* The Masses *made the liveliest reading of any American socialist journal before or since.*

Nothing could be more calamitous than for patriotism to become the established religion of this country. I do not know exactly what religion is. Every psychologist has a different theory of its origin and nature. Some say it originates in fear, others in wonder, others in the filial affection, others in gregarious instinct—a desire for infinite companionship. But I doubt if the religious emotion is any of these single things, the same in different cases. I think that any object or any idea which appeals to *a considerable number* of our instincts, and offers them a *combined satisfaction*, may become the focus of an attachment so controlling, and so *fixé*, as to gain that uncanny and

SOURCE. Max Eastman, "The Religion of Patriotism," *The Masses*, IX, July 1917, pp. 8–11.

unreasonable priority among our feelings which we call religious. The religious object *binds* us (as the Latin original of the word implies), not by a single tie, but by gathering into itself so many threads of our impulsive nature that no one motive whatever can break its hold. God is indeed a refuge to our fear, a temple to our wonder, a parent for the little child that lives in our heart. He is an infinite companion. He satisfies so many of those native cravings which the terms of life leave thwarted, that His hold upon us becomes supernormal and sovereign, and our whole being is transfixed by His name as though we were maniacs and He our obsession.

In order for this to happen, however, it is necessary that we have the gift of making God seem real. In past ages, with a Christ or a Virgin Mary giving the warmth of flesh to the picture, and a general consensus of mankind supporting the opinion that God *is* real, it was not difficult to acquire this gift. Perhaps almost a majority of mankind possessed it, and the religion of God was one of the determining forces in history. In this day, however, for many reasons, it is growing difficult to make God seem real. The money and machine character of our civilization leaves little room for miracles. A belief in supernatural causes is dangerous in a factory and impractical in a bank. And moreover, Jesus Christ expressed so many principles of conduct wholly out of accord with our industrial life, that the ministers of his gospel are forced to deny him and betray his ideals continually while asserting his godhead, and this makes them seem weak and queer, and his godhead dubious. Deity is identified with the church, and the church is hypocritical and alien to everyday life, and so deity grows slippery and unpleasant to our minds. God is a long way off. There is no sovereign motive in our lives.

That is good—It allows us to be intelligent and agile in various kinds of enjoyment and enterprise. It lets us love truth more whole-heartedly, and become acquainted with liberty. It is so lofty a state, in fact, that most people have not the strength of stem to endure it; they think they must find something to lean on and bind themselves around. And so our godless age has been characterized by a wistful hunger and search after religions. It is the age of "isms." And some of these isms have been able to bind together a number of native impulses, and hold men almost as strongly as God did. Socialism with its doctrine of universal brotherhood to be attained by the method of class war, offers almost infinite indulgence of two otherwise unreconciled impulses—pugnacity and social love. With its system of revealed economics, it offers, too, an absolute in which mental curiosity can rest. It has its gospel according to Marx. Socialism is no mean religion. But it is not a religion that binds or blesses the rich and powerful, and so it could hardly become established in a country like ours. For an established religion we needed something a little more like God—a little vaguer and more elegant and better adapted to bind in among other motives the economic self-interest of those who rule. We needed something that would give us the same emotional crystallization without greatly disturbing the profits on capital.

Quite consciously a great many good people were searching for a thing of this kind, for a new and vigorous religion. And now, through the lucky accidents of history, they have found it. For there is nothing more copiously able to bind into its bosom the multiple threads of human impulse, and establish that fixed and absolute glorious tyranny among our purposes, than military patriotism. You will see how everything that was erect in this country bows down to that sentiment. The love of liberty, the assertion of the rights of man, what little of the ethics of Jesus we had—these things must obviously yield. And not only these, either, but the common principles of morality and truth. We shall see men devoting their utmost energy to an endeavor which they declare to be evil.

"Gladly would I have given my life to save my country from war," says William J. Bryan, "but now that my country has gone to war, gladly will I give my life to aid it." This Christian gentleman, whose morality was perhaps the most rigid thing we had in the country, thus boasts that he will devote his declining years to a cause which he considers wicked. Like Abraham who would slaughter his son at the bidding of God, Bryan is ready to do murder—he has called it murder—for the sake of his country. And this seems entirely right and noble to his countrymen. To me it seems utterly ignoble.

Not only morality, either, but the ideal of intelligence itself, of truthful seeing, will be abandoned. Men will glory in the ignorance and celebrate the stupidity of what they are doing. "I shall vote," said Senator Stone, against "the greatest national blunder of history," but after that "my eyes will be blind to everything but the flag of my country."

When ordinary alert perception has been renounced, it is needless to say that the extreme ethical visions of Jesus must go, and that God—long suffering God—will be denounced from the pulpits that were his last refuge. I suppose the pew-holders of Henry Ward Beecher's church are satisfied with Newell Dwight Hillis, for they have stood a good deal from him besides his preaching, and here is his creed of patriotism:

"All God's teachings about forgiveness should be rescinded for Germany. I am willing to forgive the Germans for their atrocities just as soon as they are all shot. It you would give me happiness, just give me the sight of the Kaiser, von Hindenburg and von Tirpitz hanging by the rope. If we forgive Germany after the war, I shall think the whole universe has gone wrong."

When God is thus enthusiastically ejected from the rostrum of the most famous church in the country, to make way for the patriotic emotion, I think we are justified in the fear that patriotism may become our religion.

Patriotism indulges that craving for a sense of union with a solidary herd, which is an inheritance of all gregarious animals. It is a craving which our modern sophisticated, citified, and diverse civilization leaves unfed in normal times. There is a great swing towards war on this account even among the most pacific people. They are flocking for a drink of this emotion. Men are willing to be dead, if they can only be dead in a pile.

This quite organic and almost animal craving is what makes us talk so much about the "great spiritual blessing" that war will bring to our unregenerate characters. When a desire springs so deeply from our ancient inheritance as this gregarious hunger does, we always feel it as mystic and inscrutable, we attribute a divine beneficence to the satisfaction of it. As a matter of fact, it would be better for the progress of society, in science and art and morality and happiness, if this terrible solidarity could be mitigated instead of enlarged. For it inhibits individual experiment, and it falsifies the facts of life, always pretending the nation is more socially and brotherly organized than it is. The "great spiritual blessing" is in fact a distraction of men's minds from the pursuit of truth and from realistic progress. It is the temporary indulgence of a facile emotion.

"I pray God," said President Wilson at the dedication of a Red Cross Memorial, "that the outcome of this struggle may be that every element of difference amongst us will be obliterated. . . . The spirit of this people is already united and when effort and suffering and sacrifice have completed this union, men will no longer speak of any lines either of race or association cutting athwart the great body of this nation."

To the instinctive man, the altogether righteousness of this aspiration, and the entire beneficence of the condition outlined, is as much taken for granted as the goodness of virtue. And yet, if seriously considered, such a state of affairs would be aesthetically monotonous and morally stagnant. Aside from the mere satisfaction of the old instinct for herd-union itself, there would be no health, no beauty, no life in it.

"Liberty and Union, One and Inseparable, Now and Forever," is the watchword that adorns the statue of Daniel Webster in Central Park. And that too seems obvious—it has become a proverb. And yet if it has any meaning whatever, the meaning is false. It has become proverbial merely because it celebrates, with some show of regard for individual freedom, this gregarious instinct of mankind which is the central armature of the religion of patriotism.

According to my idea, however, the satisfaction of a single instinct, even though so arbitrary and ancient-rooted as this, cannot acquire that peculiar hypnotizing force upon us which makes us name it religious. We might love union and the monotony of the herd very much, and still continue to act morally, and exercise intelligent judgment, and perhaps love God and walk humbly with our neighbor. But it happens that the moment we declare for the herd, and let loose our enthusiasm into that vent, especially at war time, a half dozen other starved monsters of passionate desire that our lawful and cultivated life has caged and thwarted, rush to this outlet and find satisfaction.

One of them is angry hate. Men are full of it, and they get small chance to exercise it in these days of legality and respectable convention. The war liberates them. They can rage and revile and spit upon the enemy with the sanction of all contiguous society, and without immediate personal danger. I think this is what makes a declaration of war especially palatable to ministers of Christ. They have repressed so much more personal spleen, as a matter of professional necessity, than the rest of us, that they let go all the more violently into the national spout. Nobody will demand that they apply the ethics of Jesus to the relations between nations; they can go on preaching forgiveness as a personal matter, while enjoying in this national festival the emotions of implacable hate.

Here is a conversation overheard in a restaurant conducted by two innocent and colorless Germans, man and wife. The talkers are American patriots.

"Did you read what Ambassador Gerard said about the German boys torturing foreigners in Germany?"

"Yes, and it's true too. They're cruel. They're savages, the Germans. They wouldn't stop at anything."

"You bet, look at these people. I bet they're spies. We'll be over here and string them up one of these days."

The sudden and copious flow of malice which follows a declaration of war suggests that a really dire condition of the natural organs has been relieved just in the nick of time. Another and even more bursting reservoir that ordinary moral conduct never half relieves, is rivalrous egotism. Society suppresses the braggart, for the reason that if bragging is to be done, each member of society feels fully entitled to do it, and there is no other solution short of bedlam. In consequence every individual is full as a bladder with inexpressible self-esteem. And by a quickly articulated emotional device, this passion too is sluiced into the channel of patriotism. A man identifies himself with his country, and then he brags about his country to his heart's desire, and nobody observes that he is bragging about himself. Only sensitive people know that patriotic loyalty is so much less flamelike and beautiful than loyalty to a friend or an idea—they feel this cold vein of complacence in it.

The patriotic religion has a hold here that God never had. God wanted people to be humble. A religion that lets us brag without knowing that is what we are doing, is far more gratefully adjusted to our constitutions. We can love our country and make sacrifices for it, we can have all those altruistic satisfactions, and yet not suffer the self-abasement that is inevitable in loving a Supreme Being. It is our country; it is not simply Country, abstract and awful.

Our country comforts us too, even as God's fatherhood did. Our filial affection is gathered up into the bosom of the fatherland. We were conceived and born in its bosom; it is our native place, the place that sheltered us long ago when we were happy; it will still care for us (especially while we are fighting for it), and give us that sense of the Everlasting Arms without which perhaps no religion would retain its extreme dominion among our feelings.

Yes, patriotism binds us by as many ties as God. We need not be surprised at those Methodist conventioners, who denounced for treason the lowly delegate who wished to put God before his country. In the very nature of the case, if our theory of religion is true, there can be no two religions. If God will not fall in step with the United States army, God must go. That has been made plain in every pulpit in this vicinity, with the noble exception of the Church of the Messiah, where John Haynes Holmes spoke not only for the sovereignty of God, but even for the ethics of Jesus, on the eve of War.

Patriotism has, like other religions whose object of worship is a little open to question, its extreme sensitiveness, its fanatical intolerance. The ceremonial observances are enforced with zealotry, and those who blaspheme with unassenting presence are likely to be thrown out bodily or confined in jail. At one of the meeting places of patriots on Broadway, known as Rector's, one night at two A.M. the ceremonial of the national anthem was being enacted, and while all the devotees were rising or being assisted to their feet, Mr. Fred Boyd and two companions—heretics of this religion—endeavored quietly to remain in their seats. Chairs, tables and salad bowls were employed by the orthodox to enforce the tenets of their creed, and these failing, a policeman was summoned in the name of the fatherland, and Mr. Boyd and his companions arrived at the night court. Here they were severely reprimanded by a judge, who acknowledged, however, that they had disobeyed no law, not even the law of God, which is usually invoked upon such unfortunates as wish to act upon their own judgment in public.

To me patriotism, in practically all of its forms, is distasteful. And I confess to a feeling of strange solitude in these days of its divinity that no other revolutionary opinions have brought me. Much of the time I wonder what it is that separates a handful of us from the concourse of mankind. We are so motley a handful, Christians, atheists, Quakers, anarchists, artists, socialists, and a few who just have a fervent pleasure in using their brains about truth. You could bring us together, and we would not agree upon anything else under the sun—but we agree in disliking the religion of patriotism. We can not stand up when the national anthem is played, not because we have any theory about it, but because the quality of the emotion expressed is alien and false to us. We can not partake of the communion and be true to ourselves. And so many of us do not go to these meeting places at all, or we come in late, or otherwise we try to avoid the acute discomfort of sitting quiescent under the scowling malice and ignorant suspicion of a mob indulging its now fixed and habitual emotion.

As I count over the little group that I know who feel this way about committing themselves to the new religion, I find two or three traits that seem somewhat to explain it. Some of the group are platonic in their temperament—given, that is, to falling in love with ideas. And so many beautiful ideas, like justice and proportion and mercy and truth, have to be renounced and reviled in abandoning oneself to this religion, that they find it absolutely impossible. They can not tear themselves away from their loves.

Others are temperamentally solitary. They are actually lacking in gregarious impulse, or have an opposite impulse to kick out and desert whenever the herd agrees upon something. They can not even understand patriotism, and these modern days make them not only sad, but bitter and contemptuous of men.

Others are rationalistic, and have a theory about patriotism, and their emotions are controlled by a theory. But there are not many whose emotions are controlled by a theory.

The character that is most common to those who can not commit themselves to this religion, is the character of having already really committed themselves to something else. And this too is rare enough.

Most of the people in our days of nervous modernity—busy with labor, or busy with entertainment—never heartily abandon themselves to anything. Such people welcome the orgy of nation-worship merely as a chance to feel.

I think of Mayor Mitchel, for example, as a little foxlike political man, who has stepped very carefully here and there, taking a bit, giving a bit, to this and to that—church, politics, business, society, dress. He shows very plainly that he never abandoned his soul to any purpose or any experience. But now he has—and it is doing him good. One can not but smile in sympathy with the Mayor's boyish extravagance in this the first experience of his life. One can not but wish him the good luck of other experiences before he dies. And he is typical of the average man and man-of-affairs. They go in for this facile religion of the fatherland, or at least they show no resistance against it, because they not only are not committed to anything else, but they never have been committed to anything. Other religions always seemed to require courage, or faith, or loneliness, or energy-of-intent; this requires only the most social and joyful abandonment of intelligent judgment and moral restraint. It is the easiest religion under the sun to feel and feel deeply for it gives the highest quantity of satisfactions, requires no imaginative faith, and demands only at the most that physical crowd-courage which is a common heritage of our race.

I do not believe many people will ever be led to feel unpatriotic. To argue against these tribal and egoistic instincts is like arguing against gravitation. But I do hope that a fair proportion of the intelligent may be persuaded to resist the establishment, in their own minds or in American society, of patriotism as a religion. Let them understand that to indulge and satisfy some one or two of the emotions that enter into this compound, is a very different thing from binding all these satisfactions into a fixed and rigid and monumental sentiment which will exercise absolute dictatorship in their minds. Strong minds do not need any religion. They are able to bear the responsibility and the labor of thinking and choosing among the values of life anew every morning. But even for those who must have a religion, an exposure of the extreme easiness of patriotic enthusiasm, its quality of general indulgence, might make them wish to bind themselves, if they must be bound, to some god that is more arduous and demanding of personal character.

SUGGESTIONS FOR FURTHER READING

American radicalism in the late nineteenth century and early twentieth century must be understood in the context of general social thought in the United States. Two older books still essential for an understanding of the directions of conservative and reform ideas are Richard Hofstadter, *Social Darwinism in American Thought* (Philadelphia, 1944) and Sidney Fine, *Laissez Faire and the General-Welfare State* (Ann Arbor, 1956). Robert Wiebe in *The Search for Order 1877–1920* (New York, 1967) has provided the most interesting recent interpretation of American values in the period covered by this volume. On the failure of radicalism in the United States, the best starting point remains Louis Hartz, *The Liberal Tradition in America* (New York, 1954). Volumes that cover American socialism in this era reflect a variety of interpretations. These include Howard Quint, *The Forging of American Socialism* (Chapel Hill, N.C., 1953); David Shannon, *The Socialist Party of America* (New York, 1955); Ira Kipnis, *The American Socialist Movement, 1897–1912* (New York, 1953); Daniel Bell, *Marxian Socialism in the United States* (Princeton, 1967); and James Weinstein, *The Decline of Socialism in America, 1912–1925* (New York, 1967). Samuel Bernstein has told an amusing story in a sober way in *The First International in America* (New York, 1962). For European socialist interpretations of the American radical movement, consult R. Laurence Moore, *European Socialists and the American Promised Land* (New York, 1970); the concluding chapter ventures some opinions about the American Socialist party in the years before War War I. John H. M. Laslett, *Labor and the Left; A Study of Socialist and Radical Influences in the American Labor Movement, 1881–1924* (New York, 1970), is indispensable on the subject of trade unionism and radicalism. On the Industrial Workers of the World see Melvyn Dubofsky, *We Shall Be All; A History of the Industrial Workers of the World* (Chicago, 1969), and Joseph R. Conlin, *Bread and Roses Too; Studies of the Wobblies* (Westport, Conn., 1969). William Preston, Jr., has dealt with governmental responses to radicalism in *Aliens and Dissenters; Federal Suppression of Radicals, 1903–1933* (Cambridge,

Mass., 1963). The most exhaustive bibliographical guide to American radicalism, Volume II of *Socialism and American Life* (Princeton, 1952), compiled by T. D. Bassett, needs updating but is still valuable. There are biographical studies of many, though not all, of the individuals included in this volume. The best available source on Sorge and DeLeon is David Herreshoff, *American Disciples of Marx; From the Age of Jackson to the Progressive Era* (Detroit, 1967). Individual published volumes include Jonathan Grossman, *William Sylvis, Pioneer of American Labor; A Study of the Labor Movement During the Era of the Civil War* (New York, 1945); M. Marion Marberry, *Vicky; A Biography of Victoria C. Woodhull* (New York, 1967); Charles A. Barker, *Henry George* (New York, 1955); Sylvia E. Bowman, *The Year 2000; A Critical Biography of Edward Bellamy* (New York, 1958); Joseph R. Conlin, *Big Bill Haywood and the Radical Union Movement* (Syracuse, N.Y., 1969); Ray Ginger, *The Bending Cross; A Biography of Eugene Victor Debs* (New Brunswick, N.J., 1949); and Granville Hicks, *John Reed; The Making of a Revolutionary* (New York, 1936). Richard Drinnon, *Rebel in Paradise* (Chicago, 1961) is the standard reference on Emma Goldman, but her autobiography *Living My Life* (New York, 1931) also makes good reading. Max Eastman's autobiography *Love and Revolution; My Journey Through an Epoch* (New York, 1964) is useful and must serve until there is a full scholarly study. On some of the others, mention should be made of good unpublished dissertations: Harold S. Smith, *William James Ghent; Reformer and Historian* (University of Wisconsin, 1957); Edward J. Muzik, *Victor Berger; A Biography* (Northwestern, 1960); and Gerald Friedberg, *Marxism in the United States; John Spargo and the Socialist Party of America,* (Harvard, 1964).